MICHAEL THOROGOOD

SAHARA, SOUK & ATLAS

Tales from the
land of the Amazigh

First published in Great Britain in 2020

ISBN 9798568991779

www.michaelthorogood.co.uk

To those who offered us their
hospitality and made our journeys
an adventure.

ABOUT THE AUTHOR

Michael Thorogood is a young writer from London. Inspired by the likes of Michael Palin and Levison Wood, he first documented his travels over a decade ago, after climbing Ben Nevis with his family. Through his stories of adventure, Michael aims to raise awareness of marginalised groups whose stories are seldom told. His first book, *Sahara, Souk & Atlas*, tells the tale of the Amazigh, the indigenous people of North Africa, in their struggle for cultural recognition. At the time of his first journey to Morocco, he was 20 years old. He has two degrees from the London School of Economics and University of Surrey in international development and politics.

Michael Thorogood
www.michaelthorogood.co.uk

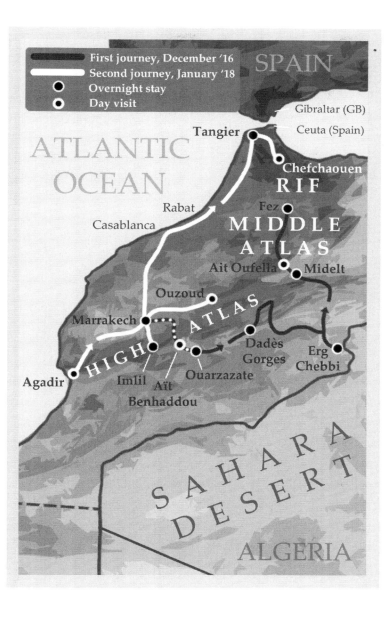

Contents

First journey

Second journey

FIRST JOURNEY

December 2016

1

Tamazgha

Marrakech

The evening is rising to its crescendo. On the eastern horizon, the snow-capped peaks of the High Atlas Mountains simmer in the embers of dusk. The mosques of the medina usher the faithful to prayer with a collective cry, as a rising wall of sound washes towards us through the souks. The grills in the square smoke with the aroma of sizzling meats and sweet nougat. Europe is a stone's throw to our north, but tonight there is the aura of a faraway land.

Storytellers and fire-eaters animate lively crowds. Wild-eyed snake charmers and magicians jostle for space with the monkey-handlers and thieves, as the beggars circle. Merchants push handcarts of walnuts and cloves, olive and fig, dates and almonds, plucked from the winter hills. The African night is a respite, but these first steps are a baptism of fire. Now the heat has subsided, the intensity of this square swells to a fever pitch. Deposited here from London just four hours ago, I have barely had time to adjust. No sooner has my empty cup of breakfast tea rustled into an airplane binbag, an elderly man in pointed slippers is wrapping a python around my neck, while a stout woman in technicolour robes clinks hand cymbals in my face.

Just moments ago, the square was empty. Marrakech had retreated to the shade. In the fiery afternoon heat, when the walls of the red city were blushed in rose, the musicians warmed with a slow melody. The flute had swelled from the cool of gardens. Percussion seeped from the shallow shade of date palms by the mosque. But tonight, in the electric evening cool, they play at their absolute zenith. A merciless melody of horns, pipes and thunderous drums pulses through the market with the restless rhythm of the east.

This is my first night in Africa and soon enough, like a shaman in a trance, I find myself drifting through a strange new world of African magic and Islamic ritual, perched on the doorstep of Europe. Ancient traditions endure in this conservative kingdom and this market square in particular, the eccentric Jemaa el-Fna, is a testament to the old ways. This is the epicentre of the old medina, the ancient core of Marrakech, and a smouldering cauldron of heat, noise and exotic smells. Sketched in the gloom to our east, the chiselled peaks of the High Atlas are now fading in the amber light. The trans-Saharan caravans once journeyed over them, carrying gold and spices, salt and slaves, Islam and wisdom, destined for Europe. Almost one thousand years ago, their merchants and camels would have halted in Marrakech for trade. We are on their trail, starting here, in a square known as the 'Mosque at the End of the World,' where they too would have been met by this carnival.

"Just remind me: how did we end up here again?" I ask Katharine, my friend from university, as we drift north from the Jemaa el-Fna and into a bustling warren of technicolour souks that are charged with the energy of night. My body has barely adjusted to the heat. The seasons have swung so abruptly and now, as the souks breathe in again and haul us deeper, I mop a river of sweat that streams off my brow.

I'm honestly not sure how I ended up here, on the northern shores of Africa. I'm not sure that Katharine knows either. Life has led us here in a blur. Don't worry: it wasn't one of those pass out drunk, wake up in Rome affairs. I have been drawn here by spontaneity, by a magnetic pull to Africa that has been pestering me since childhood. But it began just ten days ago, some 3,000 miles north of here, in the Arctic Circle. At midnight. The -20°C cold gnawing away at my skin, as my padded jacket tried with futility to beat back the breath of a Lappish night.

With me back then were the New Zealanders, Katharine and Matt, who are with me here too in Morocco. Over recent months, we have all been on a 'study' exchange in Copenhagen ... though, in truth, we are yet to locate the library. On the contrary, we have gotten to know the airport quite well and this North African journey is our last hurrah before we all return home for Christmas, the Kiwis to their rock in the deep South Pacific and I to mine in the North Atlantic. Soon we shall part ways, maybe even forever, and who could have guessed that these months of adventure would all come to an end on the northern shores of Africa? I certainly could not. You see, back then, on that fateful late night in the Arctic just over a week ago, Lapland was meant to be our final farewell.

We were out on frozen tundra, hunting for the aurora, guided by the shallow moonlight to the rhythmic whistle of rising winter winds. Matt checked the app on his mobile one last time. If we were to catch a glimpse of the so-far elusive northern lights, it would be now. After a week in hiding, they were now at their strongest. All that we needed was a break in the midnight cloud. Ahead of us lay a snowy clearing in the Arctic forest. Tall pines surrounded it, cocooning it like barricades. We were tracking the path of an animal, whose hoofprints were strung across the clearing from one side to the other, before disappearing back into the forest beyond. We followed them. I led the way.

Every footstep was tentative across the ice. The tracks looked fresh, but we did not know what the animal was, nor where it was hiding. At last, we were distant from the lights of town. The cabin was far behind us, the Arctic night a splendid black. Finally, we had found ourselves a raw isolation: enveloped by the trees, pinned down by the biting cold, our world reduced to this small clearing within the pines.

But then, in the blur of one heart-shuddering moment, our search was at its bitter end. A primeval rush consumed my being and a sharp, icy chill shot through my veins. The pines leaned in to surround us as the swirling winds let out a haunting shriek. I was chest deep in bitter water, the ice having collapsed beneath my feet. The clearing that we had been crossing was not a clearing at all. It was a thinly frozen lake.

Now my lower body hung in the icy depths, my weight hopelessly balanced between my outspread arms that rested on thin ice to either side, holding me in limbo. It was midnight, sub-zero, pitch black. One false move and who knew the depths of the gloomy void below? The Kiwis and Alan, our American friend, were frozen by indecision. Step forward and mount a rescue and they may befall the same fate as me. I had to extract myself. In mere moments I could become hypothermic, so I pressed down with one arm to lever myself out, but immediately the ice splintered away into the abyss, my limbs sent scrabbling, feeling desperately for frozen ground. We were teetering on the brink.

Matt stepped in. Boldly he was stood on ice that I had just moved over; no doubt it too was thin. By now Alan was also one leg deep and wrestling with gravity, as Matt reached down and hauled at my arm, the ice breaking away once again. Hauled onto somewhat frozen ice, we made a swift and unnerving retreat along the animal tracks the way that we had come. I felt sure as we moved that the ice would splinter again, but we made it back to the forest where I removed my ice-filled gloves, gave everything a shake and rolled about in the snow, as Bear Grylls had once told me to do.

Then, finally, we laughed. There seemed no more natural reaction in a moment like this. We had survived a close call and could return to the cabin with a tale to share. Only now did I inform the others that I cannot swim, little that it would have mattered in the icy depths of an Arctic night. Once more the pines opened up as we retreated hastily to the cabin and darted, without hesitation, for the respite of the sauna.

"That's what the Finns do, right?" I joked to the others. "Jump into an ice hole in deep winter, then dash for the sauna. Look, let's face it: I'm basically a Finn."

"You didn't do it naked," Katharine reminded me, as we poured water onto the rocks that gushed steam over ice-bitten skin. We were at the climax of a great adventure across the ice. The Arctic light show may have evaded us, but this was a fittingly dramatic conclusion to our six months of travel. But then, pumped with adrenaline from the midnight fiasco, conversation took an unexpected turn.

"Come on, when will you have the chance again?" Katharine urged me once more. Unbeknown to me, she had been planning. "It's Africa – come on! What a way to see the year out."

"I have exams," I counter.

"Yeah, and since when have we bothered with those on this study exchange?" she reminded me. "Look – we jet to Morocco next week, then, if all goes smoothly, we'll be home in time for Christmas."

"And if it doesn't?"

"Then it's tagine for Christmas dinner!"

Sweat now beaded from my warming skin, but still the prospect of Africa seemed entirely farfetched. Christmas was less than four weeks away, my travel budget was running aridly dry and I had the small task of moving all my earthly possessions from Copenhagen back home to London. Frankly, I was reluctant.

"Balek! Balek!" An overladen donkey thunders through the souks apace, its bellowing young driver parting a sea of people who dive for the cover of babouches piled high in store fronts. Less than a fortnight on from the Arctic fiasco, I am thrust back into the deep yet again. My frost-nipped skin has barely thawed out as we delve into the restless souks, where the air is piquant with the waft of hanging meats, the stench of exotic fruits and the lung-tightening choke of motorbike fumes. The soundtrack is perpetual too: enthused barter, the barking of dogs, raucous laughter, the chatter of bikes, the clatter of mules, shouts to clear the way as merchants hurry through.

While at first an impossible warren of twisting medieval streets and frustrating dead-ends, these ancient souks are, in fact, logically ordered into specialist markets. They fan from the nearby spice, carpet, leather and jewellery souks, to the dyers' souk and tanneries that brush the far northern and eastern city walls. But the logic matters little: these souks are a labyrinth and tonight we move by instinct, lured in by the madness, flooding with the masses in a blur of passing colour. One million exotic items spill from storefronts onto the dusty streets: glass lanterns, vibrant scarves, woven carpets, leather satchels, decorated earthenware, shining gemstones, wooden instruments.

We drift north, to the Rahba Kedima, the Spice Square, where our noses are under assault. Slaves used to be traded in this ancient market, but tonight it is a visual and aromatic overload. Apothecaries flog their potions and sacks of hopeful spice mixture. There is one for every ailment and the locals have turned out en masse, bartering for doubtful cures, seeking out wonder drugs. There are the skins of exotic animals, live tortoises, snakes and chameleons. They are used in spells. After all, this is the domain of witches who frequent the souks and rural markets of this kingdom, trading potions and curses, and advising on their use. Some villages will have their own fortune teller and many Moroccans believe in the existence of genies: spiritual beings that come from the Arabic word *djinn.* They are said to operate in places where you find water: in pots and pans, in drains and sinks, in the hammams.

We are lured even deeper, to a technicolour street named the Rue du Mouassine, where, even at this moonlit hour, the artisans toil. They are crafting leather and painting large urns, moulding clay and spinning wool, labouring away in the ancient courtyards of the medina's once-exquisite fondouks. At the zenith of trans-Saharan trade, these sizeable fondouks, also known as caravanserais, served as inns for the merchants and stables for their animals while halting in the red city to trade. They provided water and fodder, storage and news, a quiet oasis of serenity in the maelstrom of the souks. While the majority have fallen into sad disrepair, others have found new life in the hands of the city's artisans, whose trades and techniques have changed little over the centuries.

Quickly my mind is numbing to the unexpected. Suddenly, a man in ragged robes hurries to our sides and thrusts three steaming glasses in our direction. He is a travelling tea merchant, making his way through the souks, and beneath him, sat cross-legged in slippers on the dusty street, a roaming dentist is just setting up shop. In a country where there is just one dentist for every 800,000 people, the most common remedy for toothache is a yank at a painful molar in a back-street souk like this one. The contrasts of this city are quite astonishing. At the confluence of East and West, the Arabs have long known Morocco as *al-Magrib al -Aqsa,* the 'extreme west.' This is the final frontier of the Arab world, the last hurrah of eastern flare and Islamic tradition before Europe. Yet earlier this afternoon, in the elegant and French-built Ville Nouvelle – the 'new town' – Marrakech was an entirely different city. It was a city urgent to embrace the glamour of modernity, a metropolis ripped from the textbook of Europe.

From dust-strewn outskirts by Menara Airport, we motored down stylish boulevards that were trimmed with neat trees, broken by lavish fountains and lined with bougie hotels. They were in new Marrakech, a corner of town that screamed of the West and shimmered with neon lights of modernity. Christmas is now just two weeks away and within the all-glass façade of a shiny new shopping complex, an artificial tree had trinkled in technicolour. Neatly-wrapped presents stacked beneath its branches, alongside which the arms of an inflatable Santa spasmed as if he were wrestling his reindeer in slow-motion. This was not how I imagined the 'extreme west' of the Arab world to be. This was, quite simply, the West!

Stray just a stone's throw east however and cocooned in a beautiful cloak of pinkish-red is the ancient medina, the soul of the city, where we now stand. Pass through its rosy gates and this is a city transformed: a timeless clash of Europe and Africa, Arab and Amazigh, religion and secularism, an offensive two fingers to the glitter and modernity of the Ville Nouvelle beyond. While modern Morocco has drifted westwards to the coast, engulfing the capital Rabat and its largest city Casablanca with a sheen of the West so abrupt in the new districts here, these red city walls continue to serve the medina as they have done for centuries: keeping the outside world out and tradition within alive, the Jemaa el-Fna the pulsing epicentre of it all.

Marrakech is a feast of contradictions, an alluring cocktail of a city. Over-burdened donkeys clatter past the storefronts of Rolex and Louis Vuitton, their arch-backed drivers tapping at their sides to keep them apace. High-rise living is springing from the dust on the city periphery like palms from oasis waters, yet just six years ago, 20,000 homes here were without electricity and clean water. This evening we revel in the hysteria of the souks, yet beyond these rosy walls there is enough glass and secular appeal to slot seamlessly into any European land. Where the two worlds meet, the paradox can be confusing.

Perhaps I should not be so surprised. Marrakech has always been a crossroads of civilisations, the first major city north of the Sahara and a gateway for the desert caravans arriving from the east and West Africa. This city was founded at the country's geographical heart to defend the ancient trade routes that arrived from the passes of the High Atlas. For almost a millennium, the red city has witnessed the rise and collapse of civilisations around it and connected them through the passage of trade and ideas. Marrakech has always been a confluence, an alluring clash of worlds. The pious nomads who founded this great city, the Almoravids, built a kasbah and a mosque on this land that would some day unite all of modern Morocco and much of present-day Spain and Algeria. They emerged from the Sahara as veiled and merciless warriors, but went on to control an empire that reached 3,000 kilometres from the Sahara to Al-Andalus in modern-day Spain, where they halted the advance of the Christian kingdoms of Iberia.

Marrakech was their capital, but it was surrounded on all fronts by tribal frontiers. Just an hour's drive to our east, now veiled in the black of night, an imposing wall of rock is strung for 2,500 kilometres across the spine of the Maghreb. The Atlas Mountains, and the dusty lowlands that sprawl in their east to a desert frontier, is the traditional heartland of the Moroccan Amazigh, the indigenous people of North Africa. Yet these were long considered anarchical lands where the authority of the sultan was rejected by the local warlords and tribes, who held absolute power. It was in the red city that the so-called *'Bled el-Makhzen,'* the land of the governed, met the *'Bled es-Siba,'* the land of the lawless, as the colonial French would later know it. Even today, the northern hills of this kingdom, the Rif, are known as lawless lands with a reputation for rebellion.

For centuries, then, Marrakech was the last bastion of order before the tribal hinterlands beyond. Tomorrow we enter them, traversing the High Atlas across the notorious Tizi n'Tichka mountain pass to the red dust rock of the otherworldly Dadès Gorge: a barren and Martian land where nomads still roam. From there we journey east, across the dusty lowlands to an island of sand on the fringe of the Sahara, the beautiful Erg Chebbi, where a cameleer of nomadic roots is awaiting our arrival. Then, after two nights in the desert with our Amazigh guides, we shall traverse cedar forest and the Middle Atlas to the pious ancient capital, Fez, over mountain passes lesser travelled and prone to closure in these bleak winter months.

Yet tonight, as we return from the souks to marvel at the theatrics of the Jemaa el-Fna once again, I cannot shake a paradox that rumbles in my mind and echoes through the moon-struck square. It is a lingering question that will not leave me on this journey, nor when it hauls me back for more in just over a year from now. It concerns a place that does not technically exist, a place you have probably not heard of, but a place that almost every man and woman from across North Africa can claim to originate from. It is called Tamazgha.

I am standing in Tamazgha now. It straddles North Africa from the

Siwa Oasis in Egypt to the east, to the Canary Islands in the west, and from the Mediterranean shores up north, to the nomadic depths of the Sahara and Sahel in the south. But study the map as hard as you might and you will not find Tamazgha. If it were a country, it would be the seventh largest in the world, home to more than 20 million indigenous Amazigh people, whose ancestors have occupied its lands for millennia. But Tamazgha is not real. Tamazgha only exists in the imagination.

The Amazigh know themselves as 'free men,' or 'free people,' and Tamazgha is their imagined homeland. It symbolises the land that their forefathers ruled, where feared Amazigh kingdoms fended off invaders and fostered a culture that would stand the test of time. Since the mists of early history, the Amazigh dominated North Africa, yet, today, Tamazgha has come to symbolise a land of struggle. Despite a majority of North Africans west of Egypt being of Amazigh origin, today the 'free people' are fighting for cultural recognition and political representation in the lands where their ancestors lived. Tamazgha, as I will soon learn, is not a place, but a state of mind.

The paradox, then, lies not in Tamazgha, but in the ironic name of the 'free people' themselves. For millennia, an unparalleled knowledge of the desert and a feared, warrior-like spirit meant that the indigenous Amazigh could control a territory that straddled North Africa, enduring conquests of empires as mighty as the French, Romans, Carthaginians, and Byzantines. While these empires could conquer the North African coast, none could control its harsh desert interior, nor the unwavering spirit of the region's free men. They know themselves as the Amazigh, 'am-ah-zee-ah,' but you might have heard of them as 'Berbers,' which means 'barbarians.' Despite forming a majority, today the 'free people' are being squeezed to the fringe of society.

No one knows for sure where the first Amazigh came from. When the French ruled Morocco in the early 20th century, they claimed that the Amazigh originated in Europe, to legitimise their occupation. But when the Arabs returned to the fore across independent North Africa, they refuted this idea, arguing that the Amazigh came from Yemen, in the Middle East, and thus were one of their own. Such contestation is mirrored in early artforms, which paint a similarly confusing picture. In Ancient Egyptian paintings, the Amazigh are shown to have light skin, whereas Roman mosaics show darker skins. Early cave paintings in the

Sahara depict black figures driving cattle, but in later artworks they are joined by whiter skinned people. Yet despite the uncertainty, most can agree that the Amazigh were the original inhabitants of North Africa, who developed a sophisticated rural culture that long predates the first foreign colonisers of Tamazgha. They were a truly indominable people, with flourishing agriculture in the fertile north, nomadism in the south and trade flowing across the Mediterranean as early as 3,000 BC.

A fierce independence and rebellious spirit means that the Amazigh have never truly been conquered. Despite the endeavours of countless empires who tried to make Tamazgha their own, the Amazigh took on all comers and had an ingenious strategy to ensure their survival. When powerful empires arrived on their shores, the Amazigh would abandon their coastal towns and retreat to the desert interior, where they knew the invaders could never survive. Then, as the conquerors captured the coasts, the Amazigh would wait and regroup, until a moment arose to strike back with vengeance. Sometimes it took weeks; sometimes many decades, but the Amazigh would always fight back, emerging from the desert a renewed force that would retake the coasts when the invading empire inevitably splintered, or melted away in the fierce desert heat.

They were a seemingly unconquerable people, although Tamazgha itself was far from united. Tribal feuding and political rifts were typical of the early Amazigh communities, who owed their allegiance to clans and tribes, rather than a nation state. Internal bickering seemed certain to tear them apart, but it did not. Despite their political differences, the Amazigh remained culturally united and bound together by a common fighting spirit that endures to the present-day. They practiced the same kind of belief system, worshipping anything that gave life and connected them to Tamazgha and the open skies. Along the banks of the Nile, Amazigh worshipped the water buffalo, whereas in the sun-baked west where drought was common, they worshipped sheep. Even when Islam swept to these shores in the seventh century, the Amazigh adapted the new faith to include their existing beliefs. It meant that while invasion was common, conquests never lasted long and so the Amazigh identity could seep deep into the fabric of surrounding civilisations. At least two pharaohs of Egypt, five emperors of Rome and three popes have been of Amazigh origin.

I remember first reading about the Amazigh people at school, in a creased old textbook gathering dust in the library. I recall little of what was written, aside from the Amazigh's two names: the 'barbarians' and the 'free people.' Somewhere, in the back of my mind, they have been lingering ever since. Today, most North Africans can trace their ancestry back to Amazigh roots. It is a lineage that reaches back thousands of years, but while the Amazigh spirit has stood the test of time, today the Maghreb is bound together by another powerful identity that unites the Arab world from Oman in the east to Morocco in the 'extreme west.' That identity is a fusion of Arabism and Islam, on which Morocco and every Maghrebi nation has been grounded since independence. Where their predecessors failed, the Arabs have succeeded, binding the region from its coast to the foreboding desert interior as one.

Until recently, to espouse an Amazigh identity was severely disapproved of. It was seen to undermine the Arabo-Islamic project and thus threaten the unity of the modern Maghrebi nations. There was simply no room in the region for an alternative binding force, and so the history, language and culture of the Amazigh people, whose ancestors have occupied Tamazgha for some 12,000 years, were squeezed to the very fringe of society. Their spirits were dampened, histories falsified, beliefs disparaged and traditions quashed, the 'free people' free no more. Even their cherished language, Tamazight, was prohibited from being taught in schools and the very idea of an Amazigh identity was considered an egregious assault on the new Arab unity in the region.

Yet the Amazigh are unyielding. Since the revolutionary flames of the Arab Spring swept across the Maghreb in 2011, the Amazigh have found a voice that they have since refused to relinquish. Once again, Tamazgha is ablaze with the horns of rebellion and in Morocco, things *are* starting to change. After years of autocratic rule under King Hassan II, his son, Mohammed VI, is considered a popular and reformist king. In 2001, two years after ascending to the throne, he issued a royal decree, or *dahir*, that declared his intentions to reverse legal discrimination against the Amazigh and reinstate their place in the kingdom's history. And now, since the Arab Spring, the Amazigh can teach Tamazight in schools again and Moroccan parents are no longer forced to pick names for their children from a list of government-sanctioned Arab names.

But the sailing has not been smooth. Much was promised after the Arab Spring, but little has been realised in practice and just two months ago, in October 2016, protests erupted again in the nation's infamously rebellious northern hills: the Rif. What began as isolated anger within the coastal city of Al Hoceima has since morphed into a much broader movement that demands an end to rampant corruption, police brutality and regional neglect. The protests rage on today. The Arab Spring has ushered in the tides of change and Morocco, and Tamazgha, are stood at the crossroads again. Arabism and Islam remain the glue of this conservative kingdom, yet so much is also changing. Modernity is facing-off against tradition in the cities, while nomadism is being shunned for the security of a sedentary life in the countryside. More extreme strands of Islamism are on the rise again. So too are the Amazigh, and tonight, as the rhythm of those pounding drums rises to our ears again, I cannot shake the desire to understand that paradox and find out what all these waves of change mean for the Amazigh who inhabit this land.

Soon I can. We depart for the east at dawn, but tonight we sit and admire the wonders of another land. The Arabs have long known this region as the Maghreb, the land of the setting sun, ode to the fact that once the souks of Damascus and Mecca are struck with moonlight, the red city is blushed pink with the embers of evening. But now here too the square is lit electric white, as the masses flood to the medina souks and circle the steaming grills like pilgrims in a timeless ritual. This city is an awe-inspiring clash of worlds. A perfect metaphor, if you like, for a kingdom rooted in the sands of Africa, yet oriented east to the prevailing winds of Arabia. At dawn we depart east for the High Atlas, across the mountain passes and into the heartland of the Amazigh, at the edge of the desert plateau. My heartbeat rises with the quickening tempo of the evening.

2

Tea in a Moonlit Souk

High Atlas, Ouarzazate

This is December, but certainly not as I know it. Despite kicking off both my shoes and socks, still I roast in the front passenger seat of our rusted, dented and entirely odd-doored Citroën C-Élysée hire car. It's a slow cooker. We are headed east towards the Tizi n'Tichka mountain pass: a notorious string of asphalt draped across the High Atlas between the red city and Ouarzazate, reaching to the edge of the desert plateau. This is a formidable route. The caravan trail used to climb over these tall mountains and so wild is this place that barbary lions roamed here until the mid-20th century. Even today, as we slalom through switchbacks that clamber over the highest major mountain pass in all North Africa, we gaze down on eagles that soar beneath us.

Remote though we are, evidently the concept of window shopping has reached the High Atlas, because for mile after grueling mile, tradesmen have positioned themselves on the apex of switchback bends with their arms outstretched, wielding what appear to be rocks or some kind of gemstone, which they hold to our car window. Others stand further back at small trade stands that hug the metal railing, flogging earthenware pots, urns, or coiled fossils. Eventually, curiosity gets the better of us and we grind to a halt near the upper reaches, where a lonely trade stand teeters some 100 metres above the valley floor. I have never seen alike: gigantic ammonite fossils coil like giant vipers, frozen in wedges of dark rock, beside gemstones and geodes of quite impossible size and colour that glean in the midday sun. They come in ludicrous shades of neon blue, bright pink and deep blood red. I want to ask the tradesman if they are genuine, but as his arms flail as if conducting an orchestra as he promises the very best deals on the entire Tizi n'Tichka, I doubt the worth of such a question.

But I have good reason to believe that they are. The High Atlas and the drylands to our near east are among the most geo-diverse areas on Earth, flooded with natural history and vast mineral wealth. Discoveries of dinosaur bones and footprints are frequently made in the Kem Kem Beds, which lie along the border with Algeria, near to the Erg Chebbi desert where soon we shall journey. The remains of a Spinosaurus, the largest predatory dinosaur and the first known semi-aquatic dinosaur, were found there as well … at the very edge of the world's largest sand desert. Indeed, an astonishing array of curious, prehistoric sea creatures can be found scattered across the Moroccan Sahara, which, millions of years ago, was a shallow inland sea. Amazigh families have made a living from the restoration of these fossils for generations, while others profit from the land's mineral richness, such as its wealth of precious metals and rare gemstones.

With such an intriguing display, I can understand why my eyes had not been drawn at first to our equally curious surrounds. Almost 2,000 metres above sea level, the air is cool and rarefied and life around here is hard. Across the fall of a valley, the earthen clay settlement of Aït Ben Ammar clings to precarious tiers of dusty earth that slice up the hillside. It is almost entirely camouflaged into the solemn and umber earth upon which it stands. No wonder we had not seen it at first. This is our first glimpse of the other side of this kingdom, beyond the increasing glitz and modernity of its west. I ask the tradesman if he lives in the village and he nods with a meek smile, as his eyes drift once more towards his settlement. The occasional satellite dish hangs awkwardly from a roof-top, but that besides, I wonder if this roadside corner is their only real connection to a world beyond these mountains. No roads reach across the valley. Instead, a lonely mule track rises from a wadi and traces the contours of the terrain to the edge of the village, where a neat mosaic of colourful clothes dries on the steep and otherwise naked earth.

Once more the road kicks skyward as we journey across land that is barren. At times snow piles at the roadside and only the birds that soar beside us induce life to otherwise desolate surrounds. Suddenly, I am struck with newfound respect for the caravans who passed over these high mountains centuries ago, on their journey from across the Sahara. The High Atlas is a formidable wall of rock, strung from the Atlantic to the Mediterranean and housing North Africa's highest peaks in its midst. Today its passing is easy and at long last, we have sight of the far side of the kingdom. Once more we pause by the roadside, high on the pass, and allow our eyes to run free over a new vista. Still in the foreground there are mountains, but beyond them the dry and dusty lowlands of the east sprawl to a desert frontier. A hazy shimmer hangs on the far horizon, veiling the enormity of what lies beyond.

Here, on the roof of the High Atlas, there is a frontier feel. We have crossed a significant line, passing from the Morocco of new into what the colonialist French once knew as the *Bled es-Siba*. Before us is the heartland of the Amazigh. Now we are in desert country.

Ouarzazate, the provincial capital of the east, stands at the head of the mighty Drâa Valley, the date basket of Morocco, some 1,000 metres high on the eastern plateau. This broad valley is nothing short of a natural wonder and from here to the desert, which is now just 200 miles away, almost every single settlement clings to a string of sinuous oases that snake with the banks of the Drâa, once the mightiest river in the region. They finally run dry by Zagora, at the desert's edge.

These are tribal and nomadic lands where most speak Tamazight, the language of the Amazigh, and already its symbols are as commonly seen as the Arabic and French of Marrakech to our west. Every great ruler of the ages, from the kings of Carthage to the emperors of Rome, knew of the Drâa and the strategic importance of its valley. It was along this slice of oasis palm green that the camels of trans-Saharan trade were driven to cities across the High Atlas, laden with gold from Timbuktu and West Africa. Darkened skins in the oases to our south speak of the legacy of that trade. Many Draoui, as the valley population are known in Arabic, originate from Mali and Mauretania, and while the date palm groves may no longer thud to the march of caravans, one thing has remained constant across the years: these lands are proudly Amazigh and you can sense it instantly in their writing that emblazons many a storefront and road sign in tifinagh script.

While many great empires set their sights on conquering the Drâa, barely any lasted long enough to leave their mark in the sand. In truth, the free people of these drylands have never really been conquered and while early invaders arrived with ambition, the Amazigh rose as one to oppose them – each and every time. There may indeed have been political rifts among them, but the Amazigh were bound in unity around a proud culture and a fiercely territorial identity. When the first foreign colonisers arrived on the North African shores in the ninth century BC, Amazigh tribes were quick to make a stand. Traders from Phoenicia, a prosperous empire in the eastern Mediterranean, had been establishing trading posts along the North African coast for hundreds of years, but in 814 BC, they settled on the shores of modern-day Tunisia and intended to stay. They called their settlement Carthage.

Legend has it that Phoenician queen Dido shipwrecked her vessel off the North African coast and discovered a peninsula jutting strategically into the sea. When Dido asked the local Amazigh chieftain if she could settle a city on the peninsula, she was only allowed to purchase a parcel of land the size of the skin of an ox. Dido agreed and proceeded to slice the ox skin into fine strips that were stretched long enough to encircle an entire citadel, and the sprawling city of Carthage was born. Sure enough, the Amazigh had met their first tactful contender to the lands they knew as Tamazgha. While a treaty signed between Carthage and the Amazigh limited the expansion of the city, by the fifth century BC Carthage had ballooned and become one of the wealthiest cities in the ancient world.

At first, relations were peaceful. The Carthaginians called the shots of local trade and the Amazigh started to worship their gods, but swift expansion of Carthage into Amazigh land and along the fertile banks of the Wadi Majardah soon sparked resistance. In 241 BC, patience wore thin and the Amazigh rebelled, sweeping from the high mountains to capture swathes of Carthage's territory. It was a short-lived endeavour, but soon a number of Amazigh tribal republics begun to spawn around Carthaginian lands, where, despite the influence of the eastern settlers, the Amazigh culture and traditions continued to thrive. In their typical style, the Amazigh retreated to the hinterlands, but soon they emerged as some of the greatest horse riders of the age. The Amazigh demanded tribute from Carthage and forced the city-state to strike favourable treaties with the local Amazigh chieftains. Come the 2nd century BC and Rome was on the stage, seeking the support of the powerful Amazigh in their bid to cripple Carthage. Defeat duly followed as Carthage was razed and the land on which it fell was symbolically cursed forever.

The first foreign colonisers of Tamazgha were gone, but the legions of Rome had taken their place. Despite fighting with the Amazigh in the defeat of Carthage, the Romans found the Amazigh an unruly and rebellious people. They brandished them the 'barbarians' – later to become 'Berbers' – for their attacks on the legions as they fought to settle the expanding Roman Empire. Tamazgha was a land of fierce contest, as the powerful invaders from the north sought to subdue the rebels of the desert. At first, they tried to divide and conquer, luring tribes from the larger tribal confederations with the promise of wealth and power, until trust had been broken and unity of the Amazigh tribes crumbled. Then they switched to governance, sending rulers to each tribal region to win the loyalty of the Amazigh, before granting them autonomy.

But rebellion in the hinterlands was relentless. When the Romans had to travel across their North African empire, they would only travel by sea, because they knew the chances of tribal attack along the much shorter overland routes. The Romans had strengths to their advantage, but the pesky Amazigh would always play hardball. When the Roman Empire rejected Christianity, most North Africans embraced the faith. Then, when Rome adopted Christianity, the region's free people had a change of heart and were swayed by the tenets of Donatism. In strict contradiction to the will of Rome, the Donatists glorified martyrdom and found piety in the tombs of those who resisted Rome, as much as the churches of the Christian order. Saint Augustine, an Amazigh himself, preached against it, but it was too late; Christianity across North Africa had already been split in two.

Swathes of Tamazgha would remain under Roman grasp for some 700 years, until the constant assault of tribal rebellion became too hard to subdue. Rebellions, uprisings and religious conflict crippled Roman authority, which eventually collapsed in 429 when the brutal nomadic Vandals swept in from the east and destroyed every lasting remnant of Roman civilisation. The indominable Amazigh had weathered Roman rule with their identity almost intact, yet, already, the next protagonist was making its way to the scene. On the Arabian Peninsula, the flames of divine revelation were raging their way westwards along the North African coast, sweeping up all in their path. As it happened, Carthage, the Romans and Vandals were merely a prelude for what was soon to follow as the Arab conquests tore across this land with a new language, law and religion. More than a millennium on, the conquerors from the east remain in place today. The Amazigh would soon face a challenge unlike any they had faced before.

Remnants of the many invaders are clear to see this evening in the number of languages that adorn the storefronts in Ouarzazate, a town that sprung from the dust under Arab rule itself. Apparently, its name means 'without noise' in Tamazight, which is odd, because as my eyes drift across the street from our little roadside café, they catch sight of a market that is erupting into evening life. This is fortunate. We are only pit stopping here for mango juice en route to our overnight halt in the Dadès Gorge, but this is the last major settlement on our journey to the Erg Chebbi and we are still to acquire appropriate desert clothing. Our Western, infidel clothes will be useless if we encounter the conditions that are typical of the desert winter: hot, blistering days, tearing winds, freezing nights, vicious sandstorms. Not to forget the many long hours spent straddling the hump of a lumbering dromedary.

By sundown tomorrow, we will rendezvous with Salim, a cameleer of proud nomadic roots, who is awaiting our arrival in the dusty town of Hassi Labied at the foot of the Erg Chebbi dunes, a whipped island of shifting sand on the Sahara's western fringe. He will guide us into its depths and up to the Algerian border, which is closed. I want to discover what remains of nomadism in Morocco today and meet the hardy Amazigh who live on the geographical and societal edge.

In one corner of the market, a messy jumble of djellabas hangs outside what appears to be someone's home and, no – I didn't know what a djellaba was either. Not until the characterful little fellow who stands beside us appeared seemingly from nowhere to explain that these loose, pointy-hooded and woolen robes are, indeed, djellabas. Almost everyone in town – man, woman, child, dog, and donkey – is sporting one. Evidently, if you don't have a djellaba draping from your neck to your feet in desert country, you're a nobody.

Moroccans, like all their Arab brothers, come alive when day begins to fade, and it seems that we have just awoken this gentleman from an afternoon slumber. He rubs his eyes wearily and invites us, with sleepy enthusiasm, through a curtained door and up a dim staircase festooned with fluffy carpets in fifty shades of red. Our new friend is whirring into life like an old computer. A rather lethargic introduction is soon replaced with increasingly dramatic facial expressions, as he sniffs evening trade. As the curtained doors draw closed behind us, detaching us from the market beyond, the feeling of committal is immediate.

Up top, however, I wonder if we have strayed into the living room of an impulsive Arab hoarder. Never have I seen such a messy jumble of eccentric wares in such claustrophobic surrounds. Silver daggers and earthen plates adorn every wall, above shelves that are dotted with an assortment of pottery and strung with a tangle of jewellery that glistens in crystal and quartz. The floor is cluttered with contorting shisha pots and intriguing gold cases, grand statues and curvaceous urns, carvings of animals and mountains of silverware, African drums and decorated shields, shining mirrors and rusted teapots, all heaped upon numerous layers of thick red carpet that induce a bizarre sensation of weightlessness. It's as if we've just caught our new friend counting his loot from a heist on a lost pyramid of Giza. Then, suddenly, from amongst the muddle, a hand shoots in my direction.

"My name is Rachid," our new friend introduces himself proudly with a prolonged, wrist-snapping handshake and a smile warm enough to melt steel. He shakes us welcome to Morocco, before tweaking his moustache and returning his hands to their resting place on his belly, which bulges from beneath a pale and thinly-striped djellaba.

"Welcome, my friends, to my palace. Let's talk djellabas. But first, please!" he rubs his hands. "You allow me to make you tea." On that cue, we exchange a knowing glance. You see, tea in Morocco is the ultimate deal-maker and tourist-breaker. With tea on the table, there will be no easy way out of this barter, and that's fine. There is business to do. It is at this point that we are introduced to Khalil, co-owner of Rachid's wacky emporium, who is wielding a steaming pot of Berber whisky in his left hand. He proceeds to pour the drink into four shot-like glasses as we are seated with Rachid around a low and ornate table that is cocooned by the muddle.

"The first is as bitter as life." Khalil launches suddenly into poetry. His voice is echoey, gnarly and monotone. "The second is as strong as love, and the third …" he spears his eyes quickly past the three of us, "is as soothing as death!"

I flinch in my seat as both Khalil and Rachid howl with laughter, before they both diverge into coughing fits.

"Haha! You daft fox, Khalil," Rachid booms after a lengthy interlude, "you scare my guest! That's what we say, friends, when we pour tea. In Morocco, you will always have three glasses of Berber whisky, each with a different taste to the last. That is the magic!"

Berber whisky, as the locals know it, is sugary, sweet mint tea, but across the Maghreb, it is so much more than just a drink. Tea is a pillar of social life, like wine to an Italian or coffee to a Finn. Introductions, farewells, ceremonies and celebrations simply do not take place in the absence of tea and on my journeys to follow, barely an hour will pass without a shot or three of the sweet stuff. In a country of Islamic faith, Berber whisky is the closest most can get to an alcoholic kick. Serving tea in Morocco is a process not dissimilar to the formal tea ceremonies of Japan. It is virtually a ritual, with tea prepared in front of guests and poured from a height to improve its flavour – and, most importantly, to show respect. The higher you thrust the teapot, the greater respect you show, so much so that the King of Morocco is rumoured to have official tea pourers, who stand on ladders to pour him a glass. A day in Morocco simply cannot go on without a glass, or three, of loose-leaf, Chinese gunpowder green tea, topped liberally with sugar and stuffed with generous handfuls of mint.

Nobody knows for certain how tea found its way to Morocco, but availability spiked in the mid-19th century when the Crimean War forced blockaded merchants of the British East India Company to divert tea destined for the Baltics to ports in Morocco. Rumor says that they came ashore and evidently it proved popular, because mint tea today is an emblem of the nation. Here you will find tea being served cross-legged by the roadside, or on neat little rugs by travelling tea traders in the mayhem of a back-alley souk. Enter a family home and tea has been served, leave the hammam and a glass will be poured, wander into the lair of a rug merchant and tea is the open door for business to begin. To refuse is to neglect a cornerstone of this communal society and so, despite the feeling of irretractable commitment, we are in.

"And please," Rachid continues, "I make you dinner also. Tagine, couscous, what you say?"

Broke student ears perk up, but I lie quickly that we have just eaten. Sat beside us around the low table, a splendid blue turban spirals atop Rachid's head. His abyssal eyes grow larger as he talks and a moustache flaps like the wings of a bird at the slightest twitch of his face. With tea poured, Matt reminds our host that we are in the market for djellabas, so Rachid instantly dispatches Khalil to fetch a box that is overflowing with a tangle of heavy jewellery that he spreads across the table in front of us. Some fifty items – metal bangles, gem-encrusted necklaces, silver rings – are divided into three equisized piles, for each of us to inspect. Disturbing volumes of Berber whisky are drunk before Rachid pauses his auction, just briefly, to offer an introduction to his local area. You may not have heard of Ouarzazate, but you have almost certainly seen its surrounds. Just down the road is the world renown Atlas Studios, by size the largest film studios in the world, as well as a host of destinations that are favourites with location scouts, such as the earthen clay ksar of Aït Benhaddou.

"My friends … you have seen Gladiator. The Mummy. Star Wars." Rachid's voice has a sudden sense of mystery. He continues: "Prince of Persia. The Black Hawk is Down. Arabian Lawrence. Yes, yes! All of them filmed here. Right here, in Ouarzazate." He returns his hands to his belly and leans back in a small chair, beaming a smile of pride.

A second pot of tea is delivered to the table by Khalil. The mango juice had given me a sugar rush in the café, but now I am borderline high, no doubt part of their ploy to make a spending spree sound like an excellent idea. There is no way we are getting out of here with all our dirhams in hand, whether we like his djellabas or not. The tea has committed us and I've lost all sense of time in this dim and windowless room, where the passing of time seems to be measured not by a clock, but by the downing of shots of Berber whisky. Rachid returns swiftly to his jewellery auction, which is still struggling to gain traction.

"My friend, this one!" he turns to me with a chunky metal ring in hand, "is *perfect* for your girlfriend." His words are delivered with such conviction that it would be preposterous to decline his offer, let alone inform him that I do not actually have a girlfriend. Then, he swivels to Katharine. "This!" he lifts a shining silver bangle high above the table, "would look great on your boyfriend. He will love you … even more!" Then it is the turn of Matt, who is also single. "And you, my friend … finally! For your wife."

Considerable time and gallons of tea have come and gone, but still we sit around the cluttered table with Rachid, auctioning jewellery we never once expressed an interest in. A careful conversation must therefore begin, where we balance commending his wares with a clear indication that we are not really interested but many thanks for the tea and no, we really must not have any more. Painfully deep into the evening, talk finally returns to djellabas and Rachid leads us to a small, dark side-room that is festooned with them. It is at this moment, with sugar pulsating through my veins, that I decide it a matter of absolute necessity that I also acquire a Tuareg turban, Amazigh rug (which I'm fairly sure is a prayer mat) and desert pants so ridiculously baggy they could easily accommodate the three of us in the desert.

"Okay!" At last Khalil steps forward as Rachid retreats to a darkened corner behind the cover of shisha pots. Until now, he has been the tea boy, but now it makes sense: while Rachid is the charmer of this operation, Khalil is the dealmaker. All of this time, we have been drinking sweet mint tea in *his* lair, and now it's time to talk dirhams.

"These items. How much you pay?"

Realising how easily I could offend our hosts, I instantly break rule number one of bartering with a Berber and ask Rachid to offer an indicative price for my four items. He picks up a notepad and begins his calculations, swiping his pen melodramatically across the page as if lost in the art of calligraphy. Thirty seconds pass before the pen is put down and the pad slapped against the table.

"This is it!" he proclaims with a throaty bellow. "The absolute best price for you, my friend. A student discount! Ha, yes … you know, a student discount? You are young and we sit together and we drink tea and we talk, so I do the *velly* best price, just for you. What you say?"

Khalil, who is managing to pull off a smile that is at the same time friendly and entirely menacing, has circled, underscored and emboldened *1,250 dirhams* at the bottom of the pad. That's £100, I work out after some sluggish mental arithmetic.

"Yes, good deal, good price!" he says as I return a blank stare. His moustache droops and smile melts to a sulking frown. "Okay, friend – come. Let's talk. How much you say?"

I suggest 500 dirhams. It's way lower than his starting price and already Khalil's face is warning me to tread lightly, but rule number two of bartering with a Berber is ringing clear in my ears: start low, or else you'll have nowhere to go. Khalil lowers his tone and steps in towards me. The room is claustrophobic, the mood uneasy.

"We have to be realistic, my friend," he says bluntly. "This material is *velly, velly* good quality. You will not find a better price out there." He motions his hand towards the dim staircase, before presenting it to be shook on his asking price, daring me to launch a rebuttal. His eyes seem to burn through mine like staring at the sun. It feels like the walls of his cluttered lair are closing in as I ponder my next move, the staircase narrowing, the market beyond detached. I am now inextricably in this deal. The tea and the passing of time has committed me, but I cannot do that price. I do not have the dirhams, so I draw upon the third golden rule: move in small increments. Six hundred, I now propose, as Khalil's face morphs to that of a grumpy cat.

"Come, come, my friend," he ushers me towards the staircase, "I show you the *exact* money that the last couple from England-land pay me for these items in the cupboard. Friend – they pay me 1,250!"

Maybe. But if there is one thing more intrinsic to this culture than tea, it is bartering. Here it is a sport, a fine art, a fact of life. In a souk or the store of a merchant, the initial asking price is never a done deal … and so the evening crawls, as our figures edge slowly closer. Finally, we agree on 550 dirhams for the djellaba, desert pants and my turban, but the rug is the final hurdle. Every Amazigh rug is patterned with the design of a particular tribe, a design that speaks of its greatest battles, history and homeland. I have found one that I want, but Khalil insists that I need a bigger one.

"This one is far, far too small for your room," he cries, insisting he knows my house better than I. He won't budge, so I am forced to deploy rule number four of bartering with a Berber, the riskiest of all, yet almost universally the most effective when a deal hangs in the balance: the walkout technique.

On my travels to follow, no method will serve me better than the walkout when engaged in a hearty barter. Many a taxi driver has called back after me as I threatened to walk away, *"monsieur, okay, I accept,"* and the most stubborn tradesmen have shaken hands after a seemingly unmovable exchange. This is the last, most potent arrow in your quiver and finally, stomachs growling at the lateness of the hour, hands are shaken on 750 dirhams for the lot. Once again, Rachid emerges from the cover of decorative cacti to rejoin the fray and as we depart with more arm-wrenching handshakes, I sense, with relief, that the mounting tension was all performance to close out a hard-fought deal.

Now the moon hangs in orange-brushed mauve above the twilight souk of Ouarzazate, as we canter into the evening and head hastily for the Dadès Gorge. Here I feel how a prisoner might at their moment of release: free, yet ruing the departure from some characters left behind. What an encounter. Still my pulse races from the intensity of those eyes and the tension as we threatened to walk away. But most of all, I buzz from the fact we had been welcomed into someone else's culture with open arms and allowed to revel in it. At last, we are in the heartland of the Amazigh: audacious tradesmen, yet equally the most bounteous of hosts. There is an energy to the evening. It is much less abrupt than the Jemaa el-Fna, yet richer and more personal. I cannot tame a smile that runs loose across my face as we depart east for Dadès, the taste of sweet mint tea still coating my tongue.

3

Valley of the Kasbahs

Dadès Gorge

Night falls fast in the valley of the Drâa. Just moments ago, our increasingly rocky and arid surrounds were tinged with the glorious orange of an Atlas twilight. Groves of date palm and olive had strung a ribbon of oases that snaked through the Valley of the Kasbahs, but now the night has consumed them. There are no artificial lights here, tainting the depths of the night and illuminating the asphalt that arcs ahead above precipitous drops. We should have arrived long before now. Driving down this road is no place to be at this hour.

My senses are heightened, as I scan the road with increasing intent for one thing: maniacal cyclists, uniformly dressed in black and with no lights or sense of self-preservation on these serious, twisting mountain roads. They ride like ghosts through the night, invisible until we are almost upon them, until it is almost too late. We arc around a bend, scan the apex, our lights swooping across the valley walls opposite, and then – woah! Out of the saddle and kicking up a climb, a rider is upon us in the darkness. Settlements are few and far between, so I wonder where they have all come from and how far they are going through the valley. Trucks thunder past the other way and dimly-lit motorcycles chatter around our outside. It is as if a Tour de France stage is taking place on a live motor racing circuit – at night, on a perilous mountain road, with no floodlights.

It is therefore a welcome relief when our overnight halt, an ancient kasbah nestled deep in the Dadès Gorge, finally aligns with our GPS. Arriving in sparse Tinghir Province under the cover of night, our surrounds are shrouded in an allure of mystery.

"Salam! Bienvenu! Wilkommen! Allez, allez, allez!" A young man at the kasbah door is shouting at me in a dozen languages.

"Salam, good evening," I say back to him.

"Ahh, the Americans are here! Everybody, they're here!" he beams back, baffled by our fusion of accents. "Come on in, friends. A tagine is cooking!"

Yassine seats us for dinner in a cold and textile-laden room, where a log fire crackles in one corner. It seems to be achieving little. He disappears into the kitchen, but returns almost immediately with a basket full of bread. Soon we are to learn that the only thing as commonplace in Morocco as sweet mint tea, which has already been poured, is bread. Whatever the meal, if you have ordered food, it is coming with bread. It is the staple of this kingdom and the unifier of rich and poor, hence the Moroccan proverb: 'manage with bread and butter until God sends honey.' In fact, up until the 1980s most families would bake their own bread each morning and, even today, wander into any souk across this kingdom at dawn and your nose will be drawn to the aroma of freshly baking bread, surrounded by locals collecting their daily supply.

The tagine top is thrust skyward. Yassine perches himself across the room from us on a low wooden stool where he stokes the dying flames with fresh tinder. Retreating his arm as it crackles and sparks, waves of heat wash across the room, tingling our cold-nipped skin.

"Have you always lived here, in the Dadès Gorge?" Matt asks him, as means of introduction.

"Almost," he says. "I was born in the valley, and my father owned this kasbah. And then, when we finished our studies, he gave it to me and my brother. But when I was younger, I studied in Marrakech." He looks up from the fire and shrugs softly. "It was fine … but the city is a strange place! I did not feel natural there. There are opportunities, but not for everyone. Many are still poor, and there is little they can do."

Yassine returns to stoking the fire. He pauses, but says eventually: "I must tell you, friends. Those years I was away were very difficult for me. Dadès is a special place. You will see tomorrow! Life here is hard, but the land is very beautiful. Still the valley is rich in Amazigh culture and nomads still roam. We still follow our traditions.

"Meanwhile, in the city," he sweeps a hand away from him, as if to shoo a cat, "there is so much going on. But life here is easier to understand."

Yassine asks about our onward journey and we tell him our route: through the gorge to the oasis town of Tinghir, the provincial capital, then southeast to Erfoud, and then Merzouga and Hassi Labied, by the desert's edge. We are going right up to the border in the Erg Chebbi.

"Perhaps we'll cross to Algeria by camel," I jest.

"They will shoot you!" he says bluntly. "The border is closed and it has been for some 20 years. Our countries do not get along and it has caused so many problems for the nomads! They cannot roam the desert anymore." He shakes his head wearily. "I am not fond of change. I am sorry to tell you, friends, but you are not going to be staying with real nomads in the desert. Today, there are very few. It is unfortunate, but nomadism today is for the bold or the foolish. Many of the nomads are actually guides, who work in tourism. When the tourists are not here, they move back to the towns.

"But you will see Algeria," he says conciliatorily. "The border is a long dark wall of rock that runs across the horizon, patrolled by guards. Anyone who tries to cross, they will shoot. Beyond it is Algeria ... and the real nomads."

There has been talk of a hike into the gorge tomorrow morning. It will be led by his brother. Our stay here was only meant to be a stop-over on the long journey east to the desert, but our arrival was late and Yassine has proven to be an intriguing host with pride in his land. We want to learn more about his valley and the Amazigh families who live here, but Yassine is wary; the hike may not be possible.

"It has been weeks since I last guided in the gorge," he warns, "and now the wadis are starting to fill with the torrents of winter. The route may not be passable."

Eventually, we pencil a plan. Time is against us, so Yassine suggests an Alpine start, departing with the dawn and gauging the conditions as we go. We will hike in the understanding that the wadis may well force us to retreat. Yassine himself will guide us; his brother is staying down the valley with family and will not be able to arrive by that early hour. I am delighted with the plan.

With our desert gear piled on the table, there is a sense of impending adventure, as we hunker down for a cold and bitter night. Tomorrow, we explore a land of many unknowns. Tonight, I sleep in wonderment for what the dawn may bring.

The sun is brushing across a broad valley of moon-like proportions. Daybreak is welcome relief after a cold and rather uncomfortable night, and as I swing open the heavy wooden window shutters, which are stiff with the frost, Yassine's promise of a fine dawn vista is realised. Shadows and cuts of early day light stripe the surrounding hillsides that are daubed in shades of orange and grey, but mostly an other-worldly, dust red. Only the lone bird that swoops through the foreground and the young boy on a mule who paces slowly across the distant hills confirm that I am, indeed, still on planet Earth.

This morning Yassine is guiding us through a nearby gorge, which rises through red rock to a formation at its end known as the 'monkey fingers,' but the journey that lies ahead is far from certain. The gorges that surround us are carved by wadis: seasonal ravines and channels of water that are typically dry, but come alive with raging torrents as the winter rains set in and the spring snowmelt gushes down from the High Atlas. Winter is indeed setting in and these gorges can spring to life at the will of nature. No-one quite knows what we will discover.

Feet move swiftly through crisp morning air and I am thrilled that Yassine is our guide. It would have been great to meet his brother, but I want to get to know this humble young man that we are quickly gaining affection for. We drop down from his kasbah to the banks of the Oued Dadès and follow a faintly-beaten track on the grass that trails its edge. At times it is marshy, and at others it vanishes altogether beneath the cover of vegetation. Groves of almond, olive and fig line the route and we cross the river frequently on slick stones to follow a path of least resistance. Here in the rain shadow of the High Atlas, it appears that all natural life has congregated in this thin verdant ribbon that slithers along the river's edge. A buzzard takes flight from a walnut tree ahead. The marshy grasses around us are alive with chirping frogs, but beyond the river the valley is dry and parched. At the trailhead, a red mammoth of rock rises from the valley floor. Struck with shadows and tumbled with boulders, it looks barren and lifeless, every flank oozing rocky outcrops. It is where we head.

"Miles from here, this little river will eventually become the Drâa," Yassine says with a smile, "the longest river in all of Morocco." Come spring and the High Atlas snowmelt, the wadis that guide our direction will blossom, but now, as we pace the banks of the thin Oued Dadès, it is difficult to fathom how this slither of silvery-green water will soon rage a torrent, passed down from the High Atlas and carried all the way to its confluence with the Imini, where it forms the Drâa.

"But the Drâa is no longer the river that it once was," he continues. "Now, it is quite weak. It does not even reach the ocean and so many people who have relied on it for years have begun to struggle."

"What happened?" Katharine asks.

"A large dam was built near Ouarzazate in the 1970s," he says. "It was mainly constructed for irrigation that was desperately needed along the valley, but also to prevent floods and to provide hydroelectricity in Rabat. But since then, so much has changed down the Drâa and as the water dries up, many families in the southern oases can no longer tend to their livestock. It has become hard to grow food, and so many have had to move to the larger towns.

"It's not just the dam," he continues, "it's the climate as well. We notice it in Dadès too. The climate is definitely getting hotter."

Once the mightiest river in the region, nourishing a chain of oases strung along its valley, the Drâa now runs dry for much of the year as the desert tiptoes westwards and the mercury creeps skywards. Once it sustained a region of more than 1,000 kilometres, from the Sahara and the Atlas to the Atlantic; now it fails to reach the ocean. The climate is warming and so this land becomes ever-more parched.

The Draoui have always been a hardy bunch. Many have practiced temporal migration for generations, moving to the towns during times of crippling drought and sustaining multiple streams of income within each nomadic family to survive the harsher months. They are a resilient people, respectful of the thresholds of their environment, but in recent decades, life in the Drâa Valley has become extremely tough.

"Since the dam was built, around half the date palms in the southern foothills of the Atlas have died due to drought," Yassine explains. Date palms are the lifeblood of oasis communities, but as the water and agricultural yields dwindle in the valley, many families who have relied on the Drâa for generations have been forced to sell or consume much of their livestock. Rainfall here is sporadic at best, but is set to decrease by a further 30 percent over the next four decades. It means that many Draoui have been forced to abandon their age-old practices of circular migration and transhumance for a more secure but sedentary life in the towns and cities.

"Water in this valley is absolutely everything," Yassine says, as we ford yet another shallow wadi. "It has always decided who is powerful and who is wealthy. Things are not how they once were, but the valley is still quite divided and those who control the water have power."

Once it was the nomads who held control, both Amazigh and Arab tribes. They were militarily stronger than those who lived in the towns and ksars, who depended on the nomads for protection. In exchange, the nomads would receive food and the right to settle temporarily in their towns, and, over time, the nomadic tribes came to dominate life in this valley. In fact, up until the mid-20th century, hordes of looting nomads made life in the oasis towns a perilous existence, even under protection agreements with the more amicable tribes of neighbouring nomads. When the colonialist French arrived in 1932, the Drâa Valley was the definition of the *Bled es-Siba*, though colonial policy did little to relieve hardship for the sedentary Draoui. While the northern cities became the chosen centres for the French industrial project, the desert and drylands were mostly forgotten. Restrictions on pan-Saharan trade dealt the final blow for many Draoui, made worse by crippling annual droughts and ensuing famine.

"Today it is nomads who seek security in the oasis towns," Yassine explains, "while others leave the valley altogether for the north."

Yet the scars of the once-mighty Drâa have not faded, nor has the pride of the many Draoui who do still cut a life out here. This valley is home to some of Earth's most outrageous landscapes, and as we enter the gorge, which breaths in and narrows around us, I am struck by the starkness of this Martian land.

Slowly we climb through boulder-strewn passages and inch through narrow ravines, the trail rising and falling, the gorge twisting and narrowing, following a path cut by the wadi when it ran at its zenith. For now, it is dry. Towering red walls with jagged tops cocoon and dwarf us, as blue sky, whipped with feathery clouds, thins to a slither above. Spiky green bushes cling to red cliffs and trace the trail's edge, which is undefined and seldom trodden. Few pass through here. An enormous boulder has tumbled from above and wedged itself between the walls. It is the size of our saloon and we are forced to crawl under it, beyond which the gorge breaths in again, narrowing further still.

Millions of years ago, we would have been stood on the sea floor, surrounded by gigantic coral reefs. Over millennia, sandstone and limestone have been formed, forced skywards by movement in the Earth's crust and carving out the Atlas and this spectacular network of sinuous gorges. During the stormy season each winter, unimaginable quantities of water and debris rage through this gorge, chiselling away at its walls and forming the towering ravines through which we pass. Each winter storm widens and deepens the gorge, making the puzzle of its passage different come spring to the one it presented the preceding autumn.

We have made good ground, but are forced to pause by a problem that seems impassable. Beneath 100-metre-high walls that squeeze us into claustrophobia, a narrow right turn in the shadows ahead is filled with deep, icy water. Clearly, these seemingly dormant wadis *are* now springing into life. Yassine paces ahead of us to assess the impasse, but returns with a face of concern. He is a mountain goat, but we are most certainly not, and we have gained height slowly. Every scramble up to the next tier of the ever-rising gorge is followed by a sketchy descent through thin passages and unobvious cracks in the rock.

"I'm not sure," he says meekly. "I don't know if we can pass. The summit plateau isn't far now, but I am afraid of what lies ahead. We do not want to get stranded here."

Yassine returns once more to the icy pool, which fills the gorge to indefinite depths from wall-to-wall. He has scouted two possible routes through: we either wade into the icy water and see how deep it goes, or climb an awful wall to our left that bypasses the problem, but with a drop of some 15 metres to the sharp and water-covered rocks below, should we stumble. We test the water that rises instantly to our thighs, but quickly rule out the climb, which is of a grade I would tackle with reluctance on any bouldering wall back home.

The water quickly deepens as I pull my shorts as high as they will go and inch into the biting depths. With shoes and socks hoisted above the waterline, my balance is distorted and the stones under my feet as slick as ice, skittling about like marbles. I fully expect myself to tumble over backwards into the ice bath, dunking my shoes and evoking post-traumatic stress from Lapland.

"We cannot pass," Yassine declares abruptly. The water is just too deep, the stones too slick, the water-pooled route that arcs around the darkened corner too uncertain. Rock walls loom around us. Now I feel an isolation that I had not before. This place can come alive at the will of nature, with the arrival of a single storm, and now I can understand why this gorge is prone to flash floods that can render it impassable and deadly. I shudder at the thought of being caught here in bad weather, or without a guide. This gorge requires a local mind and Yassine knows it intimately, every scramble, passage and small gap in the rock that we pass through unexplainably.

"Let's try the climb," Matt decides. It is that or retreat and fail, but Yassine looks on with unease. In turn, we each follow Yassine up the sketchy climb and admire the height that we have gained, though our smugness is short-lived. A drop looms to our right, and now we must downclimb back to the damp gorge floor, beyond the water problem. Yassine reaches out his arms to fruitlessly stop any fall as we settle ourselves on the first tentative footholds. The wall is almost vertical, a drop teasing us below, but with our hearts in our mouths, we bundle down to a small rock ledge that eases our descent back into the gorge.

Soon the dryness of our clothes matters little, as we wade through yet more water-pooled sections that rise quickly to the furthest end of the gorge, where blue sky broadens once more and we emerge, at last, from the high red walls. This is the last push: a steep climb up the hillside to a lifeless, rock-strewn plateau of red dust rock, punctuated only by the occasional bunch of spiky vegetation, that has somehow cut an existence up here.

"I hope you agree it was worth it!" Yassine beams, as the summit plateau falls away at a balcony of rock, like a pulpit, gazing over a most astonishing vista. It certainly was. Like a ribbon of gold, one thousand gorgeous kasbahs line the road that we had driven along under the veil of darkness last night, snaking with the valley between high red walls. This morning they looked sombre, the colours of bare mountains, but now they are resplendent under the hues of a high Maghrebi sun. The kasbahs stream with the road through the dusty valley, beyond which the land kicks again to the dizzying heights of the Atlas, capped in glistening snow.

These kasbahs are proof of this valley's hostile and lawless past. One thousand years ago, when the trans-Saharan caravans flowed across this land, these remote valleys were the domain of bandits and thieves, who made its passage a perilous ordeal. So dangerous was the desert crossing that once goods reached these drylands from their exotic and far-flung origins, they were of extremely high value, and thus an appealing prize for thieves. These particular trade routes were known as 'salt roads,' as merchants would depart from the valley with salt, which at the zenith of desert trade was as valuable in weight as gold, to exchange for gold, ivory, leather and slaves in Timbuktu down south. Owing to its value, salt was even used as a currency here until the 20th century, when the French introduced paper money. In fact, that's where the word 'salary' came from. So much wealth flowed through this land that when Arab geographer Ahmad al-Ya'qubi journeyed here in the ninth century, he commented that gold and silver was 'found like plants and it is said that the wind blows it away.'

This made the caravans a prime target for the bandits of the valleys, and hence a market soon emerged for fortified compounds, where the merchants and their animals could safely stay. That is precisely why one thousand beautiful kasbahs flow through this valley today. These were fortified homes, built by the rich and powerful, defended by soldiers in four turreted corners who ensured that those inside were safe from the thieves, along with their precious cargoes. In exchange for a hefty tax, the merchants would have access to a granary, water supply, sleeping quarters – often under the open skies – somewhere to rest the animals, store wares, and a mosque. Many even had a pair of cemeteries, one for Jews and one for Muslims, as, owing to the perils of the desert crossing, not everyone survived the journey. With the tax, the kasbah owners of the valley accrued an incredible wealth and, even today, the sheer volume of caravan traffic and the enormity of the wealth that they carried through is clear to see in the panorama in front of us.

Yet most spectacular of all is the dramatic rock formation that rises diagonally from the valley floor to our left. The 'monkey fingers' stack like leaning matchsticks, each daubed in the gloriously rich colours of morning. Like a bamboo forest of rock, they jut and stack at angles, as if someone has run a knife along the hillside and sliced the rock into a thousand pieces that ooze and tumble in artistic sequence, falling to the valley floor like a landslide frozen in motion. Soon we must begin our descent across trackless ground in the rough direction of the wadi, but before we depart I still want to better understand Yassine's connection with this valley. He is a humble, educated and multilingual young man who knows of a life beyond these mountains. Clearly, it matters little. Today he has guided us with an indelible smile and an effortless stride. His land is wild and life is not easy. Perhaps that is its allure.

"There is a legend in our valley," Yassine says, "that the wind has a son who lives in Boumalne." He motions his hand down the valley, towards the provincial centre of Boumalne Dadès, which was founded to support the ancient practices of transhumance. "That is why he rips through this place each winter, to come and visit him."

Yassine's words are humbling. Come spring this valley will be alive with vibrant colour, the scurrying of young life and rushing wadis, but now the land is pale and braced for the onset of a harsh winter, which is already showing signs of imminent arrival.

"When the winter storms come to Dadès, they are very powerful," Yassine explains. "Now it is dry and for most of the year the wadis do not run. But if the snows are bad, as often they are, life will get harder for those who live in the hills." He looks at me briefly and shrugs softly. "Those who keep animals will struggle."

Untamed this valley may be, but there are great riches in these hills that have kept families settled for generations. In the mountains, they mine for silver and gemstones, like the ones flogged by the High Atlas traders, and there are acres of groves – floods of almond, olive and fig. The southernmost gorges are known for their growing of roses, which are made into rose water. In the nearby Vallée des Roses, legend has it that, decades ago, pilgrims returned from Mecca with the 'mother of all flowers,' the Damascus rose, which breathed life into the Moroccan rose industry. Then, early in the 20th century, parfumiers from France recognised the potential of this region for their industry, and the rest is history. Today roses are grown across hundreds of kilometres in the valley, which houses two distilleries for rose essence.

As we near the wadi, the little Amazigh village of Aït Ouglif is perched on a rise above the water. It is a simple settlement of earthen clay homes, where donkeys wander beneath colour washing strung on lines across dusty streets. It is Yassine's village, and he seems to know everyone. His neighbours greet us in Arabic as they complete their daily chores and kids laugh and wave, their eyes flooded with intrigue as they hurry from their yards to wish *salam* to these strangers passing through. As they do, I wonder if Yassine is their primary connection to a world beyond this valley, the man who brings outsiders with odd clothes and foreign mannerisms past their homes. There are no roads here, not one vehicle in sight. The nearest road trembles in the heat haze, across the verdant banks of the Oued Dadès, some distance away.

The complexities of the world beyond are slow to take root here. Nomadic families still reside in the surrounding mountains, some living in caves, while others move their livestock seasonally from the summer pastures of the High Atlas to their winter home up in the Jebel Saghro mountains, across the Drâa Valley to our southeast. In the spring and autumn they move across these lands with their camels and mules laden and it is here, on the edge of the desert plateau, that the land begins to rise towards the Atlas. Even Yassine's kasbah is higher than any point in the United Kingdom.

These nomads derive from once-mighty Amazigh tribes, who long ruled over these lands. Most nomads in the valley still belong to a tribe and consider themselves the people, or 'Aït,' of a shared homeland or ancestor. Notable among them are the Aït Atta from the Jebel Saghro, one of the most storied tribes of Amazigh nomads, who roamed these lands across the last millennium, dominating the sedentary populations of Draoui and becoming the valley's ruling elites. Nomadic tribes even played a crucial role in the Islamisation of the Maghreb during the Arab conquests. Or, more to the point, these Amazigh tribes almost stopped the Arabs in their tracks. No sooner had the pesky Romans been flushed out of North Africa, the first Arabian military missionaries started to march their way west – into the heart of Tamazgha.

The year was 666 AD. The Prophet Muhammed had died just three decades before and Arabia was awash with the spirit of religious fervour and divine revelation. Morocco, on the other hand, was seen in Arabia as a hotbed of backward infidels, who needed converting by the sword. While the first Islamic forays into North Africa were mostly carried out by pious groups acting alone, they were soon followed by a full-blown military campaign, intent on converting the entire Maghreb to the new faith. When the seat of the Arabian caliphate moved to Damascus from Medina, the time for religious war had come, and the order came from the caliph of the Umayyad Dynasty to begin the long march west.

Arabian general Uqba ibn Nāfi led from the front of a cavalry force that swept through deserts and mountains, to share the revelations. His horseback expedition covered some 8,000 kilometres, halting briefly in 670 to settle Kairouan in modern-day Tunisia, a strategic base for their future endeavours. Just a decade on from his departure from Arabia, he reached Morocco, crushing an Amazigh army so large that 'Allah alone could count them,' before defeating the Byzantines in rebuilt Carthage. Many Amazigh tribes were quick to embrace the new faith, which they combined with their traditional beliefs, and with Amazigh brothers by their side, the Umayyads had conquered most of North Africa by early in the eighth century. Now the region was under Arab rule, administered by the caliph's governors in Kairouan, while Uqba eventually met his fate in a battle against more resilient Amazigh in the Algerian desert. Where its predecessors failed, the Arabs had succeeded, uniting the unruly Amazigh under the banner of Islam and ensuring their compliance with the divine mission.

Yet, obviously, the rebellious Amazigh were not going to allow the Arabs to stomp across their lands without a fight. Islam was one thing, but Arab rule from a distant caliphate was quite another. Indeed, while many Amazigh embraced the new faith, many others were angry when Islam and Arab values began to replace the tribal practices and political idioms on which North African society had been rooted for millennia. For many Amazigh, Islam was not welcome at all. Prayer five times per day, the need to fast each year, pilgrimage to Mecca, and a call to jihad was a new world of discipline many were not willing to accept. These were 'free people,' doing as they pleased in the lands of their ancestors. Now they were answerable to a caliph in the distant east – and God!

Islam, then, did not guarantee the support of the Amazigh tribes at all. It sat awkwardly with their deeply matriarchal society and it was, in fact, a woman, Queen Dihyā, who led one of the most notorious Amazigh rebellions against Arab rule. Near the end of the seventh century, Queen Dihyā became the leader of the Amazigh tribes and marched in battle against the Umayyad Dynasty and its Islamic armies, which were encroaching on Amazigh lands. Once Carthage had fallen into the grip of the eastern caliphate, Umayyad general Hasan ibn al-Nu'man set out to find a new enemy worthy of his sword. Word had reached him that Dihyā, queen of the Amazigh, was the most powerful ruler in all North Africa, and so he set after her, in pursuit of her fabled Amazigh armies. They finally met in the Battle of the Camels, in modern-day Algeria, where Dihyā, true to her name, duly defeated Hasan and wiped out his entire invading army in the process.

Yet Dihyā had been badly shaken. In truth, she was no match for the sophisticated Umayyad armies, who were bound to return to exact their revenge. She panicked and turned to guerrilla warfare, beginning with a scorched earth campaign that burned Amazigh lands in order to starve the Arab armies, who were fast approaching. Her endeavour had little impact on the roaming nomads and tribes, but the sedentary oasis dwellers rose in fury. She had crippled their livelihood and in so doing hastened the enemy's advance, as allies within her own ranks started to turn against her. At the turn of the eighth century, Dihyā died in battle against the Umayyad armies, her sword in hand. According to a somewhat doubtful claim by Arab historian Ibn Khaldun, she was 127 years old. She nonetheless remains a symbol of Amazigh rebellion today, for her refusal to give in. Rebellions rumbled on for centuries, though the Amazigh would also march alongside the Arabs in battle, playing a key role in the invasion and subsequent Islamisation of Al-Andalus. But the Amazigh had already made their point: they were willing to resist Arab rule and had moulded the ways of the eastern invaders to suit their existing beliefs and culture. The Arabs may have been here for good, but soon the Amazigh were to rule Morocco once again.

Despite being a shadow of their former selves, tribes such as the Aït Atta, who predate the arrival of the Arabs and Islam, continue to shape life along the Drâa as they have for millennia. At the pinnacle of trans-Saharan trade, they were the dominant tribe of these lands. Unrivalled knowledge of the lifeless Jebel Saghro, which means 'the mountains of drought,' made them integral to the survival of the merchant caravans, and with it came power and wealth. Even today, the nomadic Aït Atta play an important role in delivering goods to some of the region's most remote communities. They form a large tribal confederation that lives, in much reduced number, across south-eastern Morocco. Anyone who believes that nomadism in this corner of Africa is resigned to the depth of the Sahara or Sahel is, fortunately, very much mistaken.

Now the Oued Dadès flows to our left, over which a stone bridge arcs to complete the loop back to Yassine's kasbah. As we cross, women wash clothes in the wadi, their faces sun-blackened and hands hardened by life in these mountains. I watch them and reflect as we drink coffee, the first of our travels here, on Yassine's leafy terrace. This valley is his identity, a pristine environment left largely unblemished by the waves of invasion and rushed furore of the world beyond these hills. I did not know that nomads still roamed here at all. While I shall soon learn that nomadic life in Morocco is being pushed to the brink, their continued presence here speaks of a kinship with the land that I so greatly admire, as well as that tenacious spirit of the Amazigh, who never accept defeat. Once more, I reflect on Marrakech: a city of chaos and charm, fighting the tides of change.

Here in Dadès, there is a much simpler soundtrack: the swishing of clothes being washed in the wadi, the cooing of birds, and the swirling whistle of those rising winter winds. This is the heartland of the Amazigh, the soul of proud people. This valley is nothing but their own.

4

Sijilmasa

Dadès Gorge, Erg Chebbi

Youssef has been a bounteous host and we are sad to be saying farewell so soon, but we need to make tracks if we are to keep to our rendezvous with our desert guides by nightfall. Already our morning escapade has put us on the backfoot and a cameleer at the edge of the Sahara is expectant of our arrival by sundown. Our journey to the desert should only take four hours, but as navigator, I have opted for a slightly longer and more interesting route, that should allow us to see more of the gorge. It involves driving north and back into the High Atlas, along roads that look joyfully twisty on our map. The extra miles should still see us arrive in time, though the journey that lies ahead will prove anything but smooth.

Not far down the road, near Todra Gorge, we come across an outrageous sequence of switchback bends, strung liberally up a mountain. The road rises swiftly from beside a metallic-blue wadi, climbing some 100 metres up five tiers of snaking asphalt between towering red walls. The road is narrow and passing other vehicles difficult, the road arcing around bare rocky outcrops that jut from the hillside, forcing the road wide. This has to be one of the most exciting roads on Earth, but soon the going gets tough. Extremely tough. When the surface runs out altogether, I know we are in trouble – but now we are committed. Deep in the valley, we quickly find ourselves on a rough gravel track where no saloon should go. Only the occasional heavy truck trundles past the other way, their large tyres spewing rocks from the loose gravel surface that falls away without distinction to a bowl of dust 200 metres below. The road clings to the mountainside above an abyss. So remote are we, here there are no barriers.

Eventually, we have to stop to admire the view, and weigh up our predicament. If we thought Dadès was lifeless, this is something else. In the cool and rarefied air at over 2,000 metres up, hardly any vegetation springs through the dry and sombre rock that coats the mountains, not a single tree for miles. The High Atlas looms in every direction, its tall peaks snow-capped and dark flanks foreboding. Almost two hours have passed and we have barely made any ground. The front bumper is torn loose – that's a problem we will come to in Fez – and we have just traversed a series of water crossings where I had to leap out and edge Matt forwards, as he tiptoed our saloon along roads the width of a truck, the depths of the valley teasing us to our right.

Soon the onward view forces a decision. We have to abandon. The surface has rendered this route impassable; a dust road snakes its way around rock-strewn mountains for unknown miles. There are no tourists here, not even locals in off-roaders, just us and the truckers daring with death in their enormous machines that are strung with beads and hung with Amazigh symbols, no doubt markers of good fortune. If we push on, we will not reach the desert today, let alone by nightfall. Painfully, we must retrace our steps for over two long hours, all the way back to Yassine's kasbah, and then Boumalne Dadès, where a left turn leads us onto smooth, sweet asphalt that arrows south to the desert.

What a fool I was to suggest such a route. Had we pushed on, soon the road would have diminished to little more than a worn dusty trace across the spine of mountains. Justice is served as I am instantly sacked from the role of navigator. Tonight we will journey into the desert like nomads: by moonlight.

Just a slither of beetroot red trims the dusky desert horizon, but though the night has beaten our arrival, we are finally nearing our rendezvous with our guide to the desert: Salim. How about it? From the notes that we have been sent, we know that we are dealing with *the* man of town. 'Once you arrive in Hassi Labied, just ask anyone around for directions to Salim,' our notes read. We are dealing with a big shot here. Everyone knows Salim. Of course!

Soon we roll into the dusty little village of Hassi Labied, at the foot of the Erg Chebbi dunes. By now the evocative image of Salim is etched firmly into our minds. Tonight, he and our camel man will forge a path through the dunes to our overnight camp, which is nestled deep in the sands. Will we share a language? Will he too ride atop a camel, or lead on foot at the head of our caravan? Soon, we shall have answers.

"Salam," I call casually from the window of our saloon as we arrive in Hassi Labied, as if everyone is expectant of our arrival. A few young men gather nearby. "Salim? Anyone know Salim?" They return blank stares, until one eventually steps forward.

"Salim?" I repeat, reinforcing my pronunciation with French gusto. "We are looking for his guesthouse, uh – *le chambre?* For the desert?" With a shoulder shrug and open hands, I give him the international signal for 'lost tourist, lost in translation.' The kind young man offers us a room in very broken English, so we thank him and move on. A short distance down the road, I make a second attempt, but with similar result. By now it is completely dark and few locals are out. The evocative vision of Salim, everyone knows him, is starting to drift away. But then, suddenly, and I mean truly out of nowhere, Aladdin appears at our car window.

"Salaaam! You found us." A man draped in full desert attire reaches his hand through the window. "Salim," he introduces himself. "Yes, you are so very welcome. Please! Follow." Salim breaks into a jog and ushers our car forward. His patterned blue and white djellaba seems to float weightless on his shoulders as he does. A wide, white turban wraps around his head, above a crevassed and sun-darkened face.

At the very edge of the village, where the streets are dusted in swirling sand, we reach a guesthouse owned by a man named Hamza, who will be our 'camel man' over the next two days. Hamza is bespectacled, turbaned, and a swooping orange robe flows splendidly down his back. He is taller and more ... how should I put it? Generously proportioned than Salim, and a bigger character too.

"Woah! Oh goodness me," he beams, staggering backwards in false amazement, before clasping Matt's right hand with both of his. "Omar Sharif is among us! Sir, it is great to meet you."

He shakes Matt welcome to the desert.

"Ahaa!" Next, he turns abruptly to Katharine. "Yeees, it is indeed! Fatima Couscous. So very welcome you are here in Africaaa. Salim, we shall buy her for 30 camels," he booms in hilarity.

Then, finally, it is my turn. I know only too well that this name is going to stick, so I am hoping for a good one.

"Ohh my!" Hamza pushes his glasses down his nose and peers over them studiously. "Mohammed Tagine!" he bellows. "Where have you been hiding? So welcome you are in Africa, Monsieur Tagine! Come, friends, come in."

Spirits lifted, Hamza generously offers each of us a spacious room in his guesthouse to change from infidel clothes into desert attire. My djellaba falls loosely over my body and offers welcome respite from the biting desert cool. My blue desert pants hang laughably low, and as for my sapphire blue turban …

"You want the Berber way or the British way?" Hamza is hovering in the doorway, ushering me over to tie my turban for me. The Berber way, obviously – although I am rather intrigued as to what the British way of tying a turban may be.

We are yet to see the dunes of the Erg Chebbi – this great island of sand on the Sahara's westerly fringe – but I know they are metres away. As we venture outside into the empty cool, our camels are tied nearby, kneeled under palms that just two hours ago would have been offering welcome respite from the torching desert sun. Now our beasts are just outlines, lurking and snorting in the darkness. Katharine claims the first animal, the largest of the three, and Matt plucks for the second. But as I near the third camel, Salim hurries over.

"No touch this one!" he says with a long wiggle of his finger. "He is … very moody! Others, fine, this one, no. Okay? No touching, just riding."

"Why is that?" I ask.

"Well, he's the youngest, and still has a lot to learn," Salim explains. "He's still at camel school! Learning how to be a camel. So, you are his teacher now, okay?" he laughs with a beat of my back. Salim darts back to the guesthouse to fill up a canteen, but I hear him call to me in the wind: "You can call him Abu. He kick and spit a lot!"

As I haul my left leg over Abu, who reciprocates with a disgruntled scuff, it suddenly becomes clear why my companions had made a dash for the camels in front. As Matt's camel once again passes wind and fires the remnants of something concerningly more solid our direction with a flick of its tail, I can also understand why poor Abu at the back here has developed a bit of an attitude. We are right in the firing line – and we've not even set off yet!

Hamza the camel whisperer works his magic on the animals one by one. With a gentle tap of a shepherd's crook and some peculiar kissing noises, each beast is up on its feet in turn – rear legs first, sending the rookie cameleer shooting forwards, before the front legs eventually rise up in sequence. We're surprisingly high up; Abu may be the youngest, but he's only an inch or two shorter than his pals in front. But at long, long last, we are finally venturing into the Sahara Desert under an inky black night sky and soon stony ground on the outskirts of Hassi Labied relents to softer sand, where our camels fall into a rhythmic plod. The peace is exhilarating, the silence of the sands empty and hollow. While I can make out little of the desert in the darkness, as the flickering lights of Hassi Labied die out slowly behind us, a canvas of stars opens above, like a necklace of glistening diamonds.

"You are travelling like nomads," Hamza calls to us from the head of the train, "like the real caravans ... by night, when it is cool."

Nomads still cross these sands and we, like them, are following in the hoofprints of merchants, warriors and missionaries, for whom these dunes would have been the last frontier of desert hinterland before the towns and villages beyond. Just down the road from Hassi Labied, near to the modern-day oasis town of Rissani, the ancient ruins of Sijilmasa sprawl along the River Ziz. Once one of the most important and busy caravan centres in all North Africa, Sijilmasa was the last desert terminus before the cities to the west of the High Atlas in the Middle Ages. It connected the Middle East, West Africa and Southern Europe through trade, religion and the exchange of beliefs, goods and ideas. Emerging from a fearsome desert crossing, merchants must have found Sijilmasa a true respite. Built around one of the largest oases in Africa, the old city was once rich in date palms, expansive gardens and tranquil backwaters that held more than enough water for some 50,000 townsfolk, and the visiting caravans. Everything that you could possibly need for the risky onwards journey was here: water, food, news, fodder for animals, new camels, lodgings, and a great abundance of dates – reputedly the best in the world. Alongside camel's milk, which is said to have medicinal properties, dates were a staple for the desert traders, who could survive on just seven a day.

It was among these tranquil date palms that cotton from Egypt, oil from Spain, and spices from Zanzibar would have been traded, as well as a quite incredulous flow of gold. In fact, so much gold was traded in Sijilmasa that a mint was soon built, exporting gold coins minted with Islamic phrases to lands as far as England, Egypt, India, and Iraq. Gold did not merely accrue wealth; it spread religion. Indeed, it was within the walls of Sijilmasa that many Amazigh merchants were first exposed to the word of Islam, carried to them from Arabia. From there it would spread north to Iberia, where it endured for around 700 years, hitching a ride with the merchant caravans who carried gold from the bountiful Ghana Empire in the south to exchange for Mediterranean salt, 'white gold,' in the north. Around nine million slaves were transported along with the caravans too, which were the backbone of regional trade from the eighth to the 16th century.

Even today, the embers of the trade are still alight, powered by the modest and single-humped dromedary, which, since its domestication some 3,000 years ago, has made more than a small dent on human history. In the 14th century, when the great Amazigh explorer Ibn Battuta journeyed with merchants across the desert, the average caravan would have had at least 1,000 animals, though on occasion as many as 12,000 camels would have been driven across the Sahara in a single caravan, to turn the wheels of the almighty, desert-straddling trade. Caravans were unable to carry enough water for survival, so runners would be sent to oases along the trail to find water and ship it back to the caravan, long before it arrived. Their survival required careful coordination, not least because merchants would often seek out deliberately dangerous routes to far-flung lands, knowing that the risk and distance would greatly increase the rarity and value of their merchandise. As Ibn Khaldun wrote, 'the wealthiest merchants are those who dare to go.'

And who guided the caravans? It was the Amazigh, of course, who as expert desert survivalists and navigators were vital to the survival of the caravans in their constant search for water, pasture, and in an often perilous struggle against the extreme desert conditions – and some less-than-friendly nomadic cousins. As facilitators of the trade, the cities of the Amazigh flourished, such as Djenné and Timbuktu in modern-day Mali to our south, cities both founded by Amazigh Tuaregs. In fact, so wealthy did Timbuktu become that when its pious king, Mansa Musa, went on pilgrimage to Mecca in the early 14th century, his entourage of some 60,000 men, all dressed in silk, and their many camels are said to have been burdened with some 30 tonnes of gold that Musa handed to the poor on his long journey east. Yet, despite his altruistic intentions, so much gold was shared out on his pilgrimage to Mecca that the price of gold fell for a decade, inadvertently ruining the economies of the nations he had travelled through, plunging them into even greater poverty. Musa was therefore left with no option but to borrow all the gold he could on his return journey at the highest possible interest rate, to rectify the economic calamity he had caused. Or, so the story goes. So wealthy was Musa, and Mali, that, according to some historians, he was the wealthiest man to have ever lived.

Tangent aside, the importance of this westerly fringe of the desert, and the role of the Amazigh nomads in facilitating this almighty trade, should not be understated. Sijilmasa and the forefathers of the nomads who guide us by moonlight tonight played a pivotal role in the course of Middle Eastern, African and European history. Today, a majority of the caravan trails are devoid of camels, though they have been replaced in some locations by heavy trucks carrying fuel and salt. A new paved route, the Trans-Saharan Highway between Algiers and Lagos, has the support of the African Union, though pan-desert trade remains a quite limited and perilous endeavour, owing to fierce sandstorms, an erratic Saharan climate, and terrorist activity.

And as for Sijilmasa, the city of gold? Well, there is an old Amazigh saying, 'where there is gold, there is trouble,' and after centuries of invasion by warring Amazigh factions, Sijilmasa and its vast wealth, both in gold and dates, finally found itself in perpetual ruins following devastation by the nomadic Aït Atta in 1818. It was a rather ironic end to a city of great riches. After all, while Amazigh feuding led to its ultimate downfall, Sijilmasa only came into existence thanks to united Amazigh resistance against early Arab rule. In fact, according to some historians, the fabled city of gold was the birthplace of modern Morocco.

Just three decades after Umayyad general Uqba ibn Nāfi had swept through the deserts with news of divine revelation, a new Arab leader arrived from the caliphate, intent on liberating the Amazigh from their backward ways. Beside him was a revered Amazigh commander, Tāriq ibn Ziyād, who was aligned with the divine mission and led his men to awaken the Amazigh with the word of God, from Tangier up north to the Tafilalt Oasis in the east, where the city of Sijilmasa would later be founded. This was religious war, and having enlightened the Amazigh with the message of Islam, Ziyād pushed north to Iberia, with an army of Amazigh men, who ushered in an era of Islamic rule that would endure for some seven centuries. Even today, the legacy of that invasion remains engrained on the peninsula: after much linguistic tongue-twisting over the centuries, the point where his army landed – Jabal Tāriq, or 'Tāriq's Mountain' – has come to be known as Gibraltar.

Yet while Ziyād was marching towards France to continue his divine mission, back in northwest Africa, rebellion was starting to flare, as the Amazigh were in revolt once again. The eastern caliph had ordered his governors in Kairouan to strengthen Arab rule of the Maghreb, and to achieve this, they would have to quash the pesky Amazigh for good. They duly delivered, levying an inordinate tax upon the 'free people,' payable in slaves, and treating them as second-class Muslims who were subordinate to their Arab neighbours, even though most Amazigh had already converted to Islam. Many were even enslaved, despite enslaving Muslims being in strict contravention to Islamic law. When the caliphate declared the Amazigh a 'conquered people' and begun to seize their property, the patience of the Amazigh wore thin. Many were inspired by an emerging sect in the east, the Kharijites, which taught that every Muslim should be treated as equals under Islamic law. Unsurprisingly, the Amazigh were eager to listen and soon Kharijite principles had penetrated their psyche and readied them for revolt.

But the Amazigh could not just come charging from the hills. The might of the Umayyad armies would crush their dissent, and so, in the time-honoured ways of their ancestors, they retreated to the hinterland and waited for a moment to strike back. When the Kairouan governors put their troops on a war footing and set sail across the Mediterranean towards Byzantine Sicily, they knew the time had come. With the Umayyad armies off African shores, the Amazigh launched their rebellion, which would go down in history as the 'Great Amazigh Revolt.' First, they made for Tangier, heads shaven in Kharijite style and spears inscribed with Qur'anic verses, and soon the northern city was in the hands of the rebels. Bearings turned south, the Amazigh raged down the west coast of Morocco and tore down Umayyad garrisons, with their armies rallying to the cries of new adherents, who had joined along the way.

In nearby Kairouan, the Umayyad governors caught wind of what was going on and ushered their men back to African shores. It was too late. The Amazigh had secured their garrisons and the central Maghreb was now under their control. Soon the news of Amazigh victory swept across the Straits to Al-Andalus, where Amazigh rebels sought to evict the Andalusian Arabs, who had come to conquer a few years before. It was to little avail, and when the Amazigh also failed in their endeavour to capture Kairouan, the Great Revolt was at its end. The rebels scattered, and with much of northwest Africa now under their control, they founded some of the first Muslim nations beyond the eastern caliphate, ruled by Amazigh tribal chieftains or Kharijite imams. Among the new states was the Emirati of Sijilmasa – a city born from Amazigh rebellion – and according to some historians, its founding marked the beginning of Moroccan independence. After the Great Revolt concluded in 743, no foreign power would rule Morocco again until the 20th century.

Perhaps unsurprisingly, the rebellious new kingdoms infuriated the caliph, Harun el Rashid, who was busy quashing a rebellion of his own at home. The Prophet Muhammad did not appoint a successor and had no surviving son, which caused great contestation in the Islamic world over the legitimacy of subsequent caliphs. Resultantly, Islam splintered into competing sects, the Kharijites among them, and in a rage over the ensuing anarchy, Rashid dispatched an army to quash an unruly group of rebels who rejected his rule. They were duly massacred near Mecca in 786, but one man managed to escape and flee in a westerly direction. His name was Idris ibn Abdullah and after a perilous two-year journey across the Maghreb, accompanied only by a loyal former slave who was also named Rashid, he arrived in Morocco, where they sought refuge.

Struck by his bravery and piety, the Amazigh decided to make the exile from Baghdad, where the eastern caliphate had moved, their new leader, and so the first Arab and Islamic dynasty in Morocco was born: the Idrisids. For the most part, the Arabs and Amazigh coexisted peacefully, but within two years, Idris I was dead, poisoned by an envoy sent by the caliph himself. Two months later, his son was born, nurtured by his former slave Rashid, and this son would later continue the dynasty as Sultan Idris II. When he too passed, the empire was divided into ten small states, one for each of his sons, which inevitably saw the dynasty spiral into extinction. The Idrisids' era was over, but modern Morocco was born and there would not be another Arab dynasty for almost 600 years. It was almost time for the Amazigh to rule Morocco again.

Sijilmasa, then, was a town spawn from rebellion against Arab rule, which helped to found the nation of Morocco. These sands are storied in history and though I am in the firing line of the animals in front, I'm glad to be at the back of our caravan, which is being led by Hamza up front and Salim at our side. As we plod deeper into the disorienting depths of the erg desert (that's a desert with sand-whipped dunes and little vegetation, as opposed to desert flatlands), all I can hear is the scuffling, snorting and farting of our camels, and the laboured plod of our desert guides alongside. Here there is a liberating energy, our steady progress unhindered by walls or the passing of time.

As we hunker down for the long ride to our overnight camp, Abu is already becoming quite a character. He is the naughty little kid at the back of the school bus, kicking the seat (or, camel) in front of him and thrusting spit balls (or, sand and the odd poop pellet) down the bus. He grunts impatiently and stomps his feet when we grind to a halt, moaning and snuffling as Hamza stops to navigate, or encourages Katharine's larger camel up the steeper dunes. I sense that if he was untied from his companions in front, he would break off into the night with a liberated canter. I am also grateful for my acquisition of desert clothing. Funnily enough, riding a camel isn't the most comfortable experience, not least for a man, and so the glow of a campfire on the inky horizon is a very welcome sight, as we kneel the camels to dismount.

Though I can only make out shapes, camp is small and shaped like an oblong, with a rudimentary wooden fence that runs around its perimeter, beaten into the sand. As Yassine had prophesised, our guides are not really nomads. The only real migration they will do is from here in the desert to the village of Hassi Labied, at the very frontier of civilisation. For much of the year their camp remains setup in the dunes, ready to welcome the next wave of tourists. As we shall soon learn, this is the reality the region over, though it's certainly not all bad. For our guides, this is the only way to sustain a life under the open skies.

Camp has five tents, each draped with a mismatch of fabrics: three for the guests, another for our guides, and a larger mess tent for dinner. A campfire roars just outside its perimeter with woollen rugs underfoot, so you can walk from dune to tent without dragging in sand. A rudimentary tap emits the occasional dribble of water in the middle of camp, and our tent is located in one corner, beyond which there is nothing – just darkness. As we finish up dinner in the mess tent, only the crackle of the campfire breaks the empty silence and offers the slightest respite from the biting cold. So, as our guides make for their tents and clouds begin to gather beneath any kind of a Milky Way, we too call it a night.

5

The Oasis

Erg Chebbi

First light in the desert and this morning my muscles are feeling a little tender. Last night I slept under a camel – or so it felt, with the weight of a dozen woollen blankets anchoring my torso into the same position all night long. In fact, so heavy were the blankets that I could only pull them up as high as my stomach to allow my lungs and other important organs to continue doing their thing. Oh – and it was still cold! Night in the Sahara had been a little uncomfortable, but we had a canvas above our heads and are, in essence, glamping (terrible word), so I'll stop sounding like a petty Westerner and hush.

As I unbutton the curtains that seal our tent entrance and tie them back, the glorious orange hues of a fierce desert morning flood in and shock my eyes. Salim is across the way, preparing breakfast.

"Hello, Africaaa," he calls to me with a smile and wave, before disappearing back into the mess tent with a steaming teapot in hand. Not for the first time, we have been called 'Africa' by our guides. I want to ask why, but for now I reciprocate with *salam*, a wave and a sun-forced grimace. Breakfast on the dunes consists of all the Moroccan treats that we have grown fond of in this country: rghaif drizzled in honey, hard-boiled eggs, melon and other fresh fruits, and a generous mountain of bread, with liberal amounts of butter and jams. It seems that nomadism is easy when town is just a short quad bike ride over the dunes.

The Oasis

"See over there, Africa?" Hamza points east. Shrouded in layers of gold, a perfectly straight ridge of dark rock lines the horizon. The ridge is so straight, it could be a man-made wall.

"Algeria," Hamza says. "We go today, yes?"

High on the dunes, I can finally gain some perspective of where we had journeyed last night. The dunes of a perfect erg desert rise and fall around us in every direction, daubed in the hues of dawn. Hassi Labied and all settled lands are now far out of sight, these sands the domain of camels and nomads. The dunes tumble unbroken to that natural border of rock to our east, beyond which the erg desert stops and the hamada and flat sands of the real Sahara begin. In fact, for all I know, we could be stood on the surface of Mars. Not only does the Erg Chebbi look a lot like the red planet, it shares geological properties too. Back in 2013, a team of Austrian space scientists conducted a number of experiments here using Martian rovers, to simulate what it might be like to live and operate on the surface of Mars.

Today our guides are leading us to a small oasis, which is around an hour's ride from camp by camel. When we arrive, I want to learn more about their nomadic roots and the reality of nomadism across Morocco today. Their way of life is one that I romanticise; movement with the seasons and kinship with the land that is left without a trace is inherent to humanity, yet in the sedentary world people have lost their fear and respect for nature. Never have we been at greater odds with our fellow creatures, land and environment. Nomadism speaks of a more amicable relationship, yet today it is dying a slow and often involuntary death around the globe. I want to find out what remains in Morocco. Are our guides clinging nobly to the life of their forefathers, or recreating their bygone ways for the sake of us tourists?

The ride ahead is warm, pleasantly so, and now my turban, wrapped like a Tuareg's, is providing shade from the sun, as opposed to warmth in the desert night. Our surrounds are movingly beautiful. Every dune has an entirely unique complexion and the colours of morning are ever changing. We are following ridgelines and Hamza, at the head of our caravan, is forging a path of least resistance for his animals. He knows these smooth arcs of sand and every rise and fall like roads, as we trace the footsteps of a solitary cameleer who passed through not long ago.

To begin with the going is easy, though as time passes I lose all sense of time, distance and direction. It feels like we have journeyed far, but as we snake through this island of sand and traverse slowly across more challenging terrain, I know that this desert can be deceiving. Soon the sun is high and beats down an onslaught. We roast in our djellabas and know the mercury is only going to climb from here, but this is winter, and our guides move with ease. For them, this heat is tame.

Suddenly, Hamza brings us to a halt.

"Fox," he says, pointing to a track dotted across the desert beneath the camels' feet. "Lots of desert fox in this area – fennec fox."

Hamza had told us last night that there are few wild animals in this region of the desert. Later we see a desert mouse scurrying into a hole, but at this time of year there are few dangerous creatures about. Snakes, scorpions and lizards are the preserve of summer months.

As we journey on, I observe more and more tracks scattered across the desert, dotted lines that scurry up dunes and dash along ridgelines. They are smaller and neater than that of the fennec fox, yet too large for the desert mouse. I wonder what they are. After much musing, it is to my great disappointment when I see a stone tumble down the dune to my left, making the exact pattern in the sand I have been observing for so long. My Attenborough moment has ground to an embarrassing halt and I am only glad that I did not open my mouth to comment on this observation any sooner.

After an hour's ride, the oasis is tucked into a basin in the sands to our left, surrounded by high dunes that dwarf the little camp below like an amphitheatre. We kneel the camels and complete our journey to the oasis on foot where a few simple tents are erected around a single palm tree. Beyond the camp, clusters of verdant shrubbery spring like magic from the desert sands. The tents, like the ones in our overnight camp, are typical of the Amazigh nomads who do still live in the Erg Chebbi and surrounding hamada. Mismatched fabrics of wool and cloth drape over a wooden truss, beating back the fiery desert heat and protecting its occupants from wind and sand. The materials are simple and easy to disassemble and manoeuvre, aiding the nomads in their constant search for water and fresh pasture.

"Tea, Africa?" Hamza offers, as he seats himself beside us in a small tent with an open side. Please. It has been hours since our last fix.

"Okay, watch this," Hamza says, "Berber WhatsApp." He puts his hands to his mouth, readying to shout. "Mansoouur, tea for Africaaa," he bellows towards the mess tent, from which a petite man with a neat moustache and rapid walk appears instantly with a steaming pot of tea, followed shortly by a Berber omelette that is brimming with chilli, tomato and paprika, the first of many on my travels. A moment presents itself to ask Hamza why he keeps calling us 'Africa.'

"We are all Africa!" he booms like a clap of thunder, his arms wide in disdain at the obviousness of my question. He runs a finger past us all: "He is Africa, I am Africa, you are Africa, she is Africa." His reply is uttered with such conviction that I do not dare probe whether this is some kind of anthropological suggestion, a notion of one-worldly togetherness, or merely something that has gotten lost in translation. Either way, our nicknames have been well and truly replaced by the universal name *Africa*, which we willingly embrace.

I want to find out more about our desert guides and the reality of nomadism in Morocco today, a way of life I know they descend from. For me it speaks of a more amicable connection between mankind and nature, a connection that has been severed almost entirely in the modern and sedentary world. The art of movement with the seasons makes perfect sense to me compared to the unnecessary complexities of urban life beyond, yet I know their way of life is dying. Yassine had told me about the nomads that still move between the High Atlas pastures and the Jebel Saghro near Dadès, the likes of the Aït Atta. I did not know that nomads still lived in Morocco at all.

"Has your family always lived here, near the desert?" I ask Hamza. He finishes a shot of tea, then begins to tell his story.

"My father was a camel driver," he says, "and he taught me everything that I know about the desert." There is not a breath of wind, his voice the only sound for miles. "He told me how life will change with every season. How to navigate with the stars. Everything that I know, he told me, and everything he knew was taught by his father, who had learned from his ancestors. Our family lived as nomads for many years in this desert. But, my father was the last."

The desert returns to eery silence, until eventually Katharine utters what we all have wanted to ask: "What happened?"

"The water!" he replies instantly with a throaty riposte. "It became less and less and so the pastures dried up. My father had no choice but to leave the nomadic life behind." Hamza shakes his head wearily, as a lone gust of wind whistles its way through the tent. "And so, he had to settle in the village, to provide for our family."

"In Hassi Labied?" I ask him.

"No, near Rissani. He had hoped to find a job, but what can you do when you have no skills in the town?" He shrugs his shoulders, then motions a hand towards the desert. "And he couldn't leave these open skies behind. You know, Africa, this has always been the most important thing for us, as desert people. When he could no longer survive as a nomad, my father moved to the town, but it just wasn't right. So, he became a camel driver in the desert, and then, when I was old enough, I helped him."

"Were there many tourists back then?" Matt asks.

"Few," Hamza replies. "Very few. But then, slowly with the years, more and more have come. When my father first moved to the town, Merzouga," the thriving local centre for desert tourism, just five miles down the road from Hassi Labied, "was just an old village, and the lake across the road had more water. In fact, there is a legend in this desert: Merzouga was once a tropical jungle, full of plants and birds. But then one day, when a wealthy family refused to help a poor woman and her son who was ill, God punished them. He buried them in sand! So, look around you. People say that is why a dry desert is here. Maybe there is a jungle under the sand! I do not think so. But, what is true is this area is now very dry. There is no water anymore.

"… but everything is okay," he reassures himself softly. "And anyway, who can change the world? Just so long as we can live under the open skies. That is all that matters. That is all."

Hamza's story is the sombre tale of nomadism across North Africa. The abandonment of a nomadic life is slow and often involuntary, but the harsh reality is that the nomads who still proudly roam this desert and surrounding hamada could well be the last generation in Morocco to do so. Only a handful of nomadic families still cut an existence in the Erg Chebbi dunes, clinging to their traditional ways thanks to the low height of its water wells, but they are a dwindling few. More live in the hamada between the dunes and rocky border wall, while others move around the Erg Chigaga near M'Hamid and Zagora in the south, the so-called 'rain nomads' who move seasonally along the western rim of the Sahara in constant search for water and pasture for their camels, goats and mules. Even many Aït Atta families now lead semi-nomadic lives, migrating with their livestock in summer, but residing in permanent homes for the rest of the year.

The climate here is peculiar, Hamza explains. Just as for the Draoui along the oases of the Drâa, life is changing as a result. Sporadic rains, droughts and increasingly unpredictable seasons are breaking the well-balanced harmony that has existed between pastoral nomads and their environment for generations. It has led to widespread poverty and famine among the nomads, as grazing lands for their livestock turn to dust and dependable water sources dry up. What results is the slow death of nomadism. Arid regions support more than a billion people worldwide, many of whom depend on livestock farming as their primary source of income, yet each year the deserts are swallowing up arable land as temperatures soar. Temperatures in North Africa are rising twice as fast as the global average and already conditions across much of the Sahara are too extreme for goats and camels, which provide the milk, meat, transport, skins and traditional medicines that are vital for nomadic life. Soon vast swathes of the Sahara will be uninhabitable, pushing human life to its settled periphery and lighting the spark for conflict over resources and water. When the remaining nomads do locate water, often it is too saline to drink.

"It's not just the climate," Hamza says. "The government does not like nomads! They send money to the cities, then blame us for all their problems. They say that the desert is getting bigger because of how we graze our animals. But mostly, the problem is Algeria. Now the border is closed and so the nomads have nowhere to go."

Moroccan law has been hard on pastoralists, who are often accused of causing desertification due to the overgrazing of their livestock. The science is unclear on whether it's true. However, souring international relations dealt the final hammer blow for many nomads. Relations between Morocco and Algeria turned cold during the Sand War of 1963, but the border was sealed following Morocco's occupation of disputed Western Sahara in 1975. Now the Algerian border is militarised, patrolled by heavily armed guards, while any hopes of migration to pastures in Western Sahara have been quashed by a 'sand wall' strung along the border, rigged with landmines. It has pinched the grazing lands of the desert nomads even tighter, and put an abrupt end to the centuries-old cycles of migration with the seasons between the Algerian Sahara in the summer and the Draoui oases in winter.

Just like our guides, many nomads have abandoned a life of movement for work in tourism, but even this has been problematic. Urbanisation across the flatlands of southern Morocco has risen exponentially as nomads settle down and tourists flood in, but this has led water consumption to skyrocket in an already water scarce region. Construction of the Atlas Film Studios and Ouarzazate's own tourism boom has only exacerbated demand and so, paradoxically, as an increasing number of nomads switch the open skies for a secure and sedentary existence, yet more are forced to follow suit as water by the edge of the Sahara becomes dangerously scarce.

Even the Aït Atta, one of the most storied tribes of these lands, are in sharp decline. The last decade has seen the introduction of so-called 'tent schools' that have sprung up in remote and mountainous corners of the kingdom to allow the children of nomads to be educated. It is a positive step given the rate of rural illiteracy, especially among girls and Amazigh in general, but to attend school requires families to stay in one place and learn new skills, such as the construction of permanent clay-brick homes. Equipped with the skills of a modern world, many young adults are understandably leaving their nomadic roots behind. After all, education is a catalyst for a more prosperous life and a sizable majority of nomadic families struggle below the poverty line. Less than one-in-five nomads has received any formal schooling, and so the statistics are unsurprising: around 25,000 nomads still roam in Morocco today, but since last decade their number has fallen by over 60 percent.

Here in the oasis camp, I sense that our guides have a romanticised view of nomadism too. They are proud and skilled desert people, who share a heritage rooted in these sands. Now their lives straddle the sand and suburbia — they have cars and houses in the villages on the fringe of the Sahara — but they refuse to leave this life behind, a life under the open skies. They, like many other nomads, have turned to tourism as a means of staying in their homelands and using the skills passed down to them across the generations. From a life of movement with the seasons, these men now move with seasonal waves of tourism, while their wives and families stay in the village.

It is a difficult one to fathom, as I sit among proud men in the oasis camp. They are living a life that they know and desire, but one that is crudely shaped to the will of those who visit. Some families of the Aït Atta now charge tourists to join them on their seasonal migrations, on the condition that paying guests help with the livestock and collection of firewood. They have quickly learned the expectations of the guests. Now the nomads travel with additional mules and muleteers, who haul sleeping bags, nylon tents, purified water, and camp toilets up to their summer pastures in the mountains. Their simple subsistence of bread, couscous, fresh cheese, dates, goat's milk and the occasional slaughtered animal has been supplemented too, with hearty tagines, soups, pastries and fresh fruit, to appease their city-dwelling guests.

Here too, as we lounge in the oasis camp and sip tea with Hamza, who periodically flicks through his mobile phone, I wonder why we are all here. Still he sits under an open sky, with his animals tied near-by, roaming freely through the desert and hosting with the hospitality that is endemic to most nomads. But Hamza is not a nomad. He would not be here if we were not. This is an honest life under the glaring sun that he leads, passed down by his forefathers, but it is an existence that is succumbing to modernity, climate change and the politics of a wider world beyond these sands. And then there is us: paying guests, parting with our hard-earned dirhams to experience a luxury life of hardship with the nomads. We have come from the world that his existence has succumbed to. We are here to embrace a way of life that we laud, one that makes more sense than our own, but one that is dying. I struggle with the paradox.

These sands have always been a place of contestation that have seen the clash of worlds old and new. This desert has long witnessed feats of great Amazigh resistance – against modernity, invaders, and a warming world – to defend their identity and way of life. The 'free people' have never been ones to roll over and die. Despite their early efforts, it was years before the Arab conquerors would extend their influence across Tamazgha. They were vastly outnumbered by the indigenous Amazigh who fiercely defended their land and culture, just as our guides today. It was only with the arrival of the Banu Hilal tribes in the 11th century that Arabisation – the spread of Arab values, language and beliefs – was firmly set in motion.

The Banu Hilal were a large tribal confederation from Arabia, sent to Tamazgha by the Fatimids of Egypt, who wanted to punish the disobedient Zirid Dynasty of the central Maghreb for abandoning Shiism. Some 300,000 Arabs – fighting men, their wives and children – set out for North Africa, where they battled Amazigh tribes and reduced the Zirids to a spattering of coastal towns. They were here to settle, and in time the arrival of thousands of Arabs ensured that the Arabic language and culture seeped deep into the fabric of the region. As chronicled by Ibn Khaldun, their savage invasion had also transformed fertile land into arid desert, forcing many Amazigh to abandon agriculture for a life of pastoral nomadism.

Yet one man, a fiery preacher cooped up in the sands of the desert, was about to change everything. He was called Abdallah ibn Yasin and having travelled to Islamic centres of learning across the region, he was ready to awaken his fellow Amazigh with a strict new interpretation of the Qur'an that would change Moroccan history. Starting from a base close to here at the westerly fringe of the Sahara Desert, Yasin formed an alliance of Amazigh tribes and, in 1054 AD, led an army of reverent nomads towards Sijilmasa. His followers called themselves Almoravids, meaning 'those bound together in the cause of God,' and they headed for the fabled city of gold with one clear mission: jihad. This was holy war, to uphold a true interpretation of Islam, waged against his fellow Amazigh. As a crossroads for the caravans carrying gold from the south and salt from the north, Sijilmasa was the envy of empires, coveted by civilisations far and wide. The Almoravids were determined to make it their own and once garrisons were secured in its vast oases, they bolted south across the desert and to the city of Awdaghust, which formed the other extremity of the trans-Saharan gold trade.

With the gold rush under their control, the Almoravids accrued an incredible wealth and assembled an army the envy of the region. Now they were ready to take their jihad beyond the Sahara, across the High Atlas and to the cities to its west. This was a perilous journey in a land of unknowns that few had traversed, riddled with bandits and thieves. These were desert warriors, raised in the heat and derived from feared nomadic tribes. Now they had to cross high mountain passes and battle with the heretics of the hills, who stood in their way. Eventually, their army of 2,000 foot soldiers, 800 cameleers and 400 horsemen arrived in the arid flatlands of the west and in 1070 they pitched their tents to settle a city as their capital. They called it the land of God – Marrakech – and with the Banu Hilal now under *their* command, the jihadis from the desert set about making an empire.

After the death of ibn Yasin, the Almoravids flourished and, for the most part, the Arabs and Amazigh thrived in unison. Under their new spiritual leader, Yusuf ibn Tashfin, the Arabs and Amazigh developed a common philosophy and Marrakech became the city we know today. In fact, the layout of the red city – its streets, palaces and souks – have barely changed since Almoravid days. No sooner had Arabisation swept the Maghreb, the Almoravids had become a dynasty and Morocco was an Amazigh empire once more. Soon Fez, Tangier and parts of Algeria fell under their control and less than three decades after emerging from the very sands that we cross today and conquering Sijilmasa, the Almoravids ruled an empire that straddled northwest Africa and Al-Andalus. For centuries, the 'free people' had dominated Tamazgha as a politically divided but culturally united people. But now, at long last, they had an empire to match and it was the barbarians from the desert that had united these Islamic lands as one.

Yet the shifting sands of the region never stand still. Up in the High Atlas, dissent was already stirring. The Almoravids had Sahara in their blood but the mountains were a place that they struggled to subdue. In fact, even when the French arrived in the 20th century, the high passes of the Atlas remained rebellious, lawless lands that the colonial leaders mostly left alone. In the hills, another group of Islamic revolutionaries named the Almohads – the 'people who believe in the unity of God' – were readying for a revolution of their own. They too were Amazigh, but they deemed the Almoravids heretics who had wrongly interpreted the Qur'an. There was a record to set straight and so they campaigned to delegitimise Almoravid rule, rallying the mountain tribes in the spirit of religious fervour. In 1130 they charged from the mountains to siege the cities of Morocco and after a long and bloody campaign, the era of the Almoravids was finally over in 1147. Soon the mosques of the land were torn down and rebuilt in Almohad fashion and the designs of the southern cities morphed from Andalusian to an opulent blend of Arab and Amazigh that still typifies the cities of today.

Just like our desert guides, then, the Amazigh were never a people to let history write itself. With the Amazigh identity on the line and a true interpretation of Islam worth fighting for, the rebellious Amazigh would rule Morocco in their name until 1554. Under the Almoravids and Almohads, northwest Africa flourished in unison and the tenacious 'free people' begun to write the next great chapter in the chronicles of Tamazgha. For now, at least, it seemed that the Amazigh were simply unconquerable.

Though the sun is at its zenith, with stomachs full Hamza invites us to explore the dunes around the oasis and suggests the use of two sandboards that wedge into the desert by the edge of camp. They are quite clearly there to appease us pesky westerners, but, after much insistence, and with great reluctance, we agree to spend the afternoon hooning around on the dunes, having an outrageous amount of fun under a fiery Saharan sun. Being the skier of the group, I reject the sandboards and opt instead for another toy perched alongside. It is nothing fancier than a simple upturned crate with a pair of rudimentary skis strapped to the bottom. I shall christen it the Berber bobsleigh and despite it looking utterly unsafe, I must have a go.

By now the heat is beating down an onslaught and any exertion is draining. Already my face is bathed in sweat, as we haul our new gear up a mammoth dune that dwarfs the oasis camp, which shrinks slowly into the sands beneath us. The exertion is such that we see little point in testing our mettle on the shallow lower slopes near camp and instead we are going all in, to the very top for a full run. Matt, an experienced snowboarder, shoulders his sandboard while Katharine pushes hers uphill from behind. For me, however, this is a case of one haul forward and a very long slide back, for each time I thrust the Berber bobsleigh from my side to my front with all my might, it proceeds to slither back down the dune. I do not dare push it up the dune with ski tips pointing forward in fear of slipping, taking out camp below and shattering both my dignity and front teeth in the process.

Eventually, we make it to the top of the dune, where it is apparent that we are stood at one of the highest points in the entire desert. Some dunes in the Erg Chebbi reach as high as 150 metres, making these the highest in all of Morocco. The Algerian border looks striking ahead of us and unbroken desert tumbles in every direction. It feels like we are raised on a pinnacle at the very heart of this island of dunes, all settled lands far removed. I have had an idea that I share with the others. Such was the effort to summit this enormous dune, I suggest we go for one run down its far side, away from the oasis camp and into empty desert, and then climb back to the top for one final run back into camp on the far side. That way we get two runs in, after which we can call it a day and retreat to our guides with the call for tea. The others agree, but as I balance the Berber bobsleigh on the precipice of the knife-edge ridge, I begin to question my own sanity. With my back to camp, I can see nothing ahead except unbroken desert, and this far side of the dune is much longer and steeper than the one running into camp.

But there can be no backing out. I have the Kiwis behind me and I am committed. I haul my legs over the crate and perch awkwardly on top, the skis of the Berber bobsleigh overlapping the knife-edge ridge. I push off with my legs. I know it's a terrible idea, but I am underway. Five seconds of joy pass by. I raise an arm in the air, a celebratory and cocky cheer to show that all is going well. The bobsleigh is picking up speed … rapidly, but soon the dunes will flatten out. I just have to endure the ride. It's a joyride, sure, but everything is going great … until I see what I am heading for.

The dune flattens out in a large bowl of sand, and the next dune is some distance away, but straight ahead of me is a small, solitary, tufted mound that rises comically from the otherwise flat and open desert. It is seemingly the only mound in this entire, smooth bowl, and now we are eye-to-eye, the mound with its stupid tuft of hair growing larger and cackling at me, willing our paths to meet.

Around me is a toxic blur of blue and yellow. The laughter of the Kiwis is now a hallucinatory whistle, lost in the wind behind me. I am a pathetic, redundant passenger. How did life lead me to this moment, charging down a dune, with a turban flapping across my face, perched on a crude and homemade Berber bobsleigh?

I am about to face my fate. I cannot steer, I cannot bail. The seconds are passing by too quickly to react. I am at full speed and my GoPro is back in camp. I'm not even going to catch this on film! This is a pointless and dignity-smashing endeavour. I elevate my legs, clench my stomach and brace for the inevitable to follow.

I take flight.

The exact details of what happens next is still a mystery to me, but a blur of sand and sky rushes past my eyes as I somersault an impossible distance through the air for what feels like an eternity. I've landed hard on my chest, my face planted comically into the sand. Never have I felt a drone through my entire body like this. I hear the Kiwis yelling from above, asking if I am okay, but I'm too winded to move let alone utter a reply and, anyway, sand is lodged down my throat. Eventually, I can flip over and give everything a wiggle to check that nothing is broken. Sand is wedged up my nose and jammed in my ears. I spit a sandcastle out of my mouth, gagging as grains irritate the back of my throat. I realise that I've lost my glasses, so my blurry eyes frantically scan the sand around me, looking for a mound of crumpled glass and plastic. To my relief, they are some three metres away and intact, although engrained with sand having taken flight mid-antics.

Once I have regained a little composure, I give the Kiwis a thumbs up and haul myself over to the Berber bobsleigh. It's cracked down one side, but fortunately still in one piece. I have landed some three metres from the crate and a further seven from the mound that launched me skywards. I am amazed that I am okay. With sandboards abandoned up top, the Kiwis join me at the foot of the dune to laugh sympathetically at my comical face. They talk me through their view of my acrobatics and I am gutted to hear that they too failed to catch it on film.

A painful, heat-beaten slog back up the dunes begins in earnest and in my current state, I care little for the expressions of discomfort that I pull. For some odd reason, the Kiwis decide not to fire themselves off this same dune, and instead we lower ourselves half way down on the camp side to have one final run on the junior slopes, where it does not take long to realise that even the sandboards are not really designed for sandy environments. On the trudge back to camp, I realise how long it will be until my next shower. My body feels like sandpaper, the desert refusing to be shaken free from my face. Every orifice streams sand like a waterfall. I have to sleep like this tonight! Hamza takes a look at my condition and instantly prescribes tea, which we down like shots as the remainder of the day passes at a mercifully easier pace.

6

One Million
Star Hotel

Erg Chebbi

Golden hour in the desert, and as we haul ourselves to the crest of a dune one last time, the oasis camp is now beneath us for good. In every direction, enormous dunes swoop and arc like a frozen ocean of crashing waves, each crowned in gold above a flood of rich orange. Nestled behind, Hassi Labied looks tiny against a broad silhouetted backdrop of the Anti-Atlas Mountains, which slice straight across the horizon in layers of darkening grey. The evening sky is a rich and intoxicating yellow, the Maghrebi sun slowly sinking.

We sit on the dunes in silent, mutual awe for the majesty of the desert sands. Even our guides, who must journey here often, sit beside us in shared wonderment, their turbans blowing gently in the wind, their smiling faces lit orange like the Sahara around us. There is total peace. Sometimes a moment like this evokes large and worldly questions, and I anticipate it, having learned of the lives of our desert guides earlier in the day. But on this occasion it does not. Instead, I find that everything makes perfect sense: the silence of the dunes, the slow passing of time, measured only by the setting sun, and the easy movement of man and animal across the land. Here there is a beautiful, timeless simplicity.

A guide arrives from the dunes beneath us, trailed by three camels for some South Korean girls who have joined our party. Some distance across the ocean of sand, a man in a flowing orange djellaba is leading another three camels on a snaking path through the dunes, with a plod that is effortless. Though they are distant in the failing light, I know it is Hamza with our animals. Eventually, I watch as his silhouetted figure halts, turns around and kneels his camels in turn. Once again, the dunes are motionless, this ship of the desert anchored in the ocean.

When we finally reach Hamza, the sun is just caressing the farthest mountains, over which the day's dying embers seep, bathing us in rich mauve. Quickly, we are returning to the mysterious depths of twilight and the energy of that sunset is matched most certainly by the inky black void into which we now sink. We mount our camels in silence and at first we ride on, Hamza at the front and occasionally by our side, but soon we must stop and dismount. Katharine's larger camel is stubborn and is refusing to descend the steeper dunes. At this twilight hour, I do not blame it; I strain my eyes to make out the terrain, which is angular, ill-defined and never flat. The camel had been threatening to throw her free as it stomped, fidgeted and protested Hamza's orders, moving only across the easier terrain – and even then at a crawl. It would have been just too risky to drive it on.

By the time we can finally remount, the night has swung to blackout and the expanse above glitters in silver. Hamza wills his great beasts on with an encouraging coo and our scarfs flutter around us in the pleasant, warming wind. Hamza points out stars and planets above, *there's Mars, that's Venus*, and tells us stories of the desert, passed down from his ancestors. The void of an empty night only enhances the poignancy of his tales, his voice the only sound for miles, as he speaks of the oasis, of mirages, of his family and forefathers moving through the desert. He reminds us that many of his tales are only folklore, but says that when he moves alone through these dunes, he can believe all of them.

"They say that a long time ago, in this place in the desert, there was a small village," Hamza begins one of his tales, "and all of the families … black. One day in the village, the people celebrate a party and after dinner, people start to play with food. You know, playing with food is something very bad. Very bad! So, the Gods sent a very big sandstorm and it covered the entire village." Hamza is getting evocative with his arms. He has halted the caravan, and moved from its head to beside us all to share this story. It must be an important one.

"Still people believe they can hear the music of these people when they sit in this desert. They say that they can hear the Gnaoua music," he continues. "Gnaoua – it means black people. Slaves. So, people still say they can hear the music of these people in this place."

There is a short silence as we ponder the moral of the story, trying to recall how eloquently we had eaten our dinner last night.

"But this is just legend!" Hamza reassures us flatly, his voice filling the void of the desert night. "Okay? So, there is logic … and legend!" Hamza taps two fingers on top of his head. "You know, Africa, a long time ago, there was just seawater here. Then the water dried and it left behind sandy rocks. Then the sandy rocks with the wind formed small dunes, you know? Then every year … bigger, bigger, bigger. So, there is the legend … and the logic!"

"Ahhh. Thank you for sharing that," Matt responds diplomatically, reluctant to pick a side between the Gods and the Gnaoua, "… that is some night sky."

When we arrive back in camp, the Koreans that we met briefly on the dunes are already sat in the mess tent. Having left just a little earlier than us, their camels must have been considerably more compliant on their journey back to camp. By now I am desperate for a shower. Sand still pours out of my ears when I tilt my head to one side and annoying little grains grit in my teeth and irritate my eyes. The Sahara has gone absolutely everywhere and even my boxers have somehow succumbed to desertification. Obviously, there is no shower for miles and the thin trickle of water that had run from the tap this morning has slowed to a pathetic drip, so I better man up and deal with it.

Food is welcome distraction and, to our delight, Hamza joins us in the mess tent for dinner. Having had the odd encounter with him thus far, I really want to get to know this curious man. I completely understand his affection for this desert that his family has roamed for generations, but Hamza is a father and a village dweller too. I want to know what is keeping him here, against the allure of greater opportunities beyond. On the dunes earlier in the evening, looking across Hassi Labied from the crashing waves of gold, I had gotten an impression of his two worlds. One is of bricks and mortar, at the very edge of civilisation and quite literally at the end of the main road. The other, meanwhile, is of timeless simplicity: animals, movement, exchange.

"You know, Africa, the name that we have for ourselves?" Hamza refills our glasses with tea. "We call ourselves 'Amazigh.' It means 'free people.'" He pulls a mobile phone from his djellaba pocket and shows us a picture of the Amazigh flag, pointing to a symbol at its centre. It is the one that I have used to divide sections in this book.

"This is the Yaz," he continues, "it means 'free man.' And Berber, what does that mean? Well, it means barbarian." A laugh seeps through his lips. "You see, Africa? We think that we are free men, but everyone that has come to conquer our lands over the years has been afraid of us and our spirit. Our free, fighting spirit! It has always been the same: the Romans, French, Arabs. You see, for us there are few things that really matter in our lives. Money? No, definitely not. Guests, like you? Yes. But most importantly, that open sky: the moon, stars, rain, sun. Today, we might live in the villages, but we are still desert people. Still we are free men."

The Amazigh flag has come to symbolise the movement calling for greater cultural and linguistic recognition for North Africa's indigenous people. It is a tricolour, with blue for the Mediterranean, a green stripe for the hills of Tamazgha, and yellow for the Sahara. But it is the 'Yaz' at its centre that stands for the unity of the Amazigh, their irretractable freedom, and endeavours for cultural renaissance. All across Tamazgha, this flag can be seen at protests, at sports events and at celebrations, as a symbol of unwavering pride in their identity and homeland. Yet, it has also become known as a flag of rebellion, and in 2019, Algeria banned the flag at protests, claiming it an assault on the nation's Arab identity.

Since 1554, Morocco has been ruled by Arab dynasties. It may have been the barbarians from the desert who united these lands in the 11th century, but tribal feuding saw the unity crumble and soon the empire splintered into a number of smaller kingdoms. No Amazigh dynasty to follow could reunify northwest Africa. In the 16th century, yet another group of religious revolutionaries claimed to be the true interpreters of Islam and revived the Kingdom of Morocco. They knew themselves as the Saadians, who claimed descendancy from the Prophet Muhammad, and they saw themselves as being ethnically Arab, not Amazigh. Just as a religious zeal had lured the Almoravids out of the desert, the Saadians legitimised their rule on a strong religious footing. Under their dynasty, Morocco thrived in a golden age, but the Amazigh were slowly forced to the fringe of society as Arabisation quickened in tempo in Morocco and in the neighbouring Ottoman Empire. Over the decades to follow, the Amazigh identity was slowly drowned out, and, in truth, it would never fully recover. Today, an Arab dynasty still rules Morocco and the Amazigh remain culturally and politically marginalised in the lands where their ancestors lived.

I ask Hamza about his wife, whom we met briefly at his guesthouse yesterday. They had an arranged marriage, he explains, after he refused the first girl his parent brought to him. He is grateful for the choice of refusal and describes the occasion when he first met his wife and visited her family. In Amazigh lands, marriage is as much about the joining of two families as it is two people, and when compared to many of their Arab neighbours, Amazigh women are given considerably more freedom and are highly valued in positions of authority.

Even across the fiercely hierarchical and tribal lands of the Amazigh Tuaregs to our south, it is women who control the tribal camps and it is often women who lead the raids. The first Tuareg monarch was also a woman and Tuareg women have the liberty to own property and decide who they marry or divorce. Most Amazigh artists are women and women are typically the public symbol of Amazigh identity. The word 'son' means 'produce of the mother' in Tamazight and unlike in some other Islamic societies, women do not have to wear the veil. In fact, in Tuareg lands it is more typically the men who are veiled. Nonetheless, while the matriarchal Tuareg have been influenced little by factors beyond the desert, most Amazigh communities have become considerably more patriarchal over the centuries, in line with Islamic tradition. As a result, it is regrettable that in this conversative and patriarchal society it can be difficult to meet Amazigh women and hear their story.

Hamza speaks of his children and his hopes for them. In a few years' time, they will be old enough for him to teach them how to orientate with the stars, understand the wind and navigate the dunes, just like his father had taught him. He does not mind if they follow his footsteps in the desert, or forge their own path in the city, just so long as they remember their nomadic and Amazigh roots. Indigenous culture has been suppressed here in Morocco. Despite around three in four Moroccans having Amazigh ancestry, their identity, rights, beliefs and culture have been squeezed to the fringe of society for decades, marginalised by the imposition of Arabism and Islam, upon which Morocco and every one of its Maghrebi neighbours has been unified since independence in the mid-20ᵗʰ century. Broadly, it has been embraced.

"But it is not natural," Hamza protests. "Still people who live in the desert believe in spirits, in stories told by our ancestors. They are very, very important in our lives, as desert people."

Many nomads do now follow Islam, but often in distinctly personal ways. Customs and beliefs die hard in this very conversative kingdom, and when Islam swept to these lands in the seventh century, it did not displace the traditional pillars of nomadic identity, nor the practices and beliefs that are intrinsic to their way of life. Many nomads believe that acts of nature, such as sandstorms or droughts, are the manifestation of divine will, and the Amazigh people are known for their reverence of marabouts: mystics and holy men who the poor, anxious or sick make pilgrimages to, seeking health, healing or answers. The worship of such idols is strictly forbidden by orthodox Islam.

"What about Tamazight?" I ask Hamza. "I hear that you can speak and teach it freely now." While suppressed in recent decades, iterations of Tamazight have been spoken in North Africa for some 4,000 years, though it evolved into a written form much later. For millennia, Tamazgha was an oral society, whose collective memory was mostly passed down the generations by word of mouth, or through various art forms such as in the patterns of Amazigh rugs, which convey the histories of great tribes, battles and victories. Consequently, Tamazight is a source of immense Amazigh pride.

"Yes," Hamza says, his eyes lighting up as he does. "We can finally teach it in schools and the children can speak Tamazight again. My son is learning. It is something very special, when he speaks to me and my wife in Tamazight. Really, we never believed it could happen."

Since 2004, children in Tamazight-speaking, 'Berberophone' areas of Morocco, which are mostly in the Atlas and other rural areas, have been required to study Tamazight, the Amazigh tongue, having long been prohibited. It was revived by the reigning king, Mohammed VI, at a time when more extreme strands of Islamism were starting to gain a foothold in Moroccan political space. It was seen as a national unifier, a stabilising force at a time of division, yet for the Amazigh it meant so much more than that. You see, following independence from colonial rule in the mid-20th century, nations of the Maghreb long held Arabic, as the only language in which the Qur'an may be recited, in a truly unassailable position, alongside Islam itself. Tamazight, on the other hand, was not deemed a national unifier, but an existential threat.

It all began decades ago, when an invading French army landed on the shores of Ottoman Algeria in 1830. They had come to colonise and soon almost 1,000 years of Islamic rule in North Africa shuddered to a halt. Recognising that few before them had ever managed to unify this region as one, the French colonisers opted for a strategy of divide and rule and immediately set about 'othering' the Amazigh from the Arabs along ethnic lines, in a bid to win their support. After all, they were in the *Bled es-Siba* and if the French colonial endeavour was to succeed, they would first have to earn the support of the region's 'free people.' It was in their interest to do so. The Amazigh had not always had a bad relationship with the Arabs, and so the French were on constant guard, afraid that the two could join forces and rally against them. When the Arabs conquered North Africa in the seventh century, they were accompanied by loyal Amazigh converts. Then, when the Arabs pushed on north to Iberia, they invaded with an army of mostly Amazigh recruits, led by fearsome Amazigh warrior Tāriq ibn Ziyād.

As such, the colonial French did everything they could to distance the Amazigh from the Arabs, to win them as colonial partners. Perhaps ignoring their rebellious history, the French deemed that the Amazigh would be easier to subdue than the Arabs, and so they began to spread the so-called 'Berber myth' that framed the Amazigh as being not true Muslims and as more biologically aligned with Europe than the Middle East. They were the favoured sons of the French, who promised to rekindle the Amazigh's more enlightened, Western, and Christian roots, while the Arabs were characterised as idle, hostile and fanatical Islamists beyond the mould of the colonial project. 'Don't associate with them,' was their plea to the Amazigh, 'you're one of us.'

After generations of repression under Arab and Ottoman rule, the 'free people' suddenly found themselves elevated to societal esteem, as the French sought to swaddle them as colonial brothers. The Amazigh were placed at the forefront of the French school system and received privileged status from colonial authorities, while Arabic was declared a foreign language of the region. The ambition was clear, but their plan backfired. Badly. For centuries, the Arabs and Amazigh had co-existed relatively peacefully and it was only with the dawn of colonial rule that clear ethnic lines were drawn between them. The French were clearly trying to sow animosity to secure their rule, and neither the Arabs nor Amazigh were fooled. Oh, and the 'free people' were not exactly eager to subject themselves to the will of a foreign power either. Soon there was upheaval and, just as the French had feared, North Africans began to rally in unison to oppose their colonial overlords.

Yet that was far from the end of it. When the French were booted out and Morocco gained independence in 1956, North Africa was still riddled with lasting remnants of that pesky 'Berber myth.' It may have proven unpopular, but it had penetrated Moroccan society. Hassan II ascended to the throne of an independent Morocco in 1961, but the elation of newfound freedom was soon replaced with contestation over the nation's new identity, and indeed that of the region. In an effort to unify their populations, every Maghrebi nation joined the Arab League and declared their nations to be officially 'Arab.' Their proud histories were realigned with the arrival of Islam in North Africa and Arabic became the sole official language of the region. Public life underwent an era of Arabisation and thousands of teachers were drafted in from the Middle East to systematically replace French as the primary tongue of education and administration with standardised Arabic. After millennia of Amazigh domination and decades of colonial rule, North Africa was now unmistakably Arab. It would not be until the 21st century that the Amazigh could speak their mother tongue in schools again.

Having long been regarded as the enlightened and autochthonous majority, the Amazigh suddenly found themselves framed as ethnically 'Arab.' Their history was falsified and identities redefined as being no different to that of the country's new ruling elites. Tamazight was declared a dialect of Arabic and school textbooks were rewritten to teach that Moroccan history began with the Arab conquests of the Maghreb, at which point the Amazigh were liberated from their backward ways. Constant rebellion, especially in the lawless Rif, aroused suspicion that the Amazigh were planning a revolution, and so with the unity of the newly independent nations on the line, the Arabs felt obliged to quash the 'Berber myth' for good. In the autocratic reign of King Hassan II, Amazigh culture was crushed under the fist of Arabism and Tamazight was abandoned by many families, fearing that speaking their language may incite colonial divisions. As Ernest Gellner wrote in 1972, 'in his heart the Berber knows that Allah speaks Arabic and modernity speaks French,' while Tamazight was the tongue of a backwards past. For the unconquerable Amazigh, these were the darkest of days.

It was therefore momentous when in 2004, shortly after ascending to the throne after the death of his father Hassan II, King Mohammed VI declared that Tamazight would become a compulsory language of education in Morocco. Not only were the Amazigh reinstated into the nation's proud history, but Tamazight was lauded as a national unifier. In 2011, its status ascended even further, becoming an official national language. This made Morocco the only nation in North Africa and the second member of the Arab League to recognise a language other than Arabic as 'official,' denying itself the cherished right to be known as a purely 'Arab' state. The king had dared to challenge the narrative upon which modern Morocco was founded. In doing so, he ushered in calls for greater rights, recognition and representation that rumble on across Tamazgha today.

"The king had little choice," Hamza tells us. "Across the border in Algeria in 2001, there were many protests and a lot of violence. It was called the Black Spring and many people died. The Amazigh protested because they had felt ignored for so long. Then, each year, on the same day, the protests began again, both in Algeria and in Morocco too. So, the king could not let it go on. He knew that things would soon turn very bad, so he had to do something."

National politics had forced his hand too. More extreme strands of Islamism were starting to gain a foothold across the region and the king knew that he needed the Amazigh as allies, despite them being a thorn in the side of the Arabs for so long. Concessions on Tamazight and the promise of reform was timely and shrewd. It enabled the king and the elites of the kingdom, known as the 'Makhzen,' to weather the storm of the Arab Spring in 2011, while regimes around them crumbled. Yet while the king survived the uprisings, the protests gave a voice to those who were previously voiceless, including the Amazigh, and they have since refused to let their voice go quiet.

71

Many have argued that the recognition of Tamazight only goes so far. Now the Amazigh are rallying for much wider-reaching rights, as well as the lessening of cavernous inequalities between urban and rural areas. Others go further, accusing the king and Makhzen of mirroring French colonial policy by inscribing Islamic laws for Arab urbanites and tribal laws for the rural and mostly Amazigh populations. This has split the kingdom along ethnic lines and sown differences in culture, rights and education that only reinforce inequalities. Arabic remains the dominant tongue of national governance, and while the cities thrive, many rural areas remain desperately poor. Up to 500,000 children are forced to work in the countryside and rates of illiteracy are among the highest across the Maghreb, almost 90 percent among rural women, and so the Amazigh's struggle goes on.

Hamza tells us of a camel race held in Hassi Labied just a few years ago. The villagers lined their camels up, a starting gun was fired and the camels shot in different directions, some charging for the desert, while others barrelled towards the village, their riders redundant passengers in a chaotic stampede. One eventually won by chance, although its rider had little to do with its victory. As I tidy a plate of couscous that Salim has prepared for us, I cannot help but think of this story as a metaphor for these proud people: nomads of this desert and Amazigh from across Tamazgha are clinging valiantly to their land and identity, though the fate of both lies only partly in their hands.

The campfire is roaring as we wander beyond the edge of camp to join Salim, who is stoking the flames with fresh wood. Only when we step away from the fire do I realise how cold the night has become. There are even more stars tonight and for the first time in my life I can see the entire Milky Way in all its streaky splendour. I attempt to take a photo, but swiftly realise my shortcomings and instead do something without precedent in the 21st century and decide to live the moment.

As the day winds down, our guides seem at ease around the campfire, although the copious amounts of hashish being smoked may have something to answer for. We warm our hands and dance to the beat of the Amazigh drums which have begun. The Korean girls join us and at last, there is a celebratory atmosphere. Storytelling and music can begin. They are pillars of nomadic life and I can feel their purpose, filling the short time that nomads have between the tasks of the day and bringing the unit closer together.

Here in our camp, four of the guides are playing traditional Amazigh instruments: one is on the tam-tams and another on the darbouka, both variants of Moroccan drum. Another is strumming an oud, like a lute, while another plays the sweet and flowing lira, a traditional, bamboo flute. Hamza, on the drums, is also in fine voice. Their percussion resonates through the camp and their rhythm is heavy, a cathartic beat that rings through the empty night, beneath a dazzling river of stars. It feels like the whole world has been shrunk to just what is lit by the fire around us, yet the vastness of the universe looms in the void above, the explosive music rising to it.

Hamza is singing songs about the nomads' homeland. One tells the tale of a shepherd, another is called the 'Camel Dance,' my favourite is simply about the beauty of Africa. They are movingly simple compared to themes of music from our own lands, and chillingly rhythmic. The beat pounds in your brain like a shaman's trance, the flute swirls high into the night with the smoke of the fire, and Hamza's booming song is the zenith of it all, thumping through the empty desert. The words may be in Tamazight, but we can sense their meaning. Our guides are invested in their music and it is a joy when Hamza hands out his drum and invites me to play. With a brief demonstration I have a feel for the rhythm, beating my hands to make a boom from the heavy wood and a sharp tap from the drumskin. Once more, I am drawn into a special moment. To the thump of my drum, Hamza is singing and the melody of that lira is ringing out through the night once more, all by the light of the fire.

Once the Amazigh music is over, Hamza invites us all to sing songs from our homelands. The Kiwis go first, chanting an indigenous Maori verse that sounds rather like the haka they perform before thrashing us at rugby in Twickenham. Then the Koreans take their turn, sharing a K-pop song from their land, all while I frantically try to muster a song from Britain. This should be easy – we virtually run the music industry!

Only *Wonderwall* is coming to mind, but that is terribly basic and my dignity has already been face-planted into the Sahara some miles from here. Plus, it is hardly the embodiment of my country's proud history. Eventually, I come up with *Hey Jude*, but I have no idea why. I barely know the words, but another British song has completely eluded me. I stutter through the few words that I know, looping it a few times with some *na na na nas* and throwing in the odd *everybody!* in the hope that someone will back me on the vocals. My prowess on the tam-tams has been rapidly undone by my lacking on the British song front. At least I am true to Eurovision form.

We beat and strum late into the night, our guides now taking their rest by the fire, their instruments handed out among us. I wish I could remember just a few guitar chords from my school days, but they too allude me and though I'm once again on the drums, that rhythm from the Camel Dance has completely slipped my mind. The racket that we make has snapped me sharply from that rhythmic, trance-like state that our Amazigh guides had induced. Earlier in the evening, Hamza spoke rather eloquently about how music is made from sounds that by themselves are simply noise, but as our Anglo-Maori-K-pop fusion shatters the aura of the desert night, there can be no denying that the sound we make classifies as nothing more than *just noise*.

7

The Beckoning Snows

Erg Chebbi, Midelt

The wind is really getting up this morning as the soft sand under our camels' hooves gives way to stonier ground on the return to Hassi Labied. A fearsome gale had been blowing raucously through the night, thrusting sand through the fabric curtains that were supposed to seal our tent entrance. Camp looked rather sand-struck this morning and now the skies over Hassi Labied are starting to grey over too. Soon, there is going to be a storm.

We are running low on dirhams, so we switch camels for Hamza's saloon and dart down the road to Merzouga for the nearest cashpoint. As we do, the sky looks menacing. The weather has swung so abruptly and now it seems that we had been extremely lucky with the weather in the desert winter. A harsh wind whips the lower dunes and a storm is clearly brewing. In an instant, the quiet tranquillity of the desert we have just emerged from has vanished completely.

"There are many sandstorms at this time of year," Hamza says as he eyes the approaching storm. "When you live in the desert, they are one of the most dangerous things you can encounter. My father told many stories of getting lost and stranded. Sometimes, he would be cut off for days. If you have to move, it can be impossible to find your way."

Storms can make life difficult and dangerous, especially for nomads in their rudimentary tents. Tucked deep in the depths of an erg desert, an already-isolated camp could get completely cut off. On the ride back from camp, I had to use my turban to cover my mouth from the spray of sand and fortunately my glasses protected my eyes. I dread to think what life is like now for the Koreans and guides who remain behind as this winter storm quickens pace. For all the tourism and merriment by the campfire, this can be a harsh and foreboding land. Just a few years ago, flash floods displaced over a thousand people and killed several in Merzouga, at the heart of desert tourism. Sandstorms can be paralysing and in the winter it can even snow. As the road ahead swirls in ripples of sand, I know that this beautiful desert can easily become a far more hostile land. After all, here we are located at the edge of the largest hot desert in the world. Journey south and you won't reach a larger village than this one for some 1,600 kilometres, until your camel stumbles on Timbuktu in the sands of Mali. This is the final frontier of civilisation, before the hinterlands of nomads and lawlessness beyond.

It's almost time to say goodbye to Hamza, but first we ask if he can recommend a place to eat in Hassi Labied. He says he does not know, but insists that we join his family for lunch, in a manner that would be impolite to refuse. Back in his guesthouse, his wife generously prepares a large Berber omelette and a plate of vegetable couscous. The food is sensational and we insist on paying, but he categorically refuses.

"Life is about doing good," he says with a final parting handshake. His wife stands beside him, his children hurry through. "Money is not important. All that matters is good people, good times," he points upwards, "and that open sky." With a call of "Bon voyage, Africaaaaaa," from behind, we are gone. The embers of nomadism may be burning across this land, but some things will never change.

Sixty miles out from the desert, at a fuelling station on the long road north to the lesser-travelled passes of the Middle Atlas, we receive news from a helpful local. It does not sound good.

Unlike in much of Europe where the process of refuelling a car is a solitary endeavour, here in Morocco it appears to be a full team effort. As we pull up at the pumps, an entire pit crew is deployed to process us as labour-intensively as possible. In fact, it is quite astonishing how many individual roles the process of fuelling a car can be divided into: as one man wields the pump, another pops coins in the machine, while his colleague readies himself to flip shut our petrol filler cap, all while a man at the window flogs us bananas. A windshield wipe is even thrown in, though I expect an undisclosed number of dirhams to slip discretely into our final fee. Back in the UK, the number of workers on this quiet backcountry forecourt could be reduced to, well – none.

But I digress. Back to that news of great concern. One of the men without a role in this particular operation has lent his arm through the window and asks where we are headed. Midelt, we tell him, nestled in the peaks of the Middle Atlas. We shall find somewhere to stay for the night, before journeying on to Fez, the ancient capital, tomorrow. He murmurs and ponders out loud for a few seconds, like an old computer processing a command, before he shakes his finger with a look of grave concern. He cannot find the English, but makes a big X with his arms and shakes his head.

"The road is closed?" we enquire in unison, to which he nods. We ask him which road is shut, the one to Midelt, or onwards to Fez. He does not understand the question, but utters something about *neige*.

Snow? Even my schoolboy French caught that but surely, he must be mistaken. Here we are stripped to single layers, endless miles of arid land, sandy crags, and rocky outcrops have been passing us by in a blur. There have been acres of hardy date palm groves. The afternoon sun is scorching us alive. The high mountains that we crossed just a few days ago were dust-ridden; only the highest of the passes had snow. All of a sudden, my mind flashes back to the guidebook that I had read on the plane journey in, its warning of mountain passes forced shut in winter months now ringing loud in my ears.

We cannot dwell on such thoughts. We have to reach our stopover town of Midelt before the night closes in, to ensure that we reach Fez in the morning. Two roads straddle this part of the Middle Atlas: one is higher and more mountainous, the other lower but far longer. Time is escaping us. Already we are racing the night to Midelt and we must avoid the darkness, given the testing conditions that may lie ahead. We do not have time for the longer route and turning back would be futile. Only the desert lies behind us, and so with thanks exchanged with our numerable pit crew, we rejoin the road under a beating African sun.

Conversation moves on quickly from the prospect of snow as dusty lowlands tremble in the heat haze around us. The road is monotonous, the miles inching by. Already I miss the easier pace of the desert, where the passing of time mattered little, and I regret being back on the road and racing the daylight. Police checkpoints line the route, as they have done across the nation. They amuse with their procedures. Some slow us down but wave us on through when they spot three weary-eyed foreigners inside. Others approach more dutifully, neatly uniformed with hands clasped behind backs, wielding mean glares.

"Where are you from?" they will demand, normally in English, but sometimes in French. New Zealand, we reply (for ease, I have become an honorary Kiwi), after which a hand shoots through the window and a cartoonish smile beams, wishing us an extremely pleasant stay. Every time I wonder what the wrong answer would be and what they are looking for. Later on, we blast through a checkpoint that we did not see coming, but the police seem unmoved by our swift passing.

The Middle Atlas passes are still an hour away as rain begins to beat down, as it threatened to do in Hassi Labied. Fortunately, it kept away. The rain is slowly changing. They have really unusual rain around here, and we all comment on it. The drops are big and infrequent, tumbling slowly from the sky. It must be the mountain climes, or a phenomena of the Saharan dust. But my mind puzzles with it, increasingly so. I am fairly sure from the silence that the others are thinking the same … but we are just too far south for it to be plausible. Perhaps I should just say it, daft as I will sound. I'm sure that it is so.

"Is that snow?"

"Nah, still too warm," Matt replies quickly with some no nonsense Kiwi common sense. The desert is still too near, the mountains just too far. Only when a dusting of white begins to pepper the arid landscape around us do we finally accept a most peculiar reality.

Daylight is fading as we drive through a land that is alien. Parched trees stand like scarecrows in the fields, their crooked arms trimmed in white, and the asphalt too is changing colour. To our relief, the locals have slowed to a cautious crawl, but at this dawdling speed we will not reach Midelt until long after nightfall. And what if the man was right? What if the road ahead is closed? Then, if we do reach Midelt, we will have to start again tomorrow, traversing high snow-clad passes that are lesser-travelled in these winter months and pictured in my guidebook, strung across the bare mountains. The journey that lies ahead is fraught with uncertainty.

Snow intensifies as we crawl north, and soon the odd mystical flake becomes a flurry of white, as we enter an area where snow has clearly been pelting for some time. Mounds of tufted vegetation that coat the lowlands are now heavy with powder, smothering our surrounds in an otherworldly yet beautiful texture. But I know we are going to make it. Our pace has been slow, but as darkness bathes the Atlas ahead, the GPS finally aligns with Midelt. I feel a sense of childish excitement for this otherwise purposeless destination, long just a stopover town on a tiresome journey north. But now, as the snow continues to tumble and the night closes in, it has become the setting for a story of its own. Are we marooning ourselves here? Fez is now within striking distance, but as we approach our kasbah and hunker down for the night, we are all solemn in the knowledge that over 200 kilometres lie ahead tomorrow over passes that will dwarf the roads of today.

In the dawn the land is frozen stiff. So too are my fingers, and indeed the heavy wooden window shutters in our kasbah room. But when I finally manage to prize them open, I cannot for the life of me understand why any sane person would decide to plonk a kasbah in the icy depths of Finnish Lapland. Certainly, as a bright green parakeet swoops down from a palm tree and sends a heavy plume of snow cascading into the ice-filled depths of a swimming pool below, the Erg Chebbi feels a terribly long way behind us. Our icy surrounds are beautiful, the skies a crystal calm, but the tranquillity is deceiving. Shimmering snow-filled plains stretch from the kasbah doors to the mountains on the far misted horizon and an overnight storm has rendered the land unrecognisable.

We part ways with our hospitable host, whose charming old kasbah was a fortuitous find on a dark and bitter winter's night. It was a place of some grandeur too, with a fountain and two striking portraits in the lobby, one of the former king, Hassan II, and another of a young regal woman that I do not recognise. Indeed, to show allegiance to the king and Makhzen, most hotels and cafés will display a royal portrait on the walls. It is usually of the reigning monarch, Mohammed VI, deemed a popular reformer by many, but occasionally a portrait of Hassan II will be on display too. Hassan II determined Morocco's path for the future after achieving independence in 1956. Heralded by some, he is widely regarded by many others as one of the most autocratic and brutal rulers in recent Moroccan history.

Ascending to the throne in his late 20s, Hassan was a leader with an obsession for power. Early in his reign, he led Morocco down the path to becoming one of the most repressive and least free nations on Earth. Three decades of his reign, from the 1960s to 1980s, have come to be known as the 'Years of Lead,' where state violence was normalised and arbitrary arrest was commonplace. While there are few official records, hundreds of political killings are believed to have been carried out, and thousands more dissidents were jailed or tortured. Many who opposed his rule simply disappeared, including in foreign cities with Moroccan and Amazigh diaspora, such as in Paris. Subversive books were banned, newspapers were forced to stop printing and even the Michelin map of Morocco was prohibited, for failing to display the disputed Morocco-Algeria border in a way that pleased the elites. In 1965, power-hungry Hassan went even further, suspending the new constitution, dissolving Parliament, declaring a national emergency and assuming the power of direct rule. In this dictatorial climate, the kingdom sunk to having one of the worst human rights records in the world.

These were dangerous years to resist the dynasty, or to make public expressions of Amazigh pride. Constant rebellion in the predominantly Amazigh Rif saw the region suffer years of neglect that even today has left the hilly northern lands decades behind in economic development. Street riots were common but brutally repressed, while others resorted to violence. In the early 1970s, Hassan narrowly escaped two attempts at his life, including one assassination attempt planned from within his own ranks. Extreme abuses of power had rendered Morocco an international outcast and, amongst the gloom of global isolation, including from France, which withdrew its ambassador from its former territory, senior officers from the Royal Armed Forces decided to attempt a coup d'état.

In the summer of 1971, when Hassan was celebrating his birthday near Rabat, armed rebels stormed his summer palace and opened fire. The assailants were almost 1,000 military cadets, who had been roped into the coup by senior officers who wanted Hassan dead. Rabat's main radio station was captured by rebels, who broadcast to the capital that the king had been killed and a new republic had been founded. But it was a bluff; Hassan was still alive. He had hidden in a palace bathroom throughout the attack, where almost 100 guests were gunned down by the cadets, many of whom got caught in the crossfire. Royalist troops soon retook the palace and a loyalist to the king, General Oukfir, who would later become the Defence Minister, set out after the rebels who were thrown into detention camps across the country. However, in an ironic twist of events, Oukfir was the mastermind of a coup attempt of his own just one year later as four F-5 military jets from the Moroccan Royal Air Force fired at the king's plane as he returned from a visit to France. Bullets ricocheted off the fuselage, but the plane would not go down. The king escaped with his life again. Legend has it that Hassan himself grabbed hold of the plane radio and yelled to the assailants in a disguised voice, 'The tyrant is dead! Stop shooting us, you fools!' after which the firing ceased.

Eventually, the tyranny of the Years of Lead was forced to an end, when international isolation forced Hassan's hand. Slowly the country saw more liberal reforms, but it would not be until the death of Hassan and the reign of his son, Mohammed VI, that Morocco's human rights record would significantly improve, to the extent that Morocco is now considered 'partially free.' In 2004, the new king decreed a number of reforms, including the officialisation of Tamazight and establishment of a commission to review atrocities in the reign of his father. However, human rights abuses remain widespread and certain topics – the king, Political Islam and the disputed Western Sahara among others – remain virtually unspeakable without fear of arrest or long imprisonment.

Yet with newfound liberties came the confidence to speak out and in the years to follow the reign of Hassan, new waves of protests would soon sweep Tamazgha and change the face of the region forever. Most, you will not be surprised to learn, first took root with Amazigh rebellion in mountains such as these across North Africa. The Years of Lead were a devastating era for the Amazigh, but soon they would rise again with rebellions on a scale not seen in generations. In fact, events in the last three decades, and especially in the 21st century, have shaken North African politics to its core.

A well-wrapped elderly gentleman de-ices our saloon with buckets of warm water and as we rejoin the ominously named 'route 13' to the north, conversation is notably muted. What if the road ahead really is closed? What if there is no way through to Fez? Here we are stranded in no man's land, with the desert behind us, the talons of the Middle Atlas ahead, and winter striking the plains that occupy the lands in between, where now we journey. Thick snowfields merge with the ice-sheened asphalt, over which clouds of powder drift and great chunks of ice fly from the heavily-chained tyres of trucks that thunder by. Apart from the odd crooked tree that juts through the powder, vegetation in these arid lands is low and buried, and soon we plough through a filthy slush that smothers the road.

But it is all in vain. Just 50 kilometres down the road from Midelt, in the sleepy little village of Aït Oufella at the foot of a mountain pass, the inevitable strikes and it seems that our gamble is at an end. A snake of stationary vehicles reaches back to us along the highway, and so we grind to a painful halt. The man at the petrol station, all the way back in the dusty lowlands, had been right. A callous wind strikes my face as we step outside and ice-skate our way to the head of the queue, where a metal snow barrier, inscribed in Arabic, obstructs the mountain road to the north. Two days ago, we would have passed with ease, but winter has struck these hills abruptly. So, with little else to do, we join the locals by the long snake of vehicles, some left idling to keep heaters ablaze and engines ticking. Mere hours ago, we were stood in the desert. How the seasons have swung.

A policeman is stood by the barrier, so I usher him over.

"Umm ... wie viel uhr?" I stutter to him, before realising that I've just asked the wrong question, and in German. He speaks no English, but after a few vigorous taps of my non-existent watch, he suggests the pass may remain closed for another three or four hours.

"Definitely reopening today?" I enquire. He shrugs.

Midday has come and gone and once more the skies are darkening. With the temperature hovering around freezing and the sun elusive, I cannot understand how the conditions could possible improve enough for the mountain pass to reopen today. At the snow barrier, Moroccans in their warm djellabas stand around in uneasy conversation. They, like us, are pondering the few available options: wait by the barrier, see the night out in Midelt, or tackle a longer route to our east that would see us arrive in Fez deep in the night.

Nobody is turning back, so we join the families, farmers, businessmen and desert folk beneath the trees by the snow-struck roadside and share the slow passing of the day in unexpected surrounds.

I've grown rather fond of this Moroccan radio station by the time the trucks and saloons in front splutter into life and flood petrol fumes back down the road towards us. It is just about early enough to call it afternoon, though I certainly wouldn't call this daylight, as a very fumy caravan of vehicles begins to motion its way through little Aït Oufella. The grey skies overhead are ominous to say the least and though we're underway, I am not counting my camels yet.

We push over the pass in renewed snowfall as a snowplough, lights ablaze, roars in the opposite direction, a stream of traffic trailing in its wake, finally freed on the far side of the pass. At last, we are traversing the Middle Atlas, a stretch of the Atlas that is far more sparse and lesser frequented than the High Atlas to our west. These are remote and wild valleys swept by the wind where golden eagles soar, and soon a gentle powdering quickens to a flurry that pounds hard against the window. Ghostly sheets of cloud wisp in the gloom of the valley below, which sinks to bottomless snow. The wipers work in overdrive, groaning and squeaking as they try to keep pace with the onslaught of white.

Some of the animals by the roadside are suited to these icy climes; others are certainly not. Powder plumes as boisterous troops of barbary macaques jostle in the depths of the snow-packed cedar forests. They swing through the canopy with ease, but the knees of the donkeys that watch their antics are sunk deep in snow, while stray dogs huddle together beneath the Christmas pines, shivery and confused, caught in the sudden swing of the seasons. The drops off the road are sickening. The truck ahead has been crabbing since we departed Aït Oufella, but now its driver wrestles for control as it squirms like a horse, bracing to kick him free. We have barely made ground since daybreak. The mountain passes slalom over the terrain with an infuriating patience, but at long last, as a frozen lake sheens on the murky horizon, the pass relents and eases through settlements that are wild and remote in their wind-swept winter white.

Eventually, our stomachs can take it no more. They demand a pit-stop in a village that is strung along the roadside. It's just like any other that we have halted at in Morocco, except here our car is pelted with snowballs, thrown by local kids. There had been no other towns along the way, so a small café with some tagine pots steaming in the snow on the pavement has become our halt for a very late lunch. In all truth, I don't trust it. Nor do I fancy our tagine when the top is whipped off, revealing a mush of vegetables and the odd strip of chicken, that looks and tastes rather like plasticine. Nor do I feel especially hygienic, after relieving myself in a hole-in-the-ground loo, contents of which were swishing around on the tiled floor, before washing my hands with a gel that I am fairly sure is just blended cucumber.

But needs must, and as my trusty companions are gladly tucking in with optimistic Kiwi spirit, I, now an honorary New Zealander, shall join them. Chur, mate.

Three days later, back in Copenhagen, I attempt to extract myself from bed. It is 10am, an ungodly late hour that I shudder at the thought of awaking at. I have been struck down with a rather horrific bout of campylobacter, which, for those who have had the pleasure of gracing life without encountering this devilish word, is food poisoning and that unearthly tagine in that snow-filled café is my prime and most reviled suspect. For four gruelling days, as I attempt to sell my bike in Copenhagen (surprisingly difficult; Morocco has clearly done little for my bartering prowess) and move all my earthly possessions back to the UK, I can think of nothing else but that goddamn filthy tagine that has wreaked such havoc with my internals.

How I felt during this week is for another book I shall never write and you shall never wish to read, but let it be known that face-planting in the Sahara or plunging into a not-so-frozen lake in the depths of the Arctic Circle pale into insignificance when compared to this, the devil's own work.

8

Fes el Bali

Fez

Not for the first time on this journey, we have stumbled upon what appears to be a filmset in the middle of an action-filled production. Surely, this impressive medieval façade will soon be torn down and a cast of some 200,000 actors who are beating metal and riding donkeys will melt back into the noise and pollution of the real metropolis that must lurk in the hills of olive beyond.

Once more, however, I am blissfully mistaken. Capital of intellect, lodestar of Islam and Morocco's second largest city this may be, but on arrival in ancient Fez you are struck instantly, and rightly, by a feeling that little has changed in 1,200 years, since the Idrisid Dynasty founded this old city on the banks of the River Fez in 789 AD. Before us is the Mecca of the West, the Athens of Africa and some of the last remnants of medieval civilisation left on the planet, still pulsing with life.

Now on foot, we pass through a splendidly ornate gate named the Bab Bou Jeloud, patterned in zellige, which crowns the western end of the medina with three keyhole-shape arches. A chaotic medieval scene unfurls within, as if homes and workshops are stacked atop one another in a disorganised sprawl. Every medina gate is patterned with a unique design, but this one in particular speaks of the people within: blue and gold on the outside are the proud colours of Fez, while green and gold zellige inside represents the permanency of Islam within these old walls.

The Fassis, as the locals here are known, are an exceptionally proud and pious bunch.

The Bab Bou Jeloud is where we meet our host: Youssef, an ever-smiling young Fassi with a propensity to giggle. He bears an uncanny likeness to our guide from Dadès in more than just name, as both men are armed with the knowledge, wit, and intrigue of a world far beyond their own. But then again, I remind myself: we have just turned up in a city that was once the intellectual capital of the world and it appears that our host is an embodiment of his city's age-old wisdom. A narrow labyrinth of back-alleys twists ever-deeper into the heart of ancient Fez – known as Fes el Bali – past family homes and workshops where music plays, en route to Youssef's riad. Tea is poured instantly on our arrival in a bright central courtyard that houses a blue mosaiced fountain and a very grand piano. A twisting staircase rises three whitewash floors to a square of open sky, beside which a narrow roof terrace peers over the medina that bursts through its ancient walls and floods the surrounding hills that cocoon old Fez like a secret.

Without doubt, this is the most dense and jumbled city that I have ever seen. A low skyline flows over the contours of the terrain like an urban ocean, crowned only by the tall minarets of mosques that reach higher towards the heavens than any other building. Aside from a mad tangle of wires and satellite dishes that pattern the panorama of rooftop terraces like a very abstract mosaic, this is a view that has changed little over the centuries. In a city where space is at a premium, rooftops are utilised to the full and only the odd tall tree in an open square offers a verdant speckling to an otherwise congested, and mostly yellow, urban sprawl.

Fez is quite shockingly dense, though as the evening adhan pinballs through the jungle of brick around us, what strikes us most of all is the realisation of just how pious this city must be. Fez is the Islamic capital of an already very devout region and on the rare occasion that you can poke your head into open sky above its congested ancient quarters, it will be met by the spectacle of more than 400 minarets jutting skyward, over half of which are squeezed within the claustrophobic confines of the old medina walls. That is like cramming 200 mosques within the coastal-hugging, two-kilometres borders of Monaco, and it's only half the mosques that this city would have had 600 years ago. Still pilgrims flood to Fez en masse, some seeking the wisdom of the many scholars who take residence here, while others, mostly from West Africa, come to pay homage at the resting place of Ahmad al-Tijani – a preacher of Amazigh origin, who brought Sufi Islamic order to much of West and North Africa. Islam is the societal glue of this kingdom, but nowhere is that more apparent than here.

Today is Friday, the most important day of prayer for all Muslims, and poking above the square just a stone's throw from Youssef's riad is the green minaret of the Kairaouine, the great mosque of Fes el Bali. Just a few moments ago, the voice of its muezzin pulsated through my being and soon it shall house more than 20,000 Fassis in worship, just as it has done for the last millennium. Yes, I said a millennium – for at least 1,100 years. According to Youssef, this mosque, one of the largest and oldest in Africa, is Fez in a nutshell.

"The Kairaouine is not just a place of worship," Youssef explains. "It is also a madrasa, an Islamic school, and the oldest university in the world!" Or, at least, the one that has seen the most continual use over the centuries. He continues: "Actually, at the beginning of the second millennium, this madrasa was the centre of education in all the Islamic world. Possibly even the most important place of learning on Earth!"

The Kairaouine is the very embodiment of Fassi wisdom and piety. While Europe was stuck in the dark ages, Fes el Bali was flourishing in intellect, which would eventually flood back across the Mediterranean to inform the Renaissance. Even in modern times, its madrasa is famed around the world for the quality of its Islamic scholarship.

"Classes are still led by a sheikh," Youssef says, "and students must learn the Qur'an in its entirety."

"So only Muslims can attend?" I ask.

"Well, yes," he replies, "but actually, I believe that a pope was one of its first graduates!" Indeed, Pope Sylvester II, who led the Catholic Church at the dawn of the second millennium, is said to be among the university's earliest, and perhaps more surprisingly, alumni, as a visiting scholar.

The mosque is easily the most impressive building in the Kairaouine quarter, a district of Fes el Bali that was settled on the west bank of the River Fez around 824 AD by pious refugees from Kairouan in what is modern-day Tunisia. Kairouan – sound familiar? The city of Kairouan was the North African base for the Umayyad governors in their seventh century conquest. Fleeing rebellion at home, the Kairouans teamed up with Idris II, son of Idris I, founder of modern Morocco, who ordered them to construct a city on the river's west bank, to rival the city built by his father on the east bank just seven years prior. They did so, constructing a modest little prayer hall in the process that would some day become the mighty Kairaouine.

"What you see across the river is still Fes el Bali," Youssef explains with a sweep of the hand, "but that is the Andalous quarter, settled by Idris I, the founder of our nation." He built it with the help of refugees who had been expelled from Al-Andalus after a failed rebellion against the Umayyads. While the Kairouans arrived with faith, wisdom and an Arabic flare that endures so prominently today, the rebels of Andalusia arrived with the skills and crafts of Europe, that would eventually spark life into the ancient guilds that still organise the medina today.

"But rather than merge as one city," Youssef continues, "the two settlements on the west and east banks began a bitter competition that would last for three centuries." Like its younger brother down south, Marrakech, Fez is not just a Moroccan conception, but the amalgam of cultures, ideas, crafts and beliefs from lands far and wide. For centuries, owing to its turbulent early history and hasty construction at the hands of refugees, Fez was not one city at all, but two. In fact, it wasn't until the 11th century and the arrival of a new dynasty, the Almoravids, that the gated walls dividing the two cities were finally razed to the ground and a bridge was built over the river to ease divisions between east and west bank. Finally united as one, the rivals formed what is now known as Fes el Bali, where religious scholarship and the guilds could flourish within new walls that kept the lawless out and the Fassis as one.

They remain that way today and more than 1,000 years on from its founding by refugees from nearby lands, an unwavering piety and thirst for wisdom endures, while Andalusian-style craftsmanship remains the lifeblood of this ancient medina, its methods having changed little over the centuries. When the French marched in and took charge in 1912, they decided to build a Ville Nouvelle, 'new town,' outside of the city limits, leaving the old walled medina and its ancient traditions intact. It was part of their ploy to keep the proud and often rebellious colonised population on side. So, while the kingdom beyond these ancient walls faces off against modernity, life for the easy-going Fassis remains just as it always has been.

We depart Youssef and descend into a labyrinth of medieval souks that sprawl from his riad, ripped straight from the pages of history. This medina is an all-consuming assault on your every sense. Carpenters toil in a wood-strewn back-alley that wafts of cedar and oak. A noisy square of large-biceped metal workers thumps with the hammering of pans. A foul-smelling district of paint-box tanneries brushes shoulders with the ancient potters' quarter, which is lit by strings of bulbs. It is perhaps so due to the holiness of the day, but the energy of these streets is cordial and calm, certainly compared to Marrakech, and swiftly our initial impression of chaos has been displaced by the realisation of age-old logic in this ancient network of souks. Together, they form the largest urban car-free pedestrian zone in the world.

In fact, every district of the medina still operates just how it would have done centuries ago, each housing its very own mosque, madrasa, hammam, fondouks (mostly used nowadays as warehouses) and bakery where the Fassis bring their dough to be baked each morning. Change in old Fez means turbulence and so is slow to take root, but Fes el Bali is also conservative by necessity. So compact is this ancient medina that many new technologies and modern amenities simply do not fit and so the medina remains dependent on the guilds and traditions first seeded by refugees centuries ago. You won't see cars on the 10,000 streets of Fes el Bali, nor will you hear the sound of heavy machinery. No – this city runs to the sawing of wood, the hammering of metal, the murmur of barter and the occasional outburst from an angry chicken. But above all, as we walk through the souks to a soundtrack of medieval life, we are struck mostly by the blissful realisation that few locals seem to care for our passing. These Instagram-worthy souks have not been preserved for us tourists, but rather for the servicing of everyday Fassi life.

Light is waning as we finally reach the most famous guild in Fez, at least in the Instagram age: its technicolour tanneries. This city is one of enormous charm. Our arrival was late and already I regret our fleeting stay here, though as we near the tanners' quarter, the feel of the streets changes abruptly. It morphs from easy to uncertain, all eyes staring our way, eager arms grabbing at ours, as youthful men loiter in doorways, ready to haul unwitting tourists to the promise of free tours, which uniformly end in the store of a 'brother.'

After much fruitless wandering in sniffing distance of the Chouara Tannery, it becomes apparent that a glimpse of this ancient industry is only attainable through one of the eager youths, who work the streets in partnership with the nearby leather shops that cocoon the tanneries and monopolise its much sought-after views. So, eventually we try our luck and disappear through a leather-filled store on the promise of *the* very best view in all of Fez. Funny that, given that we have just passed the best panorama in Morocco. And the kid with the baseball cap had the top ranked rooftop on TripAdvisor! But I digress. Mint leaves have been thrust into our hands, *'sniff, sniff, place smell like sh–,'* and we are following a man we met mere moments ago over live wires and under satellite dishes across a ... very Moroccan rooftop. Already, I have had to convince him that I really do not need new slippers.

But my goodness, this young man is most certainly not a liar. As we straddle a narrow walkway and gaze from the edge of the rooftop, the panorama that unfurls below is Fez in a nutshell, one of many medieval guilds upon which this city was built. Like a giant paint box, some 200 round tanning vats line in a colour spectrum, from deep blood red and duck egg blue, to whitish cream and chocolate brown. Around them, sun-darkened men teeter along narrow gangplanks that connect up the vats, working a fully operational medieval tannery where the methods have barely evolved over the centuries. Behind the tall yellow buildings that rise in each corner like sentry towers, draped in the hides of sheep, camel and cow, ancient Fez flows over the hills, with a million satellite dishes shining silver.

This is believed to be the oldest tannery in the world and the work is certainly a job for the youthful and athletic. In summer months, the tanners must endure temperatures of over 50°C as they squat, teeter and dunk the heavy hides in colourful vats of pigeon poop and sheep urine that, along with lime, are used to strip the skins clean, ready for dying in the nearby dyers' souk. Everything is done by hand and yes, despite the wilted leaf of mint that I clutch snug to my face and sniff vigorously like some kind of wonder drug, this foul place smells of true and utter sh–. Mercifully, despite the biblical stench and backbreaking work, this is a reasonably well-paid profession and the tanneries of Fez, like most across the kingdom, are run as cooperatives, with a foreman leading his workforce and supporting the adjacent leather shops, whose balconies peer over the hard graft below and control the tourist views. Jobs here are practically hereditary and many who work in the leather shops and nearby leather souk, where most produce is sold locally, are relatives of those dunking leather under a beating sun outside. Centuries ago, Fez would have had 200 tanneries operating just like this one; today, only three remain.

A little old lady proceeds to chase us around her leather store like a hungry stray as we pretend to browse for babouches, but, much to our surprise, and relief, we slip out of her store with a generous tip and depart with ease, back into the hordes of faux guides and tourist-snatchers promising a view like no other. Actually, we tell them, the finest view of the tannery is just along the road.

Night has charged these streets with a renewed energy, as we twist our way back through the labyrinth to Youssef's home. In typical Arab style, while commerce bustles in the souks, domestic life is hushed and discrete in quieter corners of the medina, where now we retreat. Back on Youssef's roof, Fes el Bali ripples beneath us like a rolling ocean of lights, as the heavy darkness bathes the Riffian foothills to our north in a deep blanket of mauve. Those hills are known as Morocco's last land of lawlessness, the final bastion of the *Bled es-Siba* and the heartland of the Amazigh movement. It is there that the Amazigh's cries for greater rights and recognition is louder than just about anywhere. In just over a year's time, unbeknown to me now, I shall journey there.

Indeed, after centuries of Arabisation, Amazigh culture is no longer strong across all of Tamazgha. Instead, it has retreated to small, isolated territories, where Amazigh pride and resistance is as strong as ever. One of those pockets is the Rif, and indeed much of the Atlas, which have become hotbeds of Amazigh resistance against regimes that marginalise and repress their culture. The same is true across the region: in Kabylia in Algeria, around the Siwa Oasis in Egypt, among the Tuareg lands in the Sahara and Sahel. These have all become places of Amazigh revolt, which have often lit the flames for much broader movements that have taken root across the region. In modern-day North Africa, Tamazgha is less a geographical entity than a state of mind. It represents a common heritage, a shared identity, a joint struggle that is rooted in the sands of

Africa and unites Amazigh across the Maghreb. Tamazgha only exists in the mind, but today, across the region, a proud Amazigh identity is stronger than ever.

While anthropologist Ernest Gellner concluded that there was little sense of Amazigh identity back in the 1970s as most indigenous people associated more with their tribe than other Amazigh, recent years have seen a dramatic shift. Nowadays, Amazigh from across North Africa are increasingly seeing themselves as belonging not only to a local tribe or group, but also to a large transnational Amazigh community. It has enabled the 'free people' to call upon their common identity and heritage to collectively resist their marginalisation, right across the Maghreb. In fact, while many North Africans are still quite unfamiliar with the term 'Amazigh,' an increasing number are starting to willingly embrace it. It is partly to reject the derogatory name 'Berber,' but also to distinguish themselves from North Africa's ruling elite, who they claim have failed to represent them. In fact, prior to independence from colonial rule, an Amazigh identity shared across North Africa didn't really exist. Instead it was local and specific, shaped by the particularities of geography and national history. Yet the pace of Arabisation and the marginalisation of Amazigh identity has forged a renewed sense of common struggle.

At first, the idea of a shared Amazigh identity was mostly celebrated through the arts, performance and cultural expressions, such as theatre, poetry, crafts, literature and dedicated media channels. They sought to broaden the use of tifinagh script and share stories of Amazigh history, to try and include the Amazigh in national narratives and in the history of the region. It was a noble endeavour, but it only achieved so much. Reforms were slow and promises hollow, so the Amazigh were forced to fight fire with fire. Now their movement has evolved again, from a campaign for cultural renewal, to a movement with political ambition. To offset what they see as untamed Arab hegemony, which ignores the plurality of cultures in North African society, the Amazigh have crafted a homogenised identity of their own that unites the 'free people' from the Rif to Siwa and from the Kabylie to the Tuareg as one. It includes the creation of a standardised Tamazight and a common linguistic and cultural umbrella, under which every Amazigh can claim to belong. In other words, it has allowed the Amazigh to rally in unison, right across the Maghreb, to reclaim their stake in the region.

It has been a fractious and controversial process, but one that seems to be working. In the 1980s, riots erupted in Kabylia after a university lecture on Amazigh poetry was cancelled by the authorities. It was seen as yet another attempt by the Algerian regime to eradicate the cultural traditions of the Amazigh, whose patience had worn thin. Rioters were brutally suppressed by the police, who violently cracked down on the unrest, yet, instead of giving in, the Amazigh decided to take a unified stand. Every year since, on the anniversary of the events, 'free people' from across the region have taken to the streets to rally in unity against what happened and to express their continued anguish. Then, in 2001, a student was killed in police custody in Algeria after taking part in such demonstrations and street riots erupted again, followed by yet another brutal crackdown that left 120 dead. It is known as the 'Black Spring.' For the Amazigh, these were the darkest of days, yet they also marked the first coordinated protests by the 'free people' against North Africa's post-independence regimes. Together, they had dared to challenge the new regional narratives and emerging status quo, which had refused to acknowledge them as a people.

Since then, the Amazigh have been assertive throughout the region as they endeavour to secure their rights. In the 2011 Libyan Civil War, Amazigh in the Nafusa Mountains rebelled against the Gaddafi Regime and battled with loyalists for control of the region. Then, in 2012, the Amazigh Tuareg in Mali staged a major rebellion and tried to found an independent nation called Azawad in the north of the nation, where all cultures could live in unity. And even tonight, in 2016, the foothills of the Rif thunder around us to the boots of protestors who are marching for economic justice and the release of political prisoners after decades of neglect in the mostly Amazigh region. They are calling it the Hirak Rif Movement and it began after a fishmonger was crushed to death in a garbage truck while trying to recover his swordfish, which had been confiscated by police for being sold out of season. What began as isolated anger in the coastal town of Al-Hoceima has now morphed into a far broader movement, raising grievances of the neglected north.

And that is to forget the Arab Spring, which shook the Arab world earlier this decade and changed the face of the region forever. As soon I shall learn when I return in a year, the Arab Spring was not just Arab at all. The Amazigh too surfed the wave of popular uprisings to secure a voice that they have since refused to relinquish. It is a story that is so often swept aside in the bigger picture of regional revolutions, but one that is certainly worth telling. Back in 2011, everything changed. Even here – in Fes el Bali, the ancient capital of Morocco and the last bastion of an ancient order. At first glance, it seems that everything here is just as it always was. But as we sip tea with Youssef and listen as the hectic souks rumble in the dusk beneath us, it is clear that the tides of change have reached here too.

"Overcrowding is rife in Fez," Youssef explains, as he swirls a pot of steaming Berber whisky. "Change here is slow and unwelcome, but a steady arrival of migrants from the countryside has been pushing my city to breaking point. There is just no room! No room for housing or modern industries. Our water and sewage cannot cope with any more people." He motions a hand to the north. "Look to the horizon. What do you see? Shanty towns … they are spawning on the hills."

In many ways, old Fes el Bali is a perfect metaphor for Morocco as a whole. Despite these ancient walls and the tradition within, here too, in arguably the most complete medieval Islamic city on Earth, I realise that I am stood among people wrestling the tides of change. Fes el Bali is reliant on the guilds upon which it was founded generations ago, but slowly they are crumbling. Just three of the medina's 200 tanneries still remain and in a jumbled old medina like this, there is simply no room for new industries or technologies to take root. Just like the nomads of the desert, then, Fes el Bali – a last bastion of the old order – is clinging valiantly to its traditions. But for how much longer?

"What really concerns me," Youssef places down his glass, "is that some of the ancient ways of the medina are starting to fall apart. Some of our most important industries, such as the pottery guild, are leaving the medina and moving to the more spacious hillsides." Back when the Almohads were in charge here, Fes el Bali had 188 pottery workshops, 372 mills, 47 soap factories and over 9,000 shops. This was a medina of thriving industry, which is sadly now in decline.

"It really matters," Youssef continues, "because all of the guilds rely on each other. They rely on the other guilds being close by! The dyers need the tanners to prepare the skins. Should one industry move away, everyone here will feel it."

"What can be done?" I ask him.

"There isn't much," he replies solemnly. "Now, even the tanneries are in decline and relying on tourism. It is fantastic for Fez, to have the tourists. But it also brings faux guides. And what of the fondouks! Now they are being transformed into hotels, and the old buildings are being torn down. It starts to break our communities and people will have to turn to other kinds of work. Fez will have to change. But you see, Fez does not do change!"

The northern cities of Morocco – Fez, Tangier and Meknes – have always been beacons of opportunity that have hauled migrants from the countryside on the promise of wealth inside these ancient walls.

"And I cannot blame them," Youssef continues. "They are here to start a better life, just as my family did. We moved from agriculture in the west, where there is still a lot of poverty. Now look at my life. But here in Fes el Bali, we cannot cope. There is no room."

"But what about the Ville Nouvelle?" I ask him. "Can the city not expand there?"

"Well," he says, "most wealthy Fassis do spend much of their time in the Ville Nouvelle. It is clean and modern, whereas many Fassis see the medina as a dirty place stuck in the past." He exhales sharply. "But the medina is the lifeblood of the entire city!" His arms are thrust wide open in anguish. "Thousands of Fassis still make their living here, and they come to shop, trade, or buy food. The new city is just a place to relax or live. This is the beating heart of Fez! Everybody relies on the medina, because if one domino falls, if one guild moves to the hills … everything else could go with it."

Back in the colonial days, progress and innovation was the preserve of the affluent French, who resided in the shining new Ville Nouvelle. The supposedly backwards medina, meanwhile, was preserved for the indigenous population to live and for the French to bimble through an ancient world of traditional charm. Even today, Fez is burdened with the legacy of colonial urban design. While the French planners thought they were doing the Fassis a favour by leaving their medina intact, they failed to anticipate just how fast the medina population would expand. The result is that today the medina is cocooned by the sprawling Ville Nouvelle, with any hopes of expansion or innovation boxed in by new Fez, which explodes in blandness beyond its ancient walls.

Yet as the lights of shanty towns glow like fireflies across the lawless foothills of the Rif, none of us are fools to the fact that things here *are* starting to change. Morocco, too, is a nation in flux, and the Maghreb is in upheaval. The Arab Spring just sent shockwaves through this land and, once again, Tamazgha is alive with the horns of rebellion that blare in the hills around us. On this journey, I have gotten to know the 'free people' and witnessed their remarkable fighting spirit. I have learned of their histories of rebellion and resilience, which they continue to write today. But now, at our journey's end, I feel determined to delve much deeper. I want to find out what the future holds for the Amazigh and I want to see what life is like in the hostile mountains and lawless valleys around us. In doing so, I want to better understand the political undercurrents that simmer beneath the surface of this region. Despite all that we have witnessed, I feel like we have barely scratched the surface, and now, in the darkness, the rocky bastions of the Amazigh heartlands are beckoning me deeper on our every horizon.

The eccentric red city. Don't be fooled by the calmer scenes of day …

… come night, the souks and Jemaa el-Fna market square are charged with an electric energy

Red dust rock of the Dadès Gorge, monkey fingers to the left and the Road of the Thousand Kasbahs strung along the valley to the right

Above, Yassine and I emerge from the water-filled gorge. Above left, his village of Aït Ouglif. Immediate left, switchbacks of Todra Gorge on my 'alternative' route to the desert

Four shades of sunset over the Erg Chebbi. Nomads still cross these
sands and we, like them, are following in the hoofprints of
merchants, warriors and missionaries

Nomadism is easy when
town is just a quad bike ride
over the dunes. Even here,
it seems the signal is good

Base camp. Nestled deep
in the dunes, a sandstorm
could completely cut off a
nomad camp like this one

Salim prepares the campfire for an evening of song and storytelling. They are pillars of nomadic life, bringing the unit closer together

Above, a Sahara selfie. Left, our three camels at sunset, ready to journey back from the oasis camp. Abu, my camel with attitude, is at the rear

The infamous Berber bobsleigh, pre-acrobatics

I pinch myself … we're still in Africa! Unexpected scenes on the long road north from the Sahara to Fez, over the passes of the Middle Atlas

Our gamble is seemingly at an end. A snow barrier in Aït Oufella blocks the mountain road to Fez

The Bab Bou Jeloud crowns the western end of the medina.
Blue and gold are the proud colours of Fez

Tanners toil around
paint-box vats under the
beating sun. The stench
is biblical, but mercifully
the work pays well

Artisan at work in the
pottery guild of Fes el
Bali. Overcrowding is
forcing some industries
to the surrounding hills,
threatening the age-old
ways of the medina

The El Badi Palace, the *Palace of Wonder*, was built during Morocco's golden age under the great Saadian Dynasty. Today, though, only its ruins remain in the ancient kasbah of Marrakech

I am back in Morocco, back in the red city!

A barbary macaque in front of the Cascades d'Ouzoud. This joyful
species only survives in a few small pockets of oak, cedar and pine in
Morocco, Algeria and Gibraltar

Closer, closer, nearer still
… aboard the Berber
Titanic, before my camera
(and we) got drenched

Above, Ali, our crazy
raft paddler. To the right,
Jason, Ruben, Nabil and I

Jebel Toubkal, the highest peak
in North Africa and the Arab
world, deep in the tribal and
once-hostile High Atlas

Our guide and host, Lahcen,
pours tea on his roof terrace in
Aroumd. After initial distrust,
we gain affection for this
intriguing young man

Village life in snowy
Imlil, base for trekkers,
guides, muleteers and
mountaineers

The golden-hued ksar of Aït Benhaddou, setting of blockbusters and once a strategic outpost on the ancient caravan trail from the Sudan to Marrakech

The perfect final sundown before my long journey north …

Roadside fruit sellers are everywhere in Morocco.
Many are poor, so a generous tip is warmly received

My sleeper train to Tangier.
Perhaps unsurprisingly, my
camera didn't get much use on
that long last day in Marrakech

An image of their colonial pasts, the north of Morocco
feels Spanish, while the south is notably more French

On the cacti-lined trail from Chefchaouen to the Spanish mosque.
Behind, the misted foothills of the Rif and to the east,
Morocco's last land of lawlessness

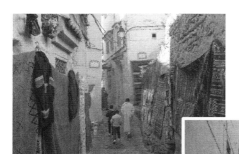

The reason for Chaouen's
many shades of blue is
contested. Some say it is to
keep away the mosquitos,
others to stay cool, or to ward
off evil spirits. Others say the
blue is merely to entice tourists

SECOND JOURNEY

January 2018

9

Drumbeat of Arabia

Agadir, Marrakech

Touchdown ... in whitewash Agadir. Where on earth is Agadir? After an eternity circling the darkened skies above Marrakech, my feet are finally reunited with Moroccan soil, but I have no clue where in the country we are. The wind was tremendous when we ventured out of the terminal and up the steps of our aircraft at Stansted Airport this morning and now it seems that the wild and stormy weather has followed us to North Africa. It was just too dangerous to land in Marrakech, so now we find ourselves under dark and humid skies in southern Morocco ... 150 miles south of where we should be.

"We're north of Marrakech," I tell the boys wrongly, not having a clue where we are. Being the one-time-Morocco-traveler, I cannot be ignorant of this simple geography. "We're near Tangier, I think – so, I will be back around here in a week."

After a sleepless night slouched in Costa Coffee and this morning's flight at the crack of dawn, this is an unwelcome delay, and as we walk beneath the aircraft wing and join the switchback queue to security, we overhear the scale of our diversion. Oh my – I am further south than I have ever been before. Ahead of us lies a four-hour coach ride north. We won't be in Marrakech until late this afternoon.

So, while the others doze off – I *cannot* sleep on *any* form of public transport – my eyes admire the arid surrounds of a rather unexpected corner of the country. This is an apt time to return. Since my last visit just over a year ago, the rallying cry of the Amazigh has been ringing out across Tamazgha once more. The 'free people' of North Africa are on the march again and through the summer last year, in 2017, protest ricocheted through the Rif: the rocky northern hills with a reputation for rebellion, where soon I shall journey. The honeymoon period that followed the Arab Spring is over. The kingdom's elites had weathered the storm of popular uprisings and some had even been strengthened by the fires of revolution that swept the Arab world, but nothing here is certain anymore. Since my last visit, over 1,000 protestors have been arrested on political charges and many have been imprisoned, but this has only fuelled the waves of disdain and in recent weeks, the Amazigh have realised important victories too. Just six days ago, the Amazigh in Algeria were able to celebrate their New Year, Yennayer, as an official paid holiday for the first time.

It's a thrill to be back among the region's free people and this time, I am determined to delve deeper, into the simmering undercurrents of the Amazigh movement and into their mountainous heartlands. I want to see for myself what changes are taking place in their hills and cities, which are sparking life into a new wave of rebellion and protest. After decades of marginalisation, Tamazgha is in the grip of an Amazigh re-awakening, which is taking hold across the region. Not in generations have the 'free people' been as vocal as they are today. I will be joined on this second journey across Morocco by four friends from university, whom I have persuaded to join me. Though, when I say 'persuade,' it was not a difficult sell. Final year studies are taking their toll, an Arabic speaker is among my recruits, and – well, we are all just rather curious about what lies south of Guildford.

So, some introductions. Joining me on this second journey will be Moe, an Arabic-speaker of Moroccan heritage who, with his local lingo and impromptu one-liners, is a vital asset on this trip. Moe will also be taking turns at the helm of our Peugeot 301 hire car (pearly white, in much better nick than our rust bucket from 2016), alongside Jason: an ever-dependable pair of hands and fellow Morocco returnee, who also happens to be my housemate. Having shared a house for two and a half years in the wild west of Guildford, Park Barn, anything that Morocco throws our way should be a doddle. Then there's Ruben: our bearded and exuberant vlogger. He's part Spanish, part Indian and full-blooded Wood Green. Over the next few days, everyone and everything in his sights will be shot, given a hilarious and deadly honest commentary and then uploaded for everyone back home in seconds. Then, last but not least, there is Nabil, who, with his Persian blood, is on a homecoming of sorts. His ancestors rode camels along the silk road and now it is his turn to live the Persian dream, albeit a little further west. He drinks tea by the gallon, clutches a transparent washbag by his side at all times and will not be seen in public without his Ray-Bans and a tailored leather jacket. In other words, we blend right in.

Once again, my finger is tracing our route across a map, beginning now in Agadir. Marrakech is our first port of call, and a springboard to the mountains that tower on its eastern horizon. I want to meet those that call these mountains home, but first our journey takes us north, to the mighty Cascades d'Ouzoud, one of the tallest and most spectacular waterfalls in Africa. Then we'll venture south of the red city, into the mountains and to a small Amazigh village that is nestled in the grasp of the High Atlas, at the foot of Jebel Toubkal, the highest peak in North Africa and the entire Arab world. We are journeying to the mountains in winter and the route that lies ahead is uncertain, but I am intrigued to find out what life is like for those that live in their midst. I hear that tourism and climate change have been transforming lives in these tribal and once-hostile frontiers, but I want to see for myself.

Then we shall passage over the great Atlas range itself, crossing the Tizi n'Tichka to the beautiful golden-hued ksar of Aït Benhaddou, the setting of blockbusters and once a strategic outpost on the caravan trail to Marrakech. Then my companions and I shall depart, they venturing east to the Sahara while I journey on alone, back across the High Atlas and then north, by train to Tangier, then bus to Chefchaouen, an ancient, fortified town nestled deep in the storied foothills of the Rif, the 'last land of lawlessness.' First world problems have forced my early departure, but more on that later.

Agadir itself is not especially interesting. A big earthquake flattened the place in 1960 and tragically killed over a third of its population, so the entire city had to be rebuilt some two kilometres further south. As such, this is a new city, something of a tourist resort. Grand, tree-lined boulevards are lined with fancy hotels, modern boutiques and cosy little cafés serving European breakfasts. But it also feels like a city built in anticipation, a city planner's city lifted straight from the textbook. It is the Paris of the south ... that no one is talking about. Copy-and-paste apartment blocks line the murky Atlantic coast like hollow, whitewash skeletons. It may be winter, but there aren't many people here.

In the hot and dusty south, Agadir therefore comes as something of a surprise. But to its north, the dull monotony of a tourist city is swept away by a thick blanket of red dust that smothers the alien land around us. The passing latitudes bring occasional stretches of beautiful fruit tree orchards, mostly lemons and oranges, that are somehow thriving in the water-scarce south, yet, despite the imminent winter rains, these southern lands are mostly barren. Dozens of fruit sellers line the road, some holding exotic fruits that I do not recognise to our window. With few settlements around, I wonder how they make a living from this simple roadside trade. Characters who remind me of the desert folk from Hassi Labied wander along the road. Many of the men here are turbaned and women veiled. Kids play football in the dust, empty jerrycans marking the goals, as adults slump in the shade of homes, chewing on nuts, watching the world pass slowly by. In this fiery midday heat, time appears stagnant. Everyone is just waiting. Waiting for the heat to pass.

As the road winds its way across hilly terrain, thick clusters of date palms spring in the narrow river valleys that snake lime green beneath us. Simple homes cling to their sinuous edges, but they are dwarfed by dark clouds that roll over the mountains ahead, veiling their summits as we motor towards the storm that diverted our flight earlier today. Time crawls and stomachs growl. Midday has gone already and we have not eaten since around 5am – in a Wetherspoons at the airport no less. My eyelids are heavy and head lulls, as the humidity chokes us alive. Surely, I can catch just a little sleep. For a moment, I wonder if I *have* drifted off, but no ... my droopy eyes are just puzzling with the scene in front of them. I take a sip of water to splash some sense into myself, but all of a sudden, I am grateful for my inability to sleep on public transport. When the boys wake up, they are not going to believe me when I tell them ... there are goats in the trees.

And please, let me get this straight: I do not mean 'in the trees' of the hooves-up-to-nibble-the-lower-branches sort. That would be *way* too mainstream! These are plucky, hardy, *African* goats. I am talking a full ten *feet* off the earth, gravity-defying goats, stood high in the spiky branches to source the lushest of the vegetation on offer. They are all along the roadside, too. For some quarter of an hour, I do nothing but gaze out of the window in awe at this wonderful and bizarre spectacle, unable to fathom how their weight doesn't send them tumbling to the ground as they bounce, boing and perch on the thinnest, least stable of the branches. The most verdant trees are each blossoming some dozen goats, defying any law of physics that I know.

Surely, I ponder, such bonkers antics are an expression of just how tough and bare these southern lands can be. Goats don't climb trees for the kicks; they are teetering on the brink for survival. This is the sparse and desolate south and the people of these dust-ridden and water-scarce lands are poor. Their simple homes, strung along the roadside, attest to it. Just two months ago, in the countryside around the nearby port city of Essaouira, 15 women died in a stampede for food aid at the weekly market in Sidi Boulaalam and almost a fifth of Morocco's rural dwellers live below the poverty line. At least 15 percent survive on less than $3 per day. All of a sudden, as we pass rivers that run dry and ramshackle homes, I have even greater respect for the tenacity of the people – and goats – who manage to cut a life down here, in a region that lays bare the challenges still facing this developing nation.

Morocco's elites may have survived the storm of the Arab Spring, but now the masses who lent them their popular support demand the realisation of promises and workable solutions for the many challenges of the 21st century. Fast. The onus is now on the Makhzen, the ruling elites of the kingdom, to find them. For their own survival, they must. The Spring gave a voice to those who were previously voiceless as well as those who speak of an alternative path for the future. More extreme strands of Islamism are on the ascendancy. So too are the Amazigh and during the Spring, people dared to speak out against the regime for the very first time and they won concessions. Morocco is not a democracy; it is a hybrid regime, but the state had no choice but to grant them. It was concede or befall the same fate as the regimes that were crumbling around them. Democratic reforms were promised, but in practice little has changed. But nothing here is definite. Nothing is permanent. Not anymore. Now the people have confidence to speak out again, regardless of the response.

Four hundred and two days have passed since I first set foot in this sprawling metropolis, but now, at long last, an orchestral ensemble of car horns welcomes me back to the mesmeric chaos of the red city. Just like a year ago, these eccentric streets are bustling. We are arriving stylishly at the back of a smoking and rusted Scania coach and now my companions are all-eyes-open as the sprawl and exoticness of this great city reveals itself at last. The heat is intense, but mercifully the thunder storm has passed, as we enter the Ville Nouvelle under darkened skies, where large portraits of the king hang from rooftops of tall hotels and official buildings, beside a parade of red national flags that flutter in the warm afternoon wind.

A large, open plaza leads to the elaborate arched façade of the Gare de Marrakech, the city's main railway station, which, in just a few days from now, will be my gateway to the north. Bougie shopping districts blur past with all the glass and al fresco eating to match any European city. Nearby, in a dusty square ringed with droopy palms, three camels kneel beside a display of fountains that rise and fall in a dazzling light-show of neon blues and pink. It appears that this city's thirst for modernity and penchant for glamour, so evident on my short visit here one year ago, has yet to be quenched. The traffic is typically unruly. Sandal clad youths ride helmet-less on motorbikes, slicing between SUVs and through a flood of yellow Dacia taxis, which in turn sweep around pedestrians with generous use of the horn and impatient gesticulations. A policeman stands amid the madness at a crossroads, blowing his whistle and waving his arms in a display that makes him look very integral, although I doubt his real relevance.

Finally, as the gloom of the receding storm is swallowed by the fall of twilight, we hire a car and navigate to our riad, which is nestled in a hectic maze of restless backstreets near the city wall. Our road is a local one, awash with evening life. A tall cream wall cascades with leaves to its left, broken only by an enormous gate guarded by the military at all hours. Behind, the secretive grounds of one of the king's royal palaces. Bright workshops spark with metal to its right and motorcycles zip up and down. Youths linger in the road and block our way. There is graffiti and clutter, life and commotion, barter and argument, all brushing against the high walls of the secret palace grounds. It is a short drive to the end of the street, where, upon reaching a mosque, we can drive no further. Hire car abandoned and now on foot, our lingering has drawn immediate attention and soon a crowd of local kids, hooded teens and elderly men surround us, warbling at Moe in a flurry of staccato Arabic as they flog their various services as guide to our riad, security guard for our poorly parked car, or host to the best restaurant in town. Quickly, we are mobbed.

"What's going on out here?" Ruben asks with a beaming smile, as he whips out his phone to record the goings on. He, like every one of us, is relishing in the madness of this hectic backstreet. "Is this normal? Why has half the street come to meet us?"

"Ha, welcome to the Maghreb, brother!" Moe replies with an aura of swagger. His Moroccan blood and Arabic chatter mean he fits in just fine, though, in truth, he's just as West London as we are. "There's no way near enough jobs in this city, so people just invent jobs for themselves." With a throaty riposte, he dispatches another teen who wanted to show us the way.

Home for tonight is a beautiful yet slightly surreal riad, owned by a warm young man named Zacharia. A swimming pool snakes through his riad like a sapphire river, over which a mosaiced bridge climbs to a sitting area adorned with African masks. Parakeets swoop above a leafy inner courtyard, though higher still cats stroll along the edge of three-story high walls, blind to their own mortality. There are at least a dozen of them, all stray, as is typical of the Moroccan cities.

"Just you … no guide?" Zacharia asks as we deposit our backpacks across the indoor river. I note that the sofa I place mine on was once a camel. We nod. "Well, then I commend the effort! Some of my guests have given away most of their dirhams before they even find me." He laughs with a playful punch to Jason's shoulder. "No, no, I joke. I ask because if you came with a guide, I would pay him. They bring guests and I pay them. We work together."

"Those kids on the streets – they're guides too?" Ruben asks.

"Yes, sadly many of them have to work as guides too, so that they can make enough to eat," Zacharia says. "Often the teens work for an adult and the kids will work for the teens. Actually, many of the young people out there have arrived from the countryside in the last year or so, wanting a better life. I have gotten to know some of them well. It's quite usual for teenage boys to leave their village and move to the city, hoping to send some money back to their family."

"That's understandable," Ruben replies.

"Yes but, really, it's all a bit of a false promise. There are not many jobs here, so instead they try to make money from tourists. You know, often it's the only way to a better life."

Here on the backstreets of Marrakech, just as across North Africa, labour is abundant but jobs are scarce, so lingering youth with little to do is a woefully common sight. Liberal economic reforms in the 1980s saw the Moroccan state scale back public sector jobs and services to a minimum, after decades of major spending that accrued crippling debt. Then, late last decade, the Eurozone crisis hit these streets hard as the market for Moroccan tourism collapsed along with the demand for Moroccan labour in Europe, remittances from which had filled up the nation's coffers. Combined, many Moroccans have been left without a viable livelihood.

It is yet another challenge that the king and Makhzen must swiftly address. While many in this modernising country have never had it so good, countless others, especially the thousands of rural migrants who arrive in the city each year, have been forced to invent work for themselves as self-appointed parking attendants, unnecessary car supervisors, impromptu tour guides, or all-singing-and-dancing tourist hasslers. It forms one dimension of the 'informal economy': lucrative but deeply insecure work that is untaxed, unregulated and ranges from the downright bizarre to the ingenious. Certainly, it's not all bad. Around a fifth of national GDP is derived from informal activity and for many of the urban poor and socially marginalised, the informal economy is a way to engage in societal life. It allows demoralised youths, hopeful migrants, travelling tea merchants and plucky street vendors to throng the same souks and medina streets as wealthy tradesmen, who flog plush carpets to thriftless tourists. As such, for the one in three Moroccans who are illiterate, the informal economy is not a nuisance at all; it is a lifeline to a more promising future.

"But still, I have to tell you – the guides have been allowed to run riot in Marrakech!" Zacharia comments. It is a reality that in one week from now, travelling solo through this city, I shall learn the hard way. "Our government does not deal with the real challenges: the poverty, or the lack of opportunities. They are too scared to get involved."

In 2010, the self-immolation of Mohamed Bouazizi, a poor street vendor in Tunisia whose small wheelbarrow of wares was confiscated by police for lacking a permit, kickstarted revolution in Tunisia and lit the fuse for the entire Arab Spring: a series of huge, popular uprisings that shook the entire Arab world in 2011. Yet for the country's elites, informal work generates a seismic $18 billion in untaxed revenue each year that the Moroccan state is unable to claim. This has resulted in a desperate shortfall in the provision of basic public services, as well as a demoralised army of frustrated youth.

"In the Arab Spring, our leaders tried to do a deal with the guides and young people," Zacharia explains, as he pours tea for us all. "They said you can continue as you wish on the streets, so long as you do not take part in the protests that were getting bigger across the country." It helped to maintain the peace while regimes in neighbouring countries tumbled, but now the Spring is over and promises have not been delivered, the masses are demanding answers again. Quite astonishingly, a survey of Arab populations conducted by the BBC in 2019 found that the Moroccans have a greater appetite for rapid political change in their country than any of their surveyed Arab neighbours. That includes the Egyptians, Yemeni, Iraqis, Lebanese, Libyans, Palestinians and Sudanese. Despite a usually conservative stance, almost half of Moroccans, 49 percent, now favour rapid change in their political system.

I want to find out more, but for now we delve back into the restless side-streets, Moe assuring the throngs of guides that we know exactly where we are headed. Of course, we don't really have a clue, and soon we find ourselves pacing electric back-alleys in a lively corner of town where fires burn, music plays and locals hang out, relishing the cool of these latest hours. There is a liberal energy on the moon-struck streets of the red city tonight. It is youthful and invigorating, but as midnight swings around, there is a certain volatility here too. You can sense it in every sparking workshop, in the eyes of every lingering youth, and in the outstretched hands of every guide, who wants to show us the way. Just like the poverty-stricken folks across the southern plains this morning, these are hopeful people, searching for answers, and for a passage out of poverty.

One of the unique charms of a night in Marrakech is that you don't need to set an alarm clock. Or, at least, not if you are staying this close to the Koutoubia Mosque, the largest in the city, whose muezzin decides that all in the vicinity must be shaken out of their beds with the dawn adhan at the first peep of light on the eastern horizon. Oh, really – I'm not complaining. We had first dibs in the breakfast room earlier and having depleted it of honey and rghaif I am now stood two stories up, where a soft haze of morning light washes over my face. It is a crisp but perfect dawn and from the stirring streets below, the heavenly waft of baking bread rises to my nose.

Nabil and I have obeyed the muezzin's orders and have risen with the storks. As for the others ... well, a forty-hour day appears to have taken its toll – and we can't blame them. A canopied roof terrace peers over the awakening medina and the Koutoubia is just a stone's throw away, bathed in gold and framed by palms that halt just short of its minaret. Behind, shrouded in mist, the jagged outline of the High Atlas is sketched across the horizon. There is snow on its highest peaks. Storks, which I do not remember from my first visit here, take flight in front of the mosque. They are impressive in stature and majestic in flight, but their enormous nests perched on chimneys – thick, neat boxes of sticks – look cartoonish and ridiculous, doubling the height of some stacks. Already, I am noticing a more cordial charm to the red city that time deprived me of a year ago, as we motion towards the Koutoubia. Being the tallest building in the medina, it's not difficult to find your way.

Those plucky Almoravids first constructed a mosque on the site of the modern-day Koutoubia, only for their successors, the Almohads of the High Atlas, to destroy it and build their own. The Almoravids had gotten it slightly wrong, building their mosque a fraction out of alignment with Mecca. This was unacceptable to the pious Almohads, who considered the Almoravids heretics. However, whereas the Almoravid mosque was five degrees out of alignment with Mecca, the Almohad's replacement faced ten degrees away. This mosque, still pointing in the wrong direction, is the one that guides our way this morning. Indeed, raging debate of the time as to the true direction of Mecca means that many old mosques across these western Islamic lands do, in fact, point the entirely wrong way.

Today is an auspicious day in Morocco. The locals of the city have spilled onto the streets in accordance and the surrounding business has come to a halt. Even the typically insatiable Jemaa el-Fna market square has been most eerily subdued. The cause for celebration is that today is Friday, an event that occurs weekly in Morocco, which can only mean one thing: couscous. Couscous on a Friday is the Sunday roast of this kingdom and in some restaurants today, there is only one thing on the menu. Already the freshest pickings from the morning souks have been sliced, diced and are now slowly steaming away in almost every home and restaurant in a couscousiere (great name, even greater design — the steam from vegetables boiling in a stockpot cooks the couscous sat in a pan on top).

Except no-one is feasting yet. As the most important day of prayer for Muslims, Friday is a day of regimented routine in Morocco and before the couscous that the women have been cooking all morning can be eaten, most men will visit the hammam, the public baths, to cleanse their bodies before joining the masses in noon prayer, Jumu'ah, which is the most important of the week. Prayer helps to set a rhythm for the day and prescribed times for worship — dawn, midday, late afternoon, sunset and night — binds the Islamic world together as one. With very few exceptions, attendance at mosque on a Friday is expected of every Muslim man, which, in Morocco, is just about all men.

The Koutoubia is quite simply bursting at its seams as the cry of its muezzin ushers us back from the souks to observe the goings-on of a Moroccan Friday. Fresh from the hammam, everyone is looking finely groomed and is wearing their very best clothes for prayer, as a piquant aroma of perfume pricks the cool morning air. The mood in the souks is one of anticipation, of the morning rising to its crescendo, but then, all of a sudden, an aura of peculiar, unfamiliar calm washes towards us like a flood through the typically hectic souks. Hurriedly, we pace towards the manic Jemaa el-Fna, expecting a scene of commotion, but it too has fallen still and Marrakech, it appears, has ground to a halt. The music has stopped, the barter has been silenced, the clatter of donkeys has been displaced by the twittering of birds and that constant, raucous ensemble of car horns is now mute.

Then, we discover why. In a wave of colour and symmetry, a vast carpet of some two hundred men rise and fall in sequence in one corner of the square. There is no wind, not a breath of movement, aside from that ocean of men and the wandering of arch-back beggars who move through the tourists by the Koutoubia behind. Evidently, there is no more room in the mosque and so the hysteria of the red city has come to a brief pause as the masses flood the square in an open-air gathering of near-silent prayer. We are moved by the moment, as this square of perpetual motion and innate insanity is transformed, just briefly, into a mosque. But then, as suddenly as the calm had washed on through the souks, there is a rupture as the great beast is stirred once more and the red city motions back into life. In a single moment, the human carpet has dissipated, the square has reorganised, the music has recommenced, and the barter begun again. Once more the floodgates of the souks are swung wide open as a river of people flow back in and the Koutoubia can breathe as the masses flood out, reclaiming the city that had fallen silent for them.

I, like all infidel, am not allowed in the mosques of this land, but I am told that even the capacious Koutoubia feels less than roomy on a Friday and that loud and large inside the grand, arched entrance hangs an arresting portrait of the king, the Qur'an in hand.

"It's a timely reminder, don't you think?" Nabil remarks.

"About what?" I ask.

"That even in prayer, the state is watching."

This does not come as any great surprise. After all, Islam, alongside an Arab identity, is one of the foundational pillars upon which modern Morocco and its Maghrebi neighbours were founded. Religion is, and long has been, as much an apparatus of state control as education or the police force. A cohesive, pious, reverent population is an obedient one and as a descendant of the Prophet Muhammad, the King of Morocco derives much of his political legitimacy from his role as a powerful and revered religious leader. To challenge the will of the king, an offence punishable with lengthy imprisonment, is to question the Commander of the Faithful.

A recent study found that the number of Moroccans who identify as non-religious has risen four-fold since 2013. It is a much faster rate of change than anywhere else in the Maghreb, yet since the 7th century, when Islam first swept to these western shores under the Umayyads of Damascus, this nation has been unified in its piety. Even in the present day, despite the many uncertainties that simmer beneath the surface of the kingdom, Islam is this society's glue and the one great constant that has lasted through thick and thin. Even when Arabisation has faltered, Islam has endured. Today I can bear witness to it: a force of togetherness, a city of motion stood still, one day of each week attuned to the rhythm of religion. Islam is the single thread that runs through king and subjects, Arab and Amazigh, rich and poor, hectic city and High Atlas village. Around 98 percent of Moroccans are indeed Muslim, most of them followers of the Sunni branch of Islam, and at a time of so many unknowns, Islam is *the* unifying certainty.

It has proven invaluable for the Makhzen during some testing times of recent years. For many decades, the rule of the kingdom's elites has been legitimised by the divine will of the king's Islamic lineage, which has made them virtually unchallengeable. It is partly so because of strict laws that forbid resistance, but also because opposing the Islamic elites would equate to heresy. Since its independence, Morocco has marched diligently to the drumbeat of Arabia and kept firmly to the dual pillars of Arab nation-building: Islam and a strong, unified Arab identity. This has enabled the Moroccan regime to unify the masses and quash dissent … but nothing is how it once was. Nothing is quite as it seemed just a decade ago.

When the fires of revolution swept across the Arab world in 2011, first unshackling Tunisia from the repressive 23-year rule of President Ben Ali, the King of Morocco and the elites of the country must have looked on with grave concern. In swift succession, regimes that seemed unmovable were duly toppled from power across the Arab world, with Egypt next to follow as mass peaceful protests in Cairo's Tahrir Square demanded the resignation of Hosni Mubarak, president for some three decades, which soon followed. In mere weeks, the Arab Spring was in full flood. Civil war broke out across Libya as protestors sought to oust the long-standing regime of Muammar Gaddafi, and then too in Syria, a costly and bloody conflict that still rages today, and within a year the Yemeni regime came crashing down as well. Fuelled by anger over low standards of living, oppressive regimes and socio-economic grievances, the entire Arab world was caught in a storm of popular uprisings unlike anything it had known before.

Throughout, Morocco was not immune. Peaceful protests over the king's powers and elite corruption had been quickening in tempo, and then, on the 20th February 2011, thousands took to the streets of Rabat while looting and disorder broke out across the infamously restless Rif. Among the protestors were informal workers and disillusioned youth, poverty-stricken farmers and marginalised groups, for whom life was a struggle, yet the Makhzen never seemed to care. Now, emboldened by uprisings in Egypt and Tunisia, they too would seize the moment and make their anguish known. The blare of revolutionary horns could be heard on the horizon, but when the Spring reached Morocco, something surprising happened. While protestors across the region had been demanding the all-out demise of their repressive regimes, few here had called for the king to abdicate. Instead, protestors called for reform, not revolution, demanding limits to the king's exhaustive powers, changes to the constitution and democratic reforms. In June 2011, realising the fate befalling his peers, the king delivered, promising a series of reforms, which, while far from realised and vastly inadequate by the account of many, were enough to hush the protesters for now.

Morocco and its elites had weathered the storm of the Arab Spring and then, unseasonably, catching commentators in the West off guard, the region fell into the grasp of an unexpected Arab Winter. No sooner had the saplings of fledgling democracy begun to take root throughout the region, absolutism and more extreme strands of Islamism begun to march again. What's more, in almost every Arab country that held elections after the Arab Spring, it was Islamist parties that rose to the fore. For the Islamists who had survived the revolutions, it seemed that the seasons had swung back in their favour. A reconfigured Morocco was among them, with the PJD, a moderate Islamist party that supports the monarchy, gaining the most parliamentary representation in the 2011 elections. In Egypt, the Muslim Brotherhood swept to power, while a Salafist party calling for the strict implementation of Sharia law became the second largest party in the country, and a democratic Islamist party took charge in Tunisia. Just as Islamism was shunned as a force capable of rallying the masses of the region, the Arab Spring had returned it to centre stage, including here in Morocco. While neighbouring regimes had tumbled, the king and Makhzen had not only weathered the Arab Spring, but seemed to have survived unscathed, owing in no small part to the enduring resonance of the king's Islamic lineage.

At least, that is how most reported it in the West. From the Spring had come a bitter winter and as the shackles of authoritarian rule were loosened across the region, it was indeed Islamism that returned to the fore. Yet there was another narrative to the popular uprisings that has gone largely unreported, swept aside in the tumultuous waves of unrest and revolution. Indeed, the so-called 'Arab Spring' was not just 'Arab' at all. It was simply a useful term to explain the common causes of protest taking place in an Arab-majority region, but it ignores the fact that many North Africans decided to join the rebellions to rally against their own, very particular grievances that were not shared by the masses. In the Spring, these forgotten people dared to speak out and challenge the very narrative upon which the modern Maghreb had been built. This was unthinkable! It shattered the veil of divine protection that had shielded the elites for generations. In mere weeks, the sanctity of regional order had been broken and voices of dissent began to flood the streets of the region.

Among them was the Amazigh, for whom the popular uprisings in 2011 marked their reawakening. For centuries, Arabisation had slowly assimilated the region and quashed any notion of Amazigh uniqueness. Their cultural particularities had been ignored and their rural heartland forgotten, but the Spring provided a rare opportunity to challenge the status quo and shake the foundations of the Maghreb. It was amidst the uprisings that North Africa's identity crisis first came to light. For years, the region had danced to the drumbeat of Arabia, but now it was clear that frustrations had been simmering beneath the surface for some time.

Repressive regimes had failed to make life better for many, not everyone shared in the new regional identity, and once the spark of the Arab Spring was lit, the inviolability of regional order burst into flames.

Now people could dare to speak of alternative paths for the future. There were just too many protestors for the authorities to suppress, and so people spoke freely – for the first time – and there was nothing anyone could do about it. This wasn't about usurping Arab rule; instead it was about envisaging a society of pluralism and tolerance, where those who did not fit the mould of the ruling elites could speak, worship and live as they please. It was about voicing anger against ignorant regimes, who had failed to listen to all those who lived in their societies. For the Amazigh, this was to be a rebellion of a modern age, and thousands of young campaigners took to the streets, flying flags emblazoned with the Yaz. They were determined to upend the idea that all North Africans were protesting for a similar reason. This, they argued, was simply not true. Indeed, as we will soon discover as we delve deeper into the cities and mountains, the Amazigh face a number of challenges that are very particular to them. In some regions, such as in the Rif, this has left their communities decades behind in economic development.

As such, with renewed wind in their sails, it was in the Arab Spring that the Amazigh movement took on an entirely new complexion. The dream of cultural renewal and recognition of Tamazight remained, but now they could dare to add new political ambition, demanding greater autonomy for Amazigh-majority regions and a more equitable share of resources between urban and rural areas. And the spirit of freedom was infectious. Rebellion was no longer the preserve of deviant tribes in far away mountains. It was now open for everyone, including urban elites, who could elevate their demands to an entirely new level – to the gates of the palace, on the streets of Morocco's largest cities. Generations of neglect had squeezed their culture to the margins of society, but it had failed to dampen their spirits. Now, buoyed by rebellious fervor across the region, the Amazigh movement could escape its strongholds in the Rif and Kabylia and, with the support of urban elites, emerge as a new political force. They organised themselves on Facebook and thousands rallied on the streets against social injustice, elite corruption and attacks on the freedom of speech. They named their campaign after the date it began – the February 20 Movement – and under its united banner, the

Moroccans marched as one: young and old, Arab and Amazigh, rural-dweller and urbanite, Islamist and liberal, rallying for change in a kingdom that once seemed unchangeable.

During the uprisings, the king and Makhzen were forced to tread a fine line. As regimes around them crumbled, the elites of Morocco had to tolerate protest to weather the storm of upheaval, while maintaining the primacy of the palace and elites. It was a game of survival that they played to perfection. Just one month after the February 20 Movement began, the king stepped in to reconcile with the protestors, in a bid to quell the unrest. He swiftly recognised that a plurality of cultures makes up Morocco, including the Amazigh's, and he even lauded Tamazight as a 'heritage belonging to all Moroccans.' Then he went even further, declaring Tamazight an official language and depriving Morocco of its cherished right to be known as a purely 'Arab' state. This wasn't just a clean break from the past, when an Amazigh heritage was considered an embarrassment to many; it was daring to unsettle the very narrative upon which his father had grounded the newly independent Morocco – and it worked. The protests stopped. The demands soon ceased. The elites of Morocco survived the Spring.

Yet, beyond the symbolism and gestures of goodwill, there can be no denying that little has really changed, and the Amazigh in particular remain neglected in the kingdom. From the exaltation of the uprisings, when it seemed that the Amazigh could reclaim their place within the nation's proud identity, has come the crushing realisation that much of what was promised to them has not come true. Rural areas remain left behind, the Amazigh have little voice in the halls of power, corruption remains rife, and arrest awaits many who dare to challenge the nation's elites. It is therefore little surprise that tensions are rising yet again, not least in the Rif where thousands rallied last summer in a new campaign: the Hirak Rif Movement. It is the largest outpouring of public anger since the Spring and it is starting to spread from the Amazigh heartland right across the kingdom.

Since the uprisings of 2011, the elites of Morocco have been unable to shake an insecurity embedded deep in their psyche. The masses had dared to speak out to oppose the regime, and they had won. While the elites survived the storm of revolutions, it now appears that the protests here may have been a mere March shower. The legitimacy of the elites has been shaken and nowhere else in the region is there greater appetite for rapid political change than here in Morocco. Now the masses who lent their support in the Spring – the impoverished farmers from across the dry southern plains, the disillusioned youth on city street corners – demand solutions to modern-day challenges and the swift realisation of all that was promised to them. And it is here too, in the kingdom that gave its elites a second chance, that the flames of disdain are starting to spread faster than almost anywhere else in the Arab world.

10

Berber Titanic

Cascades d'Ouzoud

Marrakech shrinks slowly in the rear view mirror, as we barrel towards the mountains. The morning is cold, but the vistas staggering, as we plunge into the country down roads lined with kasbahs. The asphalt may be new, the roads smooth as silk, but in the midst of World War II, a rather unlikely road trip took place down this very stretch of highway that we motor along today. It occurred in the restless winter of 1943, following the Casablanca Conference where the leaders of Britain and the United States joined two French generals, Charles de Gaulle and Henri Giraud, on the west coast of Morocco to strategize the Allied approach for the coming phase of the war. And it was here, in the African winter sun, that Winston Churchill had willed Franklin D. Roosevelt to accompany him on a short winter sojourn to Marrakech.

"You cannot come all this way to North Africa without seeing the city of Marrakech," Churchill had exclaimed to Roosevelt at the time. "Let us spend just two days there, in the Paris of the Sahara. I must be with you when you first see the sun set on the Atlas Mountains."

They did so, despite Roosevelt at first insisting that he must return to America at once – the war still raging, this being January of 1943 – and so the pair motored south, the President and the Prime Minister, wintering in the North African sunshine, on what was for Churchill a working holiday, part of a one month tour of the Arab world. The war time leaders watched as, on the farthest horizon, the peaks of the High Atlas morphed from rose to dusky purple with the setting of the sun. It was here too that Churchill, an avid painter, on a balcony of a villa in Marrakech, set up easel for the only time during the war and declared the panorama in front of them 'the most lovely spot in the world.'

So taken was Churchill, in fact, that this short winter visit of 1943 was one of six that he would make over 23 years. 'Morocco was to me a revelation,' he wrote in the *Daily Mail* in 1936. 'The newspapers or official documents afford not the slightest impression of the charm and value of this splendid territory. Here in these spacious palm groves that rise from the desert, travelers can be sure of perennial sunshine, of every comfort and diversion, and can contemplate the stately and snow-clad panorama of the High Atlas Mountains. The sun is brilliant and warm, but not scorching; the air crisp and bracing, but without being chilly.'

Churchill found a respite in the High Atlas Mountains and, 75 years on from their winter sojourn, I cannot help but wonder if this snow-clad panorama past which we drive on our long journey to the falls of Ouzoud had some small bearing on his resolve and the outcome of the war. Back then, when the wartime sojourners motored along this road, only the High Atlas would have towered beyond the stony plains and acres of earthy farmland that trim the roadside. Now there are countless kilometres of new developments, and while the red walls of Marrakech would have defined the outer city limits when Churchill painted them on canvas, today the red city has spilled through its walls to become a chaotic, sprawling metropolis, with an abrupt Ville Nouvelle and many new satellite towns that simmer in the heat haze around us.

Yet life has changed little within those ancient walls and, here too, as we motor through the country, countless rural towns pass slowly by, each an image of unchanging ways. The unmarked roadside merges into the dirt, upon which lively markets bustle with activity and produce as thirsty patrons gather in the shade of colourful canopies by the ever-busy roadside cafés. Those angled to catch a refreshing breeze earn the most custom. A minaret crests the low skyline of each rural village and motorcycles dart in every direction across the road, chased by children on the back of donkeys who cover their mouths from the dust. Young shepherds, many before their teens, tend to flocks in earthy fields, and life for the majority is still centred upon local trade and agriculture, as it has been for centuries. You are stuck acutely by the impression of a world that is unchanging, but not all is stagnant. In fact, even in these rural hills to the west of the snow-topped mountains, it is apparent on this slow drive to Ouzoud just how fast this country *is* advancing.

Above the minarets of every rural town, an abrupt new skyline has stolen the limelight. Sweeping ribbons of smooth new asphalt are now lined with construction sites of stylish, whitewash developments. Skeleton-like shells of modern apartment blocks are springing from the dust like palms from oasis waters and vast new housing districts are shooting skywards. For now, they are empty, this the vision not of today, but of the Morocco of the future.

"This is the king's side of the country," Moe explains from behind the wheel, "and this is *his* highway, from Rabat to Marrakech."

"The one he is taken down?" I ask.

"Yes. But also any dignitaries that visit Marrakech from the capital. They are taken down this highway, to impress them. That's why all the new development is here. It's a showroom!"

That is the nature of urbanisation across much of Africa today: all-glass skyscrapers, shimmering new planned cities, glitzy satellite towns plonked on the dusty earth, all to project an image of Africa on the rise and breaking away from a colonial past to forge a new destiny, even if the country beyond the whitewash glamour remains much the same. It is a similar story here in Morocco; the king is determined to show that his country is the one advancing the quickest, and brash construction is the easiest way to achieve it. Yet there is a problem. Africa is urbanising faster than anywhere else on Earth, but while its cities are expanding at breakneck speed, the urban economies are barely changing. Even here, in one of the wealthiest economies in Africa, thousands of migrants are arriving in Morocco's cities each year, only to find there are barely any jobs waiting for them on arrival. In fact, many rural-to-urban migrants, especially in cities south of the Sahara, continue to rely on agriculture and the provisions of their rural village, even after migrating to the city. It has trapped millions of Africans in a cycle of migration between their village and city, or in unpredictable informal work.

Just as in the Ville Nouvelle of Marrakech, where arch-backed street vendors hustle for custom outside glitzy new shopping centres, here in rural Morocco there is a paradox to this nation's thirst for swift, visual modernity. Some in the cities have never had it so good, and money is clearly pumping into these once-sleepy lowlands. But as we drive past ramshackle stands, rusted Mercedes saloons and rural farmers' markets where time is stood still, I wonder who will own these new homes in the skyward developments that have sprung from the dust on the doorstep of traditional rural towns. Soon a line of high-speed rail will shoot along Morocco's west coast, connecting Tangier on the Mediterranean shores with Casablanca to its south in just two hours. It will be served by 200 mph, double-decker, French-TGV-powered missiles, the first high-speed rail in Africa, funded in part by loans from France and the Gulf States. It speaks volumes of the ambition of this nation, but many have argued that this $2 billion project is as much bravado to project a picture of Moroccan progress as it is a necessary upgrade to the nation's infrastructure. The kingdom has strived in recent years to entice international business and projects like this are designed to distract investors from its detractions, such as deeply enrooted corruption.

But not everyone is fooled. In 2018, Morocco ranked lower than Iraq on the Human Development Index, much lower than neighbours Algeria and Tunisia, and many have argued that this enormous investment, which has accrued Morocco a mountain of national debt, could have found better use elsewhere. Healthcare is vastly inadequate, with one doctor for every 1,600 people, and a national coalition that aims to halt the high-speed rail project found that for every ten metres of new track that is built, a rural school could have been constructed. Oh, and then, just like the empty skeleton high-rises that line the road, there is the biggest question of all: how many everyday Moroccans will be able to afford a ride on the new $2 billion trains?

Though today is sharp and clear, the sweeping flanks of the tallest mountains around us have been thoroughly pelted in a blanket of white. Winter, it seems, has pummelled the High Atlas hard. Yet as we turn west from the range that glistens in the sun and near Ouzoud, we find ourselves sinking into red, rocky and forested surrounds where the road sweeps past citrus trees and acres of olive groves, winding its way above teasing drops. Even in the winter, these foothills are surprisingly abundant and, indeed, as our flight to Agadir revealed, while the south of Morocco is dry and dusty, its northern hills are lush and green.

It is a landscape of some distinction, though our arrival in Ouzoud, a tidy little town that rises above the murky Oued Tissakht, is nothing less than typical. A helpful gentleman in a padded and bright blue gilet reliably informs us that we cannot park behind the long line of vehicles that hug the curving roadside, but no problem. We should follow him down a long, winding track to a dusty square in the shade of a solitary oak, where a space is waiting, just for us. As the helpful man exchanges a hearty thumbs up with another man who is sat nearby, we thank him and say farewell. He will, of course, be there on our return, awaiting a generous handful of dirhams for the pleasure of supervising our car. Or, not ...

"Okay, ready, brothers? Yallah. Let's go, follow," he orders with a flick of a hand, ushering us towards the water. Ah ... it turns out that not only is our new friend an impromptu car parker, but he doubles as a tour guide and after a few short gabbles in Arabic with Moe, we find ourselves walking in the footsteps of Ahmed the Opportunist along the exceedingly brown and muddy Oued Tissakht. He appears to be a man of few words, though on his daily wander downstream to the Cascades d'Ouzoud (which, of course, is his day job), Ahmed must have plenty of time to ponder the ways of the world beyond his little town.

Just along the trail, the murky Oued Tissakht flows into the El Abid River, the 'Slaves River,' where it meets its fate with gravity. Ahmed is unsure how the El Abid came to have such a curious name, but the trades along the river are certainly more amicable today than its name suggests they may have once been. Cooperatives producing and selling argan oil, which is exceptionally pure and cheap here in its country of origin, spring from beneath the shallow shade of trees and beside farms where goats, mules and chickens wander freely. Strung along the dusty path, little shacks selling trinkets and patterned rugs lure the few passing tourists in and high above the trees across the river, on the shoulder of a mountain, an enormous and ornate hotel is still in construction. With its grand, regal qualities and various shades of pink, it would look more at home in Jaipur and in this relatively unfrequented part of Morocco, I struggle to fathom the need for its incredulous proportions. I wonder what the future holds for little Ouzoud.

I mention to Ahmed all the towering whitewash developments and sweeping new roads on the long drive in. They are considerably better than the roads in the UK, I comment truthfully. He tells me they were paid for with government money and in recent years they have helped to lure more tourists in.

"But while the roads are good, the life is not so easy, eh?" he adds. "Now there are more tourists, but it is still difficult to make money for the family. I don't own a car. I don't know the roads very well. And I won't be a millionaire soon!" He laughs. "No Ferrari."

I ask Ahmed what he thinks of the country's ruling elites. They are responsible for much of the kingdom's infrastructure and many still depend on the goodwill of the Makhzen to enjoy their basic rights and a prosperous life. A study in 2014 found that almost two thirds of people feel inequalities are rising in Morocco, while almost half feel that they themselves live in poverty. It is a steep rise on past years and the report also notes that 'intolerance towards inequalities has heightened,' while Moroccans are 'more conscious of their rights and increasingly willing to express their dissatisfaction, demands and expectations.' Notably, the study was conducted by an independent council established by the king himself in February 2011, amidst the Arab Spring, to better understand the nation's economic and social fabric.

"I do not think of them!" he retorts with a booming laugh, like an inner thunder. His head is large for his body, his chin stubbled and hair buzzed close to the skin. He is aged around 40. "No, I kid. But really, Moroccans tend to just get on with life. Actually, no one makes fun of their country or people like us. We are the best at it!

"Of course," he raises a hand to pause himself, "it is important, but many people just do not care about politics." He halts suddenly. "Why care? We aren't going to change the world!"

"Is that why the Arab Spring went relatively smoothly here?" I ask him. "Because across the Maghreb, people rose up and started to rebel. Does that mean the king is popular?"

"We are just not stupid!" Ahmed replies bluntly. "Tell me: how in God's name are people going to change the politics? Look, everywhere in the Maghreb. Look now ... what has really changed? Nothing. But, you either sit and complain, or get on with your life. Most Moroccans just carry on. I do!"

A drooping metal chain marks the end of the trail and my Western mind, attuned to the hymnbook of health and safety, searches urgently for the metal barrier that must surely guard the cliff edge and obstruct everyone's photos. Disturbingly, there isn't one, and the only high-vis around is Ahmed's bright blue gilet, so instead we walk right up to the edge of the cliff, where the muddy El Abid and Oued Tissakht, now as one, gush from the rise to our left and nosedive more than 100 metres into the vast, verdant gorge below. In an instant, the thunderous crash of the water rises to us. It pummels our eardrums, as three great plumes of water twist and spiral on their dance with gravity to the valley floor, beating the orangey-red rock of the sheer cliffs. Its power is unnerving and the gorge that it has carved spectacular: sheer rock walls, towering on every side, they, like the El Abid that rages through below, a deep, earthen brown.

Across the cascades, standing on terraces that jut up the side of the rock face, rudimentary wooden huts and simple homes cling nervously to a string of steep zig-zag paths. A ghostly haze of light falls down from above them, glistening every stray water droplet that sinks into the vast gorge below, where small colourful rafts paddle perilously close to the thunderous arrival of the falls. In an unspoken consensus, our childish minds have urged us down the cliff and to the precarious little boats by the water's edge. Ahmed leads the way along a steep, stony track that winds its way down the cliff through thick cedar forest, where barbary macaques bound around like kids on a sugar rush. It seems the young-sters are all at play, while the elder apes perch themselves in the middle of the dirt path on cuts of sun that seep through the trees, arms to their sides, chests wide open, basking in the rays, seemingly oblivious to our passing.

Ahmed had walked ahead of us, but now I catch up with him again. Our conversation fell silent on the slick and twisting descent down the cliff, but his head was down and I sense that he has been gathering his thoughts. Eventually, he speaks again.

"I do not know what the future holds," he says with a weary voice. "I have a young daughter, named Aya, who is two years old. So, often I ask myself: what kind of a life can I give her? There is a lot of change taking place in Morocco and many divisions. But I do not care for the politics! All that matters is that I can earn good money so my daughter can lead a good life. Their words do nothing."

I sense that for Ahmed, despite his intentions to turn a blind eye to the tides of the region, this is personal. Life is not easy and for many in the kingdom, himself included, divisions within Moroccan politics and society are a barrier to progress and prosperity. Since the Spring, when groups who were previously voiceless had been able to speak liberally, Moroccan politics has become increasingly divisive. Few can agree on what path the kingdom should take and North African politics at large has become increasingly polarised along both ethnic and religious lines. Many do not care for such debate; it slows down decision-making and creates rifts in society. But it is an inconvenient truth: while the Spring shook the roots of the modern Maghreb, no-one can agree how it now should move forwards. It poses a major threat to the weakened regimes that narrowly survived the Arab Spring. Now the Maghreb is caught in a new wave of religious and ethnic fervour, which is waiting to pounce should the ruling elites fail to deliver on their promises. Islamists are on the ascendancy. So too are the Amazigh, who demand greater pluralism in politics and society. Many in the Amazigh movement view Islamism was a deep suspicion, and the feeling is mutual.

Such is the emerging political force of both the Amazigh and some more extreme strands of Islamism that many North African regimes have sought to pit the two against each other. They have done so in a bid to tolerate opposition voices, while ensuring neither becomes powerful enough to challenge the incumbent elites. They act as counter-balances to control the influence of the other, enabling both to wield a voice in Maghrebi society, but never so much that they can become a threat. In recent years, the Moroccan and Algerian regimes have begun to recognise and embrace the Amazigh's resurgence, which has helped them to keep rising Islamist forces in check. While the two used to see eye-to-eye, they have now drifted far apart, with the Amazigh movement becoming much more liberal, advocating for secularism and democracy. But what results is a fierce ideological standoff that risks splitting North

African society in two, while the ruling regimes try to spin the political chess game in their favour.

For the Amazigh, it is a difficult one to weather. On the one hand, the ruling elites have begun to view their movement in an increasingly favourable light. Back in 2012, the Moroccan foreign minister and the second highest official in the ruling PJD party shocked his peers across the region when he called for the word 'Arab' to be dropped from the 'Arab Maghreb Union.' He argued that the Maghreb should be seen as a multicultural and diverse space, rather than an exclusively 'Arab' one, and just this year, Algeria too declared Amazigh New Year, Yennayer, a national holiday for the first time. It implies that the ruling elites have come to welcome the Amazigh resurgence as an important part of their national identity. But this support tends to only extend to the point that it serves the interests of the regime, and to the extent that the Amazigh themselves are counter-balanced by other forces on the political chess-board. Should the Amazigh become just too powerful, the elites would surely swing favour back towards the Islamist groups.

North African regimes aren't the only ones trying to weigh into the contestation that has emerged since the Spring. France is often accused of interfering in the affairs of its former colonies by offering support to the Amazigh – long their favoured sons – who tend to align with their liberal values. In fact, the swelling influence of the Amazigh movement has as much to do with diaspora communities in countries like France, as it does North African populations. Israel too has been accused of using the Amazigh to help realise its goals in the Arab world. It is known to have close ties with the organisers of the Kabylian autonomy movement in Algeria and, given the strong historical ties between the Jewish community and Amazigh, the Israelis have been accused of using them as proxies, to strengthen their image and foster relations with Arab nations, without having to use official diplomatic channels.

Maghrebi politics since the uprisings has therefore been messy, and even Islamism itself is splintering into a number of competing factions. Salafists are contesting elections against moderates. In Egypt, more than a dozen different Islamist parties filled the political vacuum after the fall of Hosni Mubarak, and nowhere in the Maghreb does a single party or strand of Islamism hold sway with the masses, including in Morocco. It is yet another reason why the Makhzen's rule stands on shaky ground;

nobody can agree on what form of Islamism should govern the nation. Consequently, rather than resolving the challenges facing the masses of the kingdom, Moroccan politics has become typified by bickering and division, which has failed to make life better for many.

Beneath our feet, the track is slippery and uneven. We skid and slide our way down, but as the gradient relents and sunlight bursts through to flood the trail in an ocean of yellow, the great plumes of the falls are visible in their entirety at last.

"The El Abid is low," Ahmed tells us as we near the water's edge, "and the falls are far from their fullest. When the spring comes to melt the snows in the High Atlas, the rivers will fill with the water from all the snowfields. But now, as you can see, the river is brown with earth from the fields and meadows. Come spring, the water is glacial. It will make the falls bigger, and they will run blue."

While the primary water source for thousands along its course, the El Abid is a dangerously polluted river. Deforestation and urbanisation along its banks have made it vulnerable to erosion and agricultural run-off from surrounding farmland. It is awash with pesticides and fertiliser as well as untreated domestic wastewater from the hotels and a massive dam upriver. Many along its course still rely on its water for their daily chores and livestock.

Ahmed hands us over to a young, exuberant raft paddler, who had been slumped dozily on his boat by the water's edge. Ali, whose base-ball cap is backwards, ushers us onboard. He wields a mischievous grin behind a neatly trimmed beard. He seats us down in flowery armchairs and gets us underway with two great heaves on the chunky ores, which propel us forwards through the murk. And as for his raft …

"We call it the Berber Titanic!" our young guide says reassuringly. "No, no, no," he laughs at great length, "I only joke with you. It's not like the film. This one's gone down twice."

Ali perches himself on a stool at the end of the disconcertingly low floating platform, facing the five of us who sit rather awkwardly on our sort-of-regal, certainly archaic pink thrones that balance on either side. Behind our thrones, up a couple of shallow steps, is a grand pink sofa with enough space for another three passengers. Pink, evidently, is the colour of Ouzoud. Bunches of colourful flowers sprout ridiculously on every side and an ornate wooden railing keeps it occupants securely inside, the sort that might have lined a Victorian staircase. Procedure in the event of an emergency includes grappling hold of an armchair and while Ahmed, who is chewing on some kind of nut perched high on a rock behind, looks unmoved by the spectacle unfurling beneath him, I cannot comprehend how Ali and his fellow, bonkers raft paddlers have managed to source such an eclectic concoction of décor for their floral and eloquently furnished amphibious Victorian living rooms.

As I make myself comfortable on the throne, my eyes drift skyward to the simple settlements that are strapped to the side of this staggering river valley. A ghostly sheet of light drifts past the high rock walls and descends towards us, illuminating every tiny droplet that flies by on its journey to the valley floor. A couple of young women watch the antics from beside their ramshackle home. A large, tan-coloured curtain flops from a corrugated-metal roof to a crooked wooden post with a beacon on top. I wonder what they make of this bizarre spectacle, as laughing tourists float past their homes on ancient furniture. Then again, I think of the waterfall and what life in this valley would be like without this, the tourism, their lifeblood.

Our guide is paddling us alarmingly close to the falls. Great heaves of the ores, propelling the Berber Titanic forwards through the murky water. That mischievous grin ... now it runs loose across Ali's face. He cannot control it and our laughter is simply willing him on, urging him forwards, daring us nearer.

Still we laugh, still he reciprocates. Already my ears are filled with a virulent cocktail of water-borne diseases, as the spray from the water-fall soaks our hair, pounds the raft, beats the river, floods our cameras, drenches our clothes.

Closer, closer still. Now the noise is a deafening thunder, a million gallons of water, one hundred metres of gravity, sucking the El Abid down towards us, crashing in a vortex less than a raft's length away.

How much ... closer?

I take stock of our situation. A Victorian living room, drifting and turning in the wash, crudely strapped with floats, pink flowers tickling the back of my neck. A young Moroccan, giggling, laughing, beaming like a maniac, edging us ever-nearer to impending doom. Ruben, top-less, standing up, dancing, enjoying an 'Indian shower.'

How did life lead me here? Somehow, everything that I have ever done and achieved has led me to this point, sat awkwardly in a barely-amphibious living room beneath a cascading African waterfall, flowers in my hair, my ornate armchair leaning perilously close to the gloomy waterline, the pink carpet drenched, clinging to a Victorian railing on-board the Berber Titanic.

Closer, nearer, closer still.

Now it's a power shower, a jet wash, pelting the front beams of the raft. Fingers go in ears, the thunder grows louder, a bellow, a crashing roar, an almighty onslaught. It's only sunk twice … it's fine! The noise and intensity, the insanity, edging forwards. I glance over my shoulder, expecting to meet a sight of water-soaked chaos. Ahmed, high on the rock, chewing on a nut, unmoved. Moe, Jason, shades on, slumped on a pink sofa, chewing gum.

"Photo, photo," says Ali, motioning us forward as the raft starts to drift in the wash. We laugh at his joke, until we realise … there was no joke. He stands up, still laughing; he does not stop laughing. The raft is without a paddler. We sway left. The El Abid sloshes overboard again, the Berber Titanic drifting and swaying, turning sideways, hauled into the vortex like a pathetic toy caught in a riptide.

My armchair dips to the murky waterline. I grab hold of it, readying for the emergency procedure.

Ali grapples with the ores.

11

In the Shadow of Toubkal

Imlil, Aroumd

Hissing beneath us, the Rheraya snakes through the valley in a rage of metallic blue. Hauled magnetic north, it gushes down through silvery-grey boulders with heady intent, splitting the forests of pine and juniper in two. Above the road that climbs through the hazy Ait Mizane Valley to Imlil, the earthen-clay homes of Taddart cling to a rockface above an abyss. A lonely mule trail rises to them across the scree and tiers of earth that grow maize in the summer months look naked and forlorn.

At last, there is a raw isolation. Slowly we rise above the snowline, as groves of walnut and cherry fall behind us in the valley haze. So too does the town of Asni, which just decades ago would have marked the trailhead where trekkers to the Ait Mizane would have switched from road to mule and braced for confrontation with hostile tribesmen who resided in the valleys ahead. Today, the Amazigh who dwell among the high mountains are rather more hospitable, though their environment remains harsh and soon the road twists severely, forced wide by lumps of rock that protrude from the rockface, only a low stone wall keeping us from the rage of the Rheraya below.

The forested corridor opens up and sunlight floods in to caress the snowfields on tall mountains that hold us in their embrace. To the east are the climbers' lodestars of Oukaïmeden and Jebel Angour, once fortresses of the High Atlas tribes but today an adventurer's mecca. On the southern horizon, somewhere in the looming rock ahead, is the massif of Jebel Toubkal, the highest peak in North Africa, and the entire Arab world. This arrival has a raw exhilaration: the ice-ravaged fury of the Rheraya tearing north beneath us, the buzzards that soar low through the biting cold, the hazy mountains closing in like tall barricades, their summits ringed in snow. Yet on arrival in the small mountain village of Imlil, a name that resonates in mountaineering circles, that isolation is abruptly and rudely shattered. It appears that we have stumbled upon a Berber Chamonix.

Ice axes, climbing rope and ski poles stack in store fronts alongside steaming tagines that cook on the steep and snowy pavement. We pass a young boy riding a mule up the rising road, which is dotted with the offices of mountain guides and piled high on either side with chunks of melting ice. From each rooftop dangles icicles. A young man passing us by has skis strapped to his feet and locals in their thick winter warmers are just starting to gather for lunch in the busy and snow-filled cafés. I pinch myself; we're in Africa, though typical Moroccan order is swiftly and mercifully restored.

"It okay, it okay. I show you!" A middle-aged man in a bobble hat has just volunteered himself as our parking attendant. He just happened to be stood by on the steep and snow-banked roadside, so he thought he may as well lend a hand. Parked cars hug the outside of the icy road that curves uphill, but there is no room for us.

"Here, space!" the man calls back up the hill with a flail of his arms and an enthusiastic leap in the air. Having skated down the hill the way we had come, our new friend is stood in a steep and ice-covered 'space,' just a fraction shorter than a Peugeot 301 and with an ominous bank of ice piled to wing-mirror height to its right.

Jason begins the perilous reverse down the steep and ice-slick slope towards a rusted Mercedes saloon that is parked just inches behind our allotted space. Inside the car, there is a controlled and thoughtful calm. Jason meticulously works the wheel, as we drop silent. Outside, meanwhile, our new friend is flailing frantically, his arms swinging to the left before he spins them back to the right, as if he himself is steering the treacherous reverse. Vigorous facial expressions and gritted teeth signal that Jason has strayed slightly off course, our new friend urging him on, willing him back, the Mercedes looming nearer in the mirror.

With copious dirhams handed over and large chunks of ice wedged behind the rear tyres as chocks (the scientific phenomenon of melting is not discussed), we control our breathing and begin to search for our guide, who Zacharia, our host in Marrakech, has put us in touch with. Moroccans always strike me as an exceedingly well-connected people. Whenever you speak of a village you have visited or a town where you are headed, the person you are speaking with will have indefinitely met someone from there or know just the person to put you in touch with. And so it proves again with Moe blurting away in Arabic on the phone to Zacharia in an attempt to locate his friend, who has a place for us to stay tonight. A few phone calls later and hands are shaken with Lahcen, a mild-mannered and somewhat steely-faced young man, aged late in his 20s, who will be our guide and host for the next two days. Sweet mint tea is poured in a roadside café, where we share our intention to explore the snowy foothills around Imlil.

"Brothers," Lahcen begins, before taking a sip of tea. "You will not want to stay in Imlil. This is not tourist season. Few places are open." We gaze across the main street, which is heaving with locals, but devoid of many tourists. "But it's okay," he says. "Come with me and we can climb onto the mountain. I have a gîte in a small Amazigh village, at the foot of Jebel Toubkal. You are in luck – only now can we hike there again now the recent snows have melted. For many days the trail was too dangerous to pass."

Lahcen thrusts the teapot high in the air as he pours us each another steaming glass. His voice is gnarly, slow and definite. The beard on his chin is pointed and wispy. Spearing brown eyes poke out from a black and thinly-white-striped djellaba, within which he seems to disappear. His hood is up. He does not smile.

"It is that way, high in the valley." We look where Lahcen points, towards a snow-covered hillside dashed with pockets of juniper. "It is called Aroumd. It is the highest village in the Ait Mizane Valley."

We consider Lahcen's offer. Our stay in the mountains is short and both Jason and Ruben are feeling unwell. Something has played with their stomachs and we are in search of medicine from a pharmacy; they all appear to be closed. Already the day is ageing and in just two days' time, I must depart my friends for the north. But, with the promise of adventure and our faith in Zacharia, we trust his word and agree. One final glass is poured as backpacks are lightened and readied for the hike ahead. As we drink, Lahcen paces around the concrete café sun terrace on his phone. He seems to be young, though his face, hardened by life in these mountains, makes it difficult to tell. He is certainly a good host and a proud Amazigh, yet his soft demeanour is matched with a steely calm and broken gaze as he converses that gives him an aura of suspicion, as if guarding an unspoken truth.

Wired to the wishes of the group, Nabil suggests lunch in Imlil before we depart. Lahcen agrees and says he will show us a place. He has a friend who runs a small café in town and we shall feast there. This is the heart of the valley's thriving tourism industry: a hub for mountain guides and the many porters and muleteers who work here, professions that hundreds in this cold and remote valley have embraced as a lifeline out of poverty. Small tourist inns and little souvenir shops line the long main road selling fossils and jewellery, handicrafts and carpets, sun caps and djellabas, and roadside cafés spill onto the snow-packed pavement, bustling with hungry locals. A single road runs through the steepening heart of Imlil. Trucks rumble through with their large, snow-chained tyres roaring and churning, kicking stones and storms of dust over the ice-slick pavement. Meat hangs bare outside butcher shops, fleshy legs and draping carcasses strung from metal hooks and shrouded in clouds of flies, crawling in insects.

It is a common sight, but I have history in these cold climes. Prime suspect in that dreaded case of campylobacter one year ago, memories still harrowing in my mind, was that dodgy tagine by the snowy roadside on our broken journey to Fez. How long had it been left in those testing conditions? This small café belonging to Lahcen's friend strikes of concerning similarity.

"Let's have meat!" Lahcen suggests. "Perhaps brochettes, or maybe a kebab?" His friend does a great one and will host us there before our departure.

"It's okay," we thank him. Today we will eat vegetarian. It is rude to refuse meat in Morocco, but we are deep in this snow-struck valley and already two of my companions are ailing. They will only be eating bread. It would be wise to be cautious.

"My friend only serves meat," Lahcen declares. "The meat here is good, we should eat here." We thank him, but say that we will find a café nearby.

"Nowhere is serving," he ripostes, ushering us inside as local hangouts across the road spill with noise and waft with a cocktail of pleasing aromas. "This is not tourist season. You won't find vegetarian food in town."

Our groaning stomachs relent: we will find a chicken tagine. Sure, it is what bit me last year, but they are easy to come by and we do not trust the meat that hangs by his friend's place, clouded in road-strewn dust, swarming with teems of flies.

"There are no tagines left in Imlil!" Lahcen rebuts to our bemusement, his eyes still spearing from inside his hooded robes, his face void of all emotion, his mouth unmoving. "Brothers, come!"

As the steam of tagine pots wafts in our faces from the first café that we enter, our initial trust in Lahcen begins to wane. Are tourist prices *really* high in Imlil? This isn't tourist season; prices should be low. We understand Lahcen would like us to eat at his friend's café. This nation is all about connections, doing business and helping out a brother. But now his steely demeanour is starting to arouse suspicion.

Eventually, an agreement is struck. We offer to buy fresh vegetarian ingredients from the local grocers and pay his friend to prepare it for us all. Lahcen smiles agreeably at the compromise and seats us on plastic chairs under an arched walkway before he disappears to help his friend prepare the lunch. Only now that we stop do we realise how bitingly cold it has become. It must be hovering around freezing and even here at this altitude, the air is rarefied. I shiver in my thin summer jacket. A pharmacy, which is closed, is beside us, and a store that sells mountain gear. Ice axes, crampons and skis wedge into mounds of snow outside. This is a tourist town most of the year, but I wonder just how extreme the temperature is going to be where we are headed, up onto the high mountains and to a small village perched on a precipice, almost 2,000 metres up.

Lahcen returns swiftly with two spicy Berber omelettes and a heavy basket of freshly baked bread. We thank him wholeheartedly and then bid him farewell as he departs for prayer, answering to the muezzin in the minaret over the road, who is calling across Imlil to the devout. "I will be 15 minutes," he says. We tell him to take his time.

Fifteen minutes becomes fifty, but still there is no sign of Lahcen. As the healthy among us struggle to demolish a hearty feast, our ailing companions are now rather unwell, and the cold is no help. We jog to keep warm. More than an hour later, Lahcen finally returns, unphased by the passing of time.

"Yallah," he booms with a thrash of his hand and a whip of his hip, pointing towards the mountains. "Ready?" Time passes slowly in these parts and the clock should not be taken literally. We must embrace it.

We depart Imlil via a steep, dirt road that narrows past storefronts, where signage written in English promises the finest riads, best eateries and most spectacular terraces in town. Djellabas sewn by machines are hung beside hiking poles and racks of crude sunglasses outside touristy shops, and striped Amazigh rugs drape over a long rail. Fortunately for us, though, there are few tourists about. Instead, a man in a long cloak that reaches to his feet clutches the hands of his two sons, swaddled in woolly hats and gloves, as a younger daughter in a buttoned blue coat chases behind cheerily in toe. Young men in puffer jackets watch as we pass by from the front of a café where they drink tea and smoke, and a couple in fashionable clothing shop at the butchers on the corner. Here in Imlil there is an old village feel, tainted only by the visible approach of another tourist season, which we have chosen to avoid.

But perhaps Lahcen was right. As Imlil slowly sinks into the valley of the Ait Mizane beneath us, the tacky tourist trimmings fade too and we rise into air that is silent and rarefied. Up to our right, the flank of a sun-caressed mountain is free of snow, but those that loom above the trailhead are draped in heavy snowfields, broken only by bare strips of earth on the steepest ground. A pale haze of midday light drifts past the minaret of a mosque in a settlement that clings to the near hillside. Behind it, across the fall of a valley, another small mosque crowns a tier of homes that perch on a precipice that falls in and out of sight behind curtains of mist that float on by.

The dirt trail turns to stony ground as we climb through forest high above the snowline, where our step becomes cautious. Mules are tied to our left, their backs draped in colourfully-striped coats, their owners resting by a low stone wall, chewing on nuts. We are walking beneath naked trees, ripped of all greenery by the winter, and the stepped path that we tread snakes its way past small homes and settlements of earthy adobe and stone. Colourful clothes and patterned rugs are strung along the path, luring the few tourists in.

Lahcen walks ahead of us. With his hands deep in pockets and his pointed hood still up, even he looks chilly. Sometimes I catch up with him and ask a question. Each time he responds with a simple reply and occasionally a smile. His English is good and gradually his answers are getting longer, but still he is shrouded in that aura of steely calm, as if numbed by the cold and resigned to the life of these mountains. He is a humble young man and I am warming to him, but still I am trying to understand him.

We halt by a waterfall that is alive with the season. Three spurts of icy water gush out of the snowy rockface and crash to earth in almost perfect symmetry, splintering off sharp rocks before gushing towards us at pace between large silvery boulders and broken ground. It roars and hisses, before joining a thin but lively river that soon we must ford. A broad cave opens to its right. It is furnished with Amazigh rugs, plastic chairs, decorative pillows, a crooked green sun umbrella, and sheets of mismatched material hung on a wooden frame, beating back the cold. It looks like people sleep here. I wonder who. A bridge made of wood and stone crosses another icy stream and soon, as we near the outskirts of Aroumd, the dirt path beneath our feet vanishes altogether and turns to a mush of ice and snow.

"When was the last snowfall?" I ask Lahcen. Once again, we walk together.

"Ten days ago," is his reply. "Only now can the mules use the trail again and tourists can reach the village. For several days it was just too dangerous. We did not take tourists up here." Lahcen points towards the trailhead. "We were cut off."

All of a sudden, as a ghostly veil of mist clears in the valley ahead to reveal little Aroumd, perched high on a rise in the swirling haze, I feel a renewed isolation. This lonely village could be cut off so easily from Imlil, that node of civilisation in the valley below, in these bleak winter months. A thin, dirt road clings to the opposite hillside. It arcs around a mountain, high above the snowline, and its barrier-less side falls 100 metres to the valley floor. It is the only vehicle road back to Imlil. One great peak dominates the sky at the head of the valley. Surely, it has to be Jebel Toubkal, a climber's lodestar and the highest mountain in the entire Arab world. It is the sole reason why a tourism industry exists in this remote High Atlas valley, a trade that employs guides like Lahcen and his family. I hear that tourism has transformed lives in this remote valley, but I want to find out how widely its fruits have been reaped in mountains that remain evidently poor.

"Everyone okay?" Lahcen asks as we rest on scattered boulders that litter the ever-rising trail. Our breathless murmurs are the only reply he needs.

"I'm feeling a little altitude sickness," Ruben tells me. I know he is not; we are still too low but his illness is taking its toll on the steepening trail and the thinning air is no help.

The vista offers much relief. Aside from Aroumd, the last village in the valley is now behind us and slowly we are cocooned by tall, snow-draped mountains that dwarf us and the trail. Great chiselled ridges rise and fall around us like an amphitheatre, little Aroumd raised on a huge moraine spur at its very centre on the ever-rising trail to the north face of Jebel Toubkal. We are on the trail that the trekkers will take to the summit. Most will reach base camp from Imlil in a single day, though in this winter season, they are a bold few. Rest is welcome solace. The sweet song of a lone nightingale had been flowing through the air, but now it is lost in the howl of winter gales.

Lahcen sits himself a few boulders away from us, but Nabil ushers him over.

"Have you always lived in this valley?" he asks our elusive guide.

"All my life," he replies with a slow nod. "My father and his father worked in these hills. Maybe his father too. They were shepherds. But then, one winter, they lost their flocks in some bad storms. Then they knew that farming was no longer the way."

"How so?" Ruben enquires.

"They knew it was the life of the poor and the foolish!" he rebuts. "Tourism was the better way to live. At first, a few of us, as guides or muleteers. Then everyone in the valley. Every family. Now all of them work as guides or porters, or they rent rooms in their gîte."

A sudden icy blast is our cue to depart before we can ask anymore. "Yallah!" bellows Lahcen. He has bolted along the trail before we have even risen, but we hear like a whisper carried to us in the winds: "We must reach Aroumd before sundown!"

Light is indeed ailing as we enter Aroumd and zig-zag up through the ice-strewn village to Lahcen's home. Artificial lights are beginning to flicker on in the homes around us. They are a solemn grey, the bare colour of mountain materials, distinctly rural and enduringly tribal, devoid of the Islamic and Arab designs of the lowlands below. Even the mosques are made from the bleak, grey stone of the mountains. Three hunched and stocky Amazigh women are pounding their way towards Aroumd on the hill beyond the village.

"They have been to pray," says Lahcen, "at the old pagan shrine in the mountains. They ask for healing if they or their family is sick. The imam does not like it!"

A proud grey horse is alone on the trail ahead. It seems surer under foot than I, and then, to our bemusement, we watch as it nears a large double door, thwacks it wide open with a swing of its head and passes through, before the door slams shut behind it. I have no idea if it knew what it was doing.

At last we reach Lahcen's family home. We are pausing here for tea before moving on to our overnight halt, a gîte that he owns just along the way. We climb the staircase that leads to his grey roof terrace as his wife, dressed traditionally in a veil, and waving, rosy-cheeked children pass down. It is a relief to take our shoes off and rest; only the exercise had been keeping us warm and now the cold bites our skin hard. The entire village is ice-struck and the path outside his home had been like climbing a steeply-sloping ice rink. I fully expected one of us – almost certainly Nabil, in his tailored leather jacket and still clutching his see-through wash bag – to tumble back down to the bottom.

But no. As we rest on Lahcen's concrete roof terrace, the day's last light is just caressing the tallest peaks around us, their summits glowing like orange crowns, silver snowfields shimmering upon a darkened ring of rocky fortresses that surround us. Imlil is now out of sight down the valley, the Rheraya has long fallen silent in the juniper below and here, with the winter cold closing in and a solitary trail weaving its way back to the nearest road, I feel an isolated peace.

Lahcen pours glasses of tea high in the air and serves a bowl of nuts, as the ailing among us take rest. I join Lahcen, who is watching the last embers of the day fade away behind the mountains, as one final haze of evening orange smudges on the far horizon.

"It's beautiful, your valley," I say to him.

"Nowhere is more beautiful," he says softly as we sip Berber whisky together. I sense that now business is secured, which must be hard to come by in these bleak winter months, he can relax. At last he seems at ease and his pride in this untamed valley can unfurl.

"This is the highest village in the Ait Mizane," he tells me. "Fewer than 2,000 people live here." At almost 2,000 metres above sea level, little Aroumd is also the deepest settlement in the valley. Further along the trail, only the small pagan shrine stands between us and the refuges on the higher flanks of Toubkal.

Lahcen points towards a silhouetted massif. "The highest peak," he begins with a widening smile, "that is Toubkal!"

I have been eyeing four peaks that loom on the southern horizon all evening, but it is a thrill to know that the highest among them is, of course, Jebel Toubkal. Not only is Jebel Toubkal impressive in stature at 4,167 metres, its summit is also notable for having first been reached as late as 1923 – and this lateness does not owe to its challenge. Instead, it speaks volumes for the tribal fortress that was the High Atlas valleys until late last century. Indeed, it remains a relatively recent phenomenon that us infidel should walk these stony trails where today signs read 'terrace views' as opposed to 'death to outsiders.' In fact, until the end of World War II, it is believed that fewer than 1,000 foreign travellers had ever journeyed beyond Marrakech and Fez to penetrate the High Atlas valleys. Amazigh tribes have occupied these hostile mountains for millennia, where they long maintained a fierce independence and un-wavering distrust of outsiders.

While those in the lowlands slowly adopted the tenets of the many conquerors, most notably the Arabs who brought Islam in their seventh century conquest, the isolated High Atlas tribes fiercely defended their territory, language, culture and identity. For centuries, it was warlords who ruled these valleys, rejecting the authority of the Arab sultans and French colonialists. In some regions of the kingdom today, such as the remote hills of the Rif where soon I shall journey, they still do. In fact, even under the French Protectorate, that lasted until independence in 1956, these remote High Atlas valleys were designated as tribal hinterlands, left to the de facto control of the local warlords. So remote and hostile were these mountains, the French simply kept away.

One of the earliest foreign expeditions into the High Atlas in 1871, led by British explorers Sir Joseph Hooker, a botanist, and John Ball, a geologist, travelled under the direct protection of the Sultan. However, owing to the distrust of the local tribes, in their account they describe a concerted effort on the part of their escort and local chiefs to prevent the party from accomplishing its objective of passaging into the proud and sacrosanct High Atlas interior. They went on to note that: 'While the climate here is admirable, the natural obstacles of no account, the traditional policy of the ruling race has passed into the very fibre of the inhabitants and affords an obstacle impassable to ordinary travellers.'

Six decades later, an entry in the 1931 Alpine Journal tells of much the same story. 'There are no records of any visit to the High Atlas between the years of 1875 and 1928,' it begins, suggesting that a political reason must be to blame for the neglect of interest in travelling to these alluring mountains. 'The native population was fanatical,' it continues, 'and, as a still more serious obstacle, the greater part of the country was inhabited by independent tribes, descendants of the indigenous Berber population, which has never been subjugated.'

Years after Toubkal was first summitted and under French colonial rule, the Alpine Journal still regarded the Atlas as being 'practically off the list of mountain ranges that is feasible for climbers,' chiefly because 'authorities have not yet pacified the whole country and so the traveller is very liable to be confronted.' Early accounts mention the positioning of 10-foot-high noticeboards along the few trails, reading *'limite de la zone de sécurité,'* beyond which lay hostile mountain passes and tribal valleys under the absolute control of local warlords. Until not so long ago, these mountains were, definitionally, the *Bled es-Siba.*

It would be decades until the High Atlas came under the control of central authorities, though in recent years hostile mountain tribes have become the most hospitable of entrepreneurs, who laud the enormous money-making potential of outsiders arriving in their isolated valleys. Marrakech is no longer a five-day journey from London, Europeans no longer need to disguise themselves in djellabas, and the village of Asni, which we passed through on our journey to Imlil, no longer marks the trailhead and the last real bastion of order and security. Today thousands flood to Imlil after the spring snowmelt to climb Jebel Toubkal or trek in its foothills during the late spring or early summer months.

Yet, as my eyes drift across Aroumd, which is comprised mostly of harsh grey buildings made from concrete, adobe and stone, it is difficult to imagine the colours that spring will bring to these mountains. In just a couple of months these bare foothills will be flanked with tiered fields of potato, barley and terraces of purple iris, while swarms of mosquitoes swirl in the dusk around the flowing rush of spring wadis. But now, as the snaking dirt road arcs around the bare, snow-brushed mountainside across the valley, I realise how vulnerable entire villages can be in these bleak winter months, that have rendered the land around us naked.

"Brothers, drink!" Lahcen orders as he thrusts the tea pot high into the air once more, the steam spiralling through the biting evening cold. "And eat, please – but not too much! I will phone my brother. He will prepare a tagine. You will eat like kings tonight!"

A smile runs loose across my face as Lahcen's face is lit up too. He beams as his eyes drift to the flanks of Toubkal once more. At last, we are all at ease. Just decades ago, we would have been unwelcome outsiders here. Tonight, it is a privilege to share this rarefied air.

12

Gîte in the High Atlas

Aroumd, Imlil, Aït Benhaddou

The last trekkers of the day are still marching their way towards Toubkal, passed by the occasional smoking motorbike or man on a mule. They will be camping on its lower flanks, though few will be summitting. I ask Lahcen if he has ever climbed to the top. There is a glint in his eyes that finally meet with mine as I do.

"So many times," he replies. He cannot help another smile. "Often I guide people, though never in winter. In the spring you can climb in just two days. One to the refuge, and another to the summit and back down to Imlil. But I never climb in winter. It is too dangerous. There are many avalanches. On a good day you can see the desert behind you and Marrakech ahead." He reaches into a djellaba pocket and pulls out a mobile phone to flick through photos. He is rightfully proud to have this great mountain towering above his village.

Sipping Berber whisky on the roof terrace of his family home, now I regret our tone over lunch. Lahcen may indeed be a sharp, connected businessman, but any true Amazigh is and this is a hard and honest life that he leads. He has been guiding and hosting in the Ait Mizane since he was young, for some 16 years. He must have been a teenager when he began. I want to know if his children will do the same.

"Maybe. Inshallah," is his reply. For a moment his eyes drift to the mountains, as if lost in a distant thought, until he says finally: "Unless they want a better life elsewhere." He motions a hand back down the valley towards Marrakech. Here, in Aroumd, we are at a dead-end: to our left is Jebel Toubkal, the life that he knows; to our right is a world of uncertain opportunity.

While most villages now have electricity, even in the chilly heights of these remote mountains, the disparity between rural and urban areas of Morocco is more pronounced than ever. Children still tend to livestock, donkeys still draw water from wells, and life for many remains a daily struggle for subsistence. Illiteracy in rural Morocco is amongst the highest in all the Maghreb, as high as 90 percent among rural girls, and around half of rural families in the kingdom struggle to meet their basic needs. Our journey here has laid bare the poverty that endures today: mud brick homes strapped to isolated hillsides, villages where time has stood still, livelihoods on the brink, a warming climate.

Tourism has thrown this particular mountain community a lifeline and it is testament to the resourcefulness of the Amazigh who reside in this valley that hostile tribespeople have become the most bounteous of hosts in the space of a mere few decades. Yet, as Zacharia had said, the reality of modern-day Morocco is that most boys will leave their rural homes and migrate to urban areas, or indeed Europe, in the search for a more prosperous life in their teens, even if such a move is ultimately a false promise. With an average per capita income of just $3,000 per year, thousands of educated Moroccans emigrate to Europe or the US each year, while the less affluent majority take whatever work they can find in the cities of Morocco, often in the informal economy. Africa is urbanising faster than anywhere on earth and Morocco is no exception. More than 60 percent of Moroccans now live in urban areas, but only the middle class is flourishing, with shanty towns and unemployment a reality of life for many urban youth.

A number of mosques are calling out for evening prayer. There is a mosque in every village, but I am still surprised to hear so many in this remote pocket of the mountains. Here in the rarefied evening air, their sound echoes through the valley with enhanced poignancy as muezzins on far-strung hillsides call back to us in chorus.

I ask Lahcen if his children attend school in Aroumd. Yes, he says. A third school was built in the village last year. This one is free. It was paid for by the government. There is a new clinic for children too, and new bridges and roads. He points to infrastructure that has sprung from the dust in recent years. Toubkal, this imposing mammoth that looms in the ailing light above us, is hauling government investment to these small Amazigh villages that dwell at its foot. Though school is free and attendance is compulsory for all children until the age of 15, the reality of rural Morocco is, again, not so rosy. Many rural children are unable to attend school at all and will work in the fields or family business. In a predominantly agrarian society where crop yields are falling each year with a changing environment, children are sometimes just too valuable to send away to school.

A rosy-cheeked girl in a buttoned coat joins us on the roof terrace. She looks cold and hugs herself warm with tightly crossed arms. Steely brown eyes peep out from beneath a snug woollen hat. They look just like Lahcen's.

"This is my daughter, Adilah," Lahcen says softly, placing his hand on her back. "She has been to school today."

"That is wonderful," I reply. "Does she enjoy school?"

"Very much," he says. "She has been going for one year now, to a new school in the village. Her brother, Zahir, attends a different one. He has been going for three years."

"Is his school in the village too?" I ask.

"Yes," Lahcen says. "But they speak in Arabic. Before this year the teacher at the other school only spoke in Arabic too. They didn't have a teacher that could speak to the children in the Berber language. And so, many Berber children did not go."

"Is that why Adilah only started last year?" I ask.

"You are right," he replies. "Adilah does not speak Arabic, so what would she have learned?" Lahcen sighs. "I must tell you, friend, many girls in Morocco do not go to school. Especially Berber girls. We really are the lucky ones. Adilah is lucky."

While education is free and compulsory in Morocco, that does not make it accessible, especially for girls in rural areas. Six years of primary schooling has been compulsory since 1962 and most children do enrol, yet almost two thirds of rural girls will not enrol in a secondary school. The reasons are myriad. Most families in rural areas are agriculturalists, many of whom have barely enough money to sustain their families and heat their homes. Books and backpacks are a luxury few can afford and while Aroumd is fortunate to have three local schools, many villages do not have a school and parents are often reluctant to send their girls out to attend them along dark and dangerous roads. Educational attainment is therefore split along gender lines, which has also served to widen the gap between rural and urban areas. Even in villages that have a school, families often have to strike a difficult balance between schooling their girls, or keeping them home to perform vital domestic labour, or work in the fields.

Then there are the barriers in society at large. In a deeply patriarchal and Islamic society, there is often an expectation that women and girls should be foremost dedicated to the home, family and husbands. Many girls are expected to look after their siblings while the adults work, and in some more traditional and isolated areas education can even make a girl less attractive to potential husbands and their families, owing to her perceived lack of commitment to family life. Some are even forced to marry as young as 12. The statistics speak for themselves. While four in five rural boys attend primary school, just one quarter of rural girls can say the same. The challenge is especially acute for the Amazigh. While schools are being built throughout the mountains and other rural areas, the authorities will often provide a teacher that can only speak Arabic, the language of institution, even though many rural children only know Tamazight. It means the Amazigh do worse at school when compared to their Arabic-speaking classmates on average, while many parents see little point in sending their children to school at all, given the linguistic barrier. Offered the choice of sending a son or daughter, it is girls who will more often than not stay behind.

It means that building new schools is not the answer. Even remote rural areas have schools, but linguistic and cultural barriers are a major obstacle to girls' education. Transport is uncertain too, roads are unsafe and given that many rural schools do not have a dormitory where girls can safely stay, many parents simply do not let them go. Yet educating girls is one of the most important objectives for any developing nation that seeks a highway to modernity. Reducing gender gaps would help the economy and improve the nation's competitiveness, but education also empowers women to better understand their legal rights and make decisions for themselves and their families. Educated women are more politically active and less likely to marry early or die in childbirth. They are more likely to have healthy children who will live longer and go to school. Female literacy is a good way to predict when a girl will marry and have their first child and how healthy they will be. Educating girls breaks the cycle of poverty, empowering women who will pass on the benefits through the generations.

Fortunately, things are moving in the right direction. Liberalisation under Mohammed VI and protest movements such as the Arab Spring have unleashed a national dialogue about gender issues for the very first time and issues that were once taboo and little spoken of have now become positively mainstream. Moroccan women are increasingly aware of their rights and while two thirds are illiterate, that has fallen to just a quarter among women aged 15 to 25. Yet while the cities steam ahead, rural Morocco is being left behind. Challenges such as rising inequality and female illiteracy have fuelled recent protest movements, and while many teenage boys migrate from the valleys to the city every year, few are finding opportunities on their arrival and many carry with them the stories of a rural world left behind. It is no coincidence that recent unrest in Morocco has typically stemmed from its rural hinterlands, or has involved recent migrants who have experienced how tough life can be both in the cities and countryside first hand.

"What do your children want to be one day?" I ask Lahcen. "What are their dreams?"

"Zahir wants to be a guide in the mountains," he replies. "I hope he will do it. I would like it, but it is his choice. Adilah I do not know. School gives her many ideas! But I think she will stay in the valley too. Tourism is our life, you know?" Lahcen sweeps his hand across dusky Aroumd. "Everyone here works in tourism. It is what we do. In every home, around three to five people will do this work. They are guides, porters or muleteers. Or they work in hotels."

Tourism is the lifeblood of these people and it is drawing wealth to their valleys, though I wonder how much it truly helps a family such as Lahcen's. Richard Branson has a hotel down the valley. Apparently, he once spotted a hilltop kasbah while hot air ballooning in the valley and now he has converted it into a luxury retreat for the rich. Guests fly in by helicopter. Lahcen sees them fly over.

"They come to see the mountains from afar," he explains, "just for two or three days. Then they fly home."

That is the new reality of life in these once-hostile mountains. Just like our desert guides from one year ago, the people of the Ait Mizane have embraced a strange new world that has enabled them to shoulder the burden of poverty. Here in Aroumd, the fruits of valley tourism *are* clear to see. Lahcen explains that life in the village is centred on a local charity that is run by the village elders and funded by income from the tourism trade. It has enabled the community to resurface and widen the mountain roads and bring electricity and clean water to every home in the village. It's a similar story back down the mountain in Imlil, where a tourist tax agreed upon by the local businesses helps to run a Village Association. Now they have an ambulance so locals can reach the nearest hospital in Marrakech quicker, and at last there is refuse collection. Proceeds from tourism have even helped to fund the construction of a community hammam.

Dusk is smudging the sky behind Toubkal in purple, as we debate our plan for the morning. We want to explore the foothills around the village, but in the afternoon we must traverse the High Atlas across the Tizi n'Tichka to Ouarzazate, where my friends and I shall part ways. I am journeying with them across the mountains because I want to visit Aït Benhaddou: once a strategic outpost on the pan-desert caravan trail, but it is a shame to be leaving Lahcen so soon. He asks if we will join him on a trek to the pagan shrine that stands along the mule track between us and Toubkal, at around 2,300 metres.

"It's around two hours, that way," he says, pointing south towards the dimming valley. "It is called Sidi Chamharouch. They say it is the tomb of the king of the jinns! They sacrifice animals up there. Women go for healing, or men who are mad. At dawn we can trek there."

Gloomy snowfields cocoon us like a cloak. They tempt me, luring me towards their bleak and enticing midst. There is adventure in these mountains, but my companions are unwell and the short hike up from Imlil has worsened their condition. The rarefied air is no help and they are reluctant to journey on. We should not make tomorrow any more difficult and so, regrettably, we must turn his offer down. I ask Lahcen if we can ride mules back down the mountain to Imlil in the morning. It will save my ailing companions the walk and allow us to explore the shallower forested track that winds through the valley. He will have to see. Since the last heavy snows, the mule man has been refusing to rent out his animals; the trail is not yet safe. He will ask again tonight.

Cold bites hard as darkness flicks like a switch over the Ait Mizane, the glorious last embers of day succumbing to the highest mountains in the west. Lahcen leads us through his family home and along the ice-sheened track to our overnight halt, a gîte that he owns, nestled in the grip of the village. It is a slightly perplexing place. Uniformly grey and proudly Amazigh this village may be, but inside his gîte it feels like we have stumbled into a Swiss hunting lodge. Sheepskins line the hallway and long rifles pin either side of a photo of the Matterhorn that hangs paradoxically above a mosaiced urn and decorative tagine. Alpine-style window shutters open inwards above a roaring fire and woven baskets hang on the walls.

The temperature is not dissuading either. As the night closes in, we hunker beneath heavy woollen blankets that cover our bodies and take turns to rise and warm by the blistering fire that rumbles in one corner. Then the evening turns to debate: mostly life, faith and Islam. Lahcen sits opposite us throughout, his djellaba hood up and his eyes closed or flicking through his mobile phone. I wonder how much he can understand and how these big debates in the context of our peculiar, hectic urban lives communicate to someone who rarely leaves the confines of this valley and who appreciates the simplest elements in life.

"Brothers," Lahcen rises abruptly. "I must leave soon and return to my family for the night, but first I have to show you something. If you must leave at dawn, you must at least see how special these mountains are by night!"

We rise immediately. Actually, that's a hollow lie. We very slowly extract ourselves from the warmth of a dozen blankets and chase after Lahcen, who has fled through the rear door and hurried up an external staircase. Up top, he is beaming once again.

"God has willed it," he says looking skywards. His smile is as wide as the expanse above. "A clear winter's night."

I am struck by how bright the mountains are. It is like the day had not faded at all and the oranges and yellows of late evening had simply morphed into one thousand shades of white, grey and deep, mysterious black. Free from city lights and despite the aching, bitter cold, we stand together beneath a ceiling of one million stars. It is no streaking Milky Way, but a myriad sparkling diamonds are strung across the night sky like a sequined dress, arcing across the void of darkness to the cols and ridges of the surrounding mountains, which, lit by moonlight, cocoon us in a renewed isolation.

Once more, conversation turns to the bigger questions in life: this infinite void above us, how small we all are. In these tribal mountains, under *that* sky, you cannot help but feel small and insignificant, maybe even overpowered.

"One tiny leaf … it has thousands of microscopic cells, each one so detailed and made up of tiny, perfectly functional components." I have begun my usual story. "Yet that leaf is just one of hundreds on a single branch … and that branch is just one on a solitary oak, in one corner of a forest, on the outskirts of a city, in a region of one single country, on this solitary, drifting earth. That tree is tiny, let alone a cell on one of its many, many leaves.

"And then this!" I lift my hands to the night above. I am having a moment. "This *infinite* universe. Our tiny planet, amidst all that space. How small are we? Tell me: how miniscule is that leaf? How is this all by chance?"

Moment over, I await the response. Flames had been stoked earlier in the evening, but now I have poured on gasoline. Some do not need convincing. "Mashallah, yes my brother," applauds Nabil. Moe stands in silent agreement, Ruben ever the diplomat.

"You know what, Mike?" Jason begins. "This night sky proves to me that there is no God!" You cannot win them all.

Back inside the gîte, Lahcen has news. The snow is still too deep in the forest, so we cannot use the mules to journey down the mountain tomorrow. We will have to go on foot with our backpacks shouldered. It is unfortunate news and with Jason and Ruben both getting an early night with their illness, I feel relieved that we decided not to hike into the deep mountains in the morning.

As we bid Lahcen farewell for the night, my eyes drift to a map on the wall behind us. Tomorrow we are crossing the High Atlas towards Aït Benhaddou, but while the map shows that we will have to return almost to Marrakech to pick up the Tizi n'Tichka east, Lahcen had told us earlier that a right turn just down the valley will allow us to slice across the lowlands, cutting the corner. I search for a date on the map. There isn't one, but it looks fairly new. A new highway, straddling the dusty lowlands to the foot of the Tizi n'Tichka? Either something has gotten lost in translation, or this proves just how fast this once-quiet corner of the kingdom is changing.

Though the infirm had been locked in a darkened room at the end of the corridor all night, even the healthy among us have awoken this morning feeling a little groggy. The window in our room did not shut properly and so I slept last night with a mound of snow just inches from my face. I was fully expecting an avalanche to go off in the night, pushing through the window and burying my head in the process. Although, come to think of it, a thick layer of snow over the head might have made things warmer than they were. Last night, despite burying myself beneath a dozen thick blankets, was bloomin' freezing.

This morning we are saying farewell to Lahcen and trekking back down the mountain to Imlil. It's a really sad moment. From initial distrust yesterday, we have grown fond of this humble young man and his family. Lahcen has been a bounteous host and life in these parts is truly hard. That steely face that I had badly misread at first … it comes from life in this remote, ice-chilled valley. These isolated mountains are no longer the hostile abode of feared tribal men. They are brimming with warm hospitality, even in the midst of a bitter winter. These are hardy and resilient mountain people, battling the elements – and poverty.

Last night, while the less healthy slept early, we had been discussing how much to pay Lahcen. This is no book online, pre-charge-my-card arrangement. Our short stay with Lahcen was setup through Zacharia, and there are numerous meals to account for, as well as guiding up and back down the mountain. We settle on a figure. Moe recons it will be enough to support his family for two weeks, which sounds excellent – but in this off-peak season and with the summit trekkers not returning until the spring snowmelt, I wonder how long it will be until his next guests arrive.

We say farewell to Lahcen with a double embrace outside his gîte, placing our heads to each other's left and then embracing again on the right. He is moved by our tip and we thank him sincerely for all of his generous hospitality. We will remember this man for a very long time. Lahcen hands us over to his friend, Rahman, another mountain guide who is wearing a padded jacket reading 'ESF': Ecole du Ski Français, a union of French ski schools. Evidently, there is a thriving ski scene in these mountains and, indeed, just down the valley is the resort town of Oukaïmeden, the highest ski resort in Africa. Annual snowfall seldom exceeds 20cm, but if there *is* enough snow then the season should run from late December to somewhere around the end of March. Just don't expect piste-grooming, or much in the way of rescue services.

On the slow trek back to Imlil, it is quickly apparent why the mules could not ride with us this morning. The twisting switchback road that sinks into the forested valley beneath Aroumd is slick as ice, and while Nabil with his wash bag in hand is skating down the mountain in city shoes, even in my hiking boots I am finding the going underfoot a little tricky. A new day is just beginning in settlements that trim the shallow trail. Even the smallest villages have their own mosque, all a stony grey, the colour of the bare mountains. They are distinctly different from the clean pale yellows and pasty oranges that are more common in the cities and less isolated countryside.

On the edge of Imlil, we get a sobering reminder of how wild and untamed this touristy valley can be. An enormous boulder around the height of a bus has wedged itself beside a stone bridge, as if it had just tumbled down the mountainside. Clearly too big to shift, the wall beside it has simply been built through it, with the boulder overlapping its edges and forcing the surrounding buildings to wrap around it.

"The boulder came down from the mountains in 1995," Rahman tells me when I mention it, shaking his head wearily. "Some people in the valley say it was an act of God. An enormous, powerful rainstorm beat our valley for just two hours, but the flood that followed it was so severe that the Rheraya swelled to a monster!" In an instant, the river was raging with 27 times its normal discharge, and a deadly torrent of water some six metres high was bearing down on Imlil.

Rahman points to a rockface of sprawling scree and a glacier above. "Boulders as large as trucks were thrown down the mountainside," he continues. "But in truth, they were the least of the problem." Rahman can only have been a young boy when the storm hit, but he speaks as if it were yesterday.

"The boulders forced the Rheraya to change course," he says, "and then the river raced towards Imlil itself, gushing down the main street. You cannot imagine how it was! Even today, I struggle to believe that it was real! But it was and in Imlil around 150 people died."

Then, as quickly as it had come, the storm passed and the Rheraya returned to its normal level. Now we walk alongside it, raging a glacial flurry through the tumbled rocks below, callous and untamed.

"Still we ask 'why?'" Rahman says flatly. "Why did it come? Why was the storm sent to us? For what? We had little and then, in just an instant, we had almost nothing."

"How long did it take for your community to recover?" I ask him, wondering if this was the storm that destroyed the flock that belonged to Lahcen's family.

"Only now have we recovered," he replies solemnly, with another long shake of his head, "two decades on. All our maize and the fodder for the animals was gone, and so the mules and goats that survived the storm we lost as well."

Some blame a divine force. Rahman is among them, although deforestation on the surrounding slopes was certainly a factor too. These mountains hold poverty in their midst and people rely on the forest for firewood, but the loss of trees had left the soil impermeable and so the river had nowhere to go but into the town itself. The terraces were all destroyed, so too the traditional irrigation channels. Only now is valley agriculture bouncing back.

"But now the environment is changing too," Rahman says. "Snow does not fall like it used to. The weather is very unpredictable. Floods and droughts are now common and they are becoming more extreme, every year. The mountains are slowly being turned into desert! Since I was a boy, it has rained less and less, each and every year."

The Atlas Mountains form a vast dividing range, splitting the desert flatlands of the east from the fertile plains of the west. Yet since 1960, the climate here has warmed by some 1.5°C, double the global average, while rainfall has dropped by around 50 percent. While the High Atlas was once covered in rich forest cover, it is now being transformed into the desert that it is supposed to be holding back. It is partly so because of climate change at a planetary scale, but also human activity, especially unsustainable logging practices. The result is that many valley families have been forced to abandon their villages and way of life altogether as greater opportunities beckon in the city.

"I have been up to some of the Amazigh villages in the surrounding valleys," Rahman says. "Many of them are now empty, or only have a few families still living there. They are like ghost villages! The terraces that used to grow vegetables are now bare and empty. It is just too dry, but also the traditional markets where the women can sell their goods are disappearing too. It means that people are forced to move and with them the traditional skills and knowledge are lost as well.

"Things in the Ait Mizane are not so bad," he continues. "We are lucky because we have tourism. With tourism comes work, money and better infrastructure, because the government is interested in the valley. We have opportunities! But in valleys around us ..." he shrugs. "There is no work. It becomes just too hard to survive."

"So, you welcome the tourism in your valley?" I ask him.

"Yes. Very much so! Even those who do not speak other languages can work as porters or mule drivers to carry equipment to the refuges, high on the mountainside. And with the tourism comes money, roads, hospitals, like in Aroumd. And people will take care of the mountains, because no tourists want to see a desert in the mountains! They want a nice place to visit. And for the children, it is a way for them to know a bigger world and maybe learn some new skills. Elsewhere, in the other valleys, many of them work as shepherds or on the street and their life is hard. Many of them get sick. But with the tourists they can learn new things and earn some money. It is good for everyone."

As the trail eases our weaving descent to Imlil, we pass a small grove of walnut trees that look hardy but immature. Rahman wields a broad smile, as he brings our party to a brief halt.

"The walnut is very important to my valley," he says. "I cannot tell you how much joy it brings me to see these trees again. They take years to grow and mature. Decades. But now they are returning to us and at last the community can thrive again."

The walnut tree is a vital cash crop for many in the Ait Mizane and now, two decades after the devastation caused by the great flood, they can finally provide a source of income once again. Down the valley, I know there are many more. In the interim, many Amazigh families in this valley have turned to tourism and my reservations about its impact in the Ait Mizane are now being shaken free. Not only does Rahman guide trekkers in the valley, but he is an instructor in the burgeoning ski scene too.

"Without it we would be poor and reliant on agriculture," he says as a parting remark. "Now we have both and the girls can go to school. Thank you for coming. And please, tell your friends to come too!"

Our departure from Imlil is a rather smoother affair than our arrival had been. There are just two other cars left on the steep and icy slope, whereas yesterday there had been some three dozen. Evidently, almost everyone who visits this small mountain village in winter is just a day-tripper from Marrakech or has been deposited here by grand taxi before trekking up onto the mountain. Again, I think how keen Lahcen must have been to host us for the night and how good Zacharia was to secure business for his friend. Tourism is the lifeblood of this valley, but it is a seasonal business.

Lahcen was right. Sure enough, as the market town of Asni shrinks in the rear-view mirror and we arrive in the town of Tahnaout, a new highway takes us charging east across trembling dusty lowlands, as the peaks of the High Atlas tower on the horizon again. It must be market day in a town near Ourika where we slow to a crawl as several hundred pedestrians and accompanying donkeys take charge of the road as if we had taken a wrong turning and ended up driving through the souks of Marrakech. Women in burkas brush against our car as massive cartloads of goods trundle by precariously on the back of motorcycles. Men stroll the dirt road, resting enormous sacks of produce on their shoulders, and to the right some kind of jumble sale is going on: a mound of clothing and mass of pots and pans, sprawled across the rocky earth like a waste pit, except with women and men sifting through, bartering for wares.

It is astonishing just how many people have flocked to this rural market strung along the road. It takes 20 minutes to move half a kilometre.

Then, as the land finally kicks skyward, the dizzying Tizi n'Tichka follows, slicing across the spine of the High Atlas where I am reminded of sights from a year ago: gem traders, precipitous drops, tiny Amazigh villages strapped to hillsides. One year on, I feel fortunate to have gotten into these mountains and met the people at their heart.

Rising before us is Aït Benhaddou, shimmering in the resplendent golden hues of evening. The High Atlas peaks are now shrinking to the north and the land down here is stark. It is almost Martian, akin to Dadès to which we are quite near, with rolling terrain dusted in red and strewn with boulders for unbroken kilometres, right to the foot of the mountains. Domesticated camels, looking rather out of place in this rocky environment, dot the way.

The land around Aït Benhaddou itself is rather more enriched. The famous settlement perches on a rise above a river valley that fans across the area, trimmed with pale trees and crowned by explosive palms that rise high above the buildings of earthen clay. A jumble of rocks tumble to my left, as Aït Benhaddou, bathed in gold, sprawls across the hillside to my right. This settlement was once an important trading post along the ancient caravan route from the Sudan to Marrakech, though more recently it has become known as setting of countless blockbusters, from *Prince of Persia* and *Gladiator*, to shows such as *Game of Thrones*. The Atlas Studios, the largest in the world by size, are just along the road in Ouarzazate and tonight we shall stay next door, in a hotel dedicated to the region's proud cinematic history.

Light shrinks away slowly in these lowlands; it is a fitting final sundown. Tonight, Aït Benhaddou is quiet beneath an ailing sun that has draped our surrounds in a rich late day light, that runs liberally over the earthen clay buildings like a coating of honey. Tomorrow we shall part ways, my friends journeying east to the desert as I journey to the west, back across the Atlas to Marrakech, before I journey to the kingdom's intriguing northern tip, the so-called last land of lawlessness, the Rif.

But this evening we stand together in mutual, silent awe. The river below shines silver, but it is dwarfed by the breadth of the mighty river valley, trimmed green, that it had forged at its zenith. Intricate earthen clay buildings stand beneath us like sandcastles, some crumbled by the passing of time, and others neatly turreted. As darkness takes over, it is as if this curious place of great imagination has been washed away by a midnight tide, returning to the valley from which it had sprung.

13

A Day on the Other Side

High Atlas, Marrakech

It's been good, friends, but I must go. This morning I'm leaving my companions and heading in the direction of home. Exams beckon, but before I collapse back into the world of essays and 2am coffee, there are some loose ends to Morocco that I first need to tie up. I have a flight out of Tangier on the northern coast in just two days' time, and that's an issue: I am on the wrong side of the Atlas, on foot and around 1,000 kilometres from the city where I need to be. Have I worked out how I'm gonna get there? Umm … no.

As I shoulder my backpack at the roadside, I cannot help but feel a little stranded. The Peugeot coughs into life and disappears slowly into the hazy morning sun, my companions setting out on their long drive east to the desert. They wave ceremoniously from the air-conditioned cool of their rather more spacious saloon, myself a shrinking silhouette at the dusty roadside in their rear-view mirror.

Actually, that's not entirely accurate. My real departure is rather less Hollywood, or, should I say, 'Atlas Studios.' Instead, it's five to seven in the morning, my alarm forced me out of bed ten minutes ago, and I am creeping around a cluttered room in complete darkness, scrabbling to find my toothbrush. Zombie-like, my out-stretched hands caress the walls around me in search of the bathroom light switch. Already I have abandoned the prospect of breakfast. Last night I had vowed to make it down for a luxurious and most likely private feast overlooking the pool at the film studios hotel, but as I stumble over yet another washbag and squeeze into what I hope are my own clothes, I just want to be out of here. And what's that burning at the back of my head? Ah – it must be all of those angry, sleep-deprived eyes peering over bed sheets, cursing me for making a less-than-dignified exit.

Fumbling towards the thin slither of light that has been seeping into the room all morning, I swing open the creaky double doors and I am thwacked round the head by a sheet of morning light. Already my two backpacks weigh heavily on my shoulders. Having failed a game of re-packing Tetris last night, my possessions are now spread across two uneven loads, which are doing wonders for my neck muscles. But, as my eyes adjust to the burning light, I am able to ignore the discomfort, as surrounding me is the film studios hotel in all its bizarreness and splendour. Great Egyptian mummies, invisible in the darkness of our arrival, tower as columns beside idyllic palms that curve round the edge of the pool. A lone cleaner sweeps the smooth and shiny floor that surrounds it, as a gentle soundtrack of Arabic music rises from the breakfast room. And then my eyes drift across sights that puzzle with my in-need-of-a-morning-coffee brain: a poolside double poster bed that is draped with silk curtains, what looks like a giant upside-down pineapple, and quotes from Caesar and Cleopatra engraved on the walls.

Oh, and the most puzzling thing of all? There seems to be nobody else staying here. It is a place of peculiar imagination, and no wonder: rising to my right is the Atlas Studios, birthplace of some of humanity's most lauded cinematic creations. The great and the good of the cinema world have been here and I could dwell all day, but there is a road to hit and the journey ahead is long. My taxi driver is a man typical of his region, with a face that is dark and crevassed. His smile and laugh are nervously large, perhaps compensation for his basic English (vastly better than my Arabic) and our somewhat limited exchanges. He offers to put my backpacks on the roof of his Dacia for the short journey to the bus station, but I politely decline and take a seat behind him. Amazigh rugs drape over the seats and heap on the front dash, tassels tickling his knees, and lucky charms dangle from the rear-view mirror. Moroccans are an exceptionally superstitious bunch, not least when it comes to the perils of road travel.

In fact, dangerous driving appears to be a national sport here and it seems that any man and his donkey can be a participant. My chuckling new friend is certainly among them and his signature move happens to be the 'daring slice,' which he conducts against every passing truck and bus as we leap across roundabouts and brake abruptly for speed humps. My belts are stuck, so I don't use them. Pleased with the entertainment value of the ride, I shower my driver in dirhams, which he reciprocates with a strong handshake and one final parting giggle.

The bus terminal is airy and smart, reassuringly so given the nature of the journey ahead, and 90 dirhams gets me to Marrakech. That's less than £7.50 for a twisting five-hour journey across the high mountains. The bus should depart around 8:30, which is just enough time to watch Louis Theroux's *'The Most Hated Family in America'* on the waiting room TV, narrated in Arabic. As the Westboro Baptist Church booms to an audience of elder Moroccan men that God hates homosexuals, it is a slightly puzzling paradox.

The hold is open, so I deposit my more cumbersome backpack and locate seat 37 near the back, alongside an elderly gentleman aged in his 70s, who looks distinctly like a short, dark Bruce Forsyth. The likeness is uncanny. A neat grey moustache sits below his snug black beanie and a faded brown jacket hugs his equally brown djellaba. I will not be the least surprised if he gets up mid-journey and begins to dance. I am the only foreigner on board the bus and, more to the point, I seem to have accidentally joined a coach tour of Moroccan Saga. Aside from myself, the next youngest person seems to be a gentleman in the row ahead in his 50s, who periodically flicks through his phonebook to make a very short call to a seemingly randomly selected individual.

The engine coughs into life and as we ready to depart at 8:45am, a man walks down the coach, squeezing a foolishly large backpack down the narrow aisle … it is mine. With no explanation, he hands it to me, and I force it in front of my knees. Then, as we depart, a voice comes over the loudspeaker in Arabic and everyone shuffles at once, as if they are about to stand. Shall we pray? Sing the national anthem? Praise the king? Is Berber Bruce about to dance? Ah, yes, Arabic – not my strong suit. Everyone responds in unison to a request to plug in their seatbelt, which I had obviously not understood. Then Berber Bruce begins his first of many long rambles to me in French, which also happens to be a language that I am useless at. Eventually, I work out that he wants me to plug in his seatbelt, so I do, which he reciprocates with another long chatter in French.

For the first two hours I do nothing but stare out the window. The view is simply sensational. Desert flatlands run out at a crust of snow-capped peaks that fill the horizon and lonely earthen-clay villages cling nervously to hillsides above broad, green river valleys. Life around here passes slowly and people flag the coach constantly but to no avail. Soon the asphalt winds as we climb higher into the Atlas, before we halt at a small truckers' stop in its midst, where Berber Bruce suggests *café*. He departs for 15 minutes, but returns still clutching a big brown envelope with blue Arabic handwriting. Where is he going? The bus will journey beyond Marrakech. Is he delivering the letter by hand? I want to find out, but we do not share a language.

The views seem even better than they had done heading the other direction yesterday, but the journey is long and I tire, though I do not sleep. I *cannot* sleep on *any* form of public transport. The drops off the road are sickening and when the surface disappears altogether, we slow to a crawl, but go for daring overtakes around the outside of big trucks at other times when the pass opens up. Our arrival time has come and gone as we approach the outskirts of Marrakech. Berber Bruce chatters again in French as we arrive. I don't have a clue. It sounds like a question, but ends in *au revoir*, so I say it back. He stays on board as I leave. He is heading on towards Casablanca. We have shared a journey, some mimes and simple interactions, but I would still like to know where he is from, where he is going, and what he was trying to say. Not for the first time, language has deprived me.

I depart the bus terminal and promptly reject a gaggle of taxi drivers who swarm around me at once, like a film star swatting away the pesky paparazzi. The heat climbs higher and soon I am stripped to single layers as the ten kilos strapped to my back slowly shatters my spine. According to tales that flood tourist guidebooks and online forums, I am walking into the jaws of a bear pit. On my journey so far, encounters with scam artists, faux guides, touts, and pesky opportunists have been cordial and rare, but now, with a mountain strapped to my back and heading into the souks alone, I brace for what my guidebook warns is the inevitable to follow.

The pavement runs out frequently as I head in the rough direction of the Gare de Marrakech, the city's rail station, to purchase tickets for a sleeper train to Tangier, so I switch sides and straddle the traffic with uncertain ease. Marrakech is now a reasonably familiar city, but today I want to tie some loose ends and explore the further medina quarters, before setting out for the north tonight. Tangier is my destination, but the real reason for my journey is the so-called 'blue pearl' of the north: Chefchaouen, a striking blue-wash settlement strapped to a cacti-lined hillside in the midst of the lawless Rif, a region with an intriguing story to tell, at the heart of the Amazigh movement.

Inside the station, I purchase my ticket for a second-class bunk on tonight's sleeper, which concerningly costs a measly 370 dirhams. That can't be right, surely? That is around £30 for a journey more than 500 kilometres in length, with accommodation for the night thrown in too. Concerned that something must be wrong, I head, without hesitation, to Segafredo where I order an authentic ham and cheese baguette with an Americano, just a little milk please, to research the journey (strange things happen when you travel solo). It's just a 45-minute walk to the Ben Youssef Madrasa – once the largest Islamic school in North Africa and now a museum – which is my rough goal for the day. I want to be back here in five hours, ready to board at 20:40.

With my bearings set towards the medina, I prepare myself for the attention that I know I will soon attract. At first there is little, but then, sure enough, I see a shadow approaching on the wall to my left. I slow down and move to one side to let the individual pass, but I know what is to follow.

"Bonjouuuur, monsieur. Ça va?" says a man. What for it? This man is walking the same way as me and with a smile as broad as his, turning a blind eye would be like slapping a kitten across the face. Oh, and let us not forget – I am British.

"Bonjour. I am good, how are you doing?" I concede. The man is dark with fuzzy hair and a crooked but kindly smile. He says he is from Ouarzazate, but he studies photography and art in Rabat. I am curious.

He is around 45, maybe less, but he will not say why he is here, in the red city.

"Where are you from?" he continues. As is the norm, he has friends from London and I am very, very welcome here in Morocco. I share where I have been and where I am going. He is from the High Atlas; I was there this morning. We exchange simple pleasantries, but his reason for walking with me is still unclear. Eventually, he brings us to a halt.

"Brother, let's get tea, please," he says, ushering me left. "We shall stop at this café, so I can show you my website."

I thank him but decline. My day here is short and I know too well that tea in Morocco is the ultimate dealmaker and tourist-breaker. Tea means commitment and the more that is drunk, the harder it can be to extract yourself from a sticky situation, especially if conversation swings and the real reason for your befriending becomes clear. Pausing for tea in Morocco is rarely *just* about exchanging stories. More often than not there is … business involved. We continue, together. Still he walks beside me, moving ever-further from where he began. We're at least one mile down the road.

"Today is warm," I say to him. "Back in London, we'd call this a heatwave. Is it unusually so?"

"Yes," he says, "this is climate change … but only for the last three days."

His English is remarkable and I certainly believe his story about his studies. He likes speaking with tourists. It's good for his English, which I complement. But then it comes. With a smile, he brings us to a pause once more.

"I have a question that I have been wanting to ask you," he says. I wonder if it is one of intrigue about my country; he seems intellectual, well-spoken, curious. "Can you help me with my journey back home to Ouarzazate? I need only 80 more dirhams."

I have few left, I tell him honestly, as I am going home soon. With no fight he smiles, says *au revoir* and crosses over the road. I will never know if he really did want to stop for tea.

Near the medina wall, a little market is teeming with life and overflowing with fruit, mostly oranges and bananas, that spills from wooden stalls. With my excess baggage shouldered, I decide not to head straight through the souks ahead. Picking a path through its labyrinthine streets would be like trying to thread the eye of a needle. On a busy street you are liable to be bothered in a tourist hotspot. On a quieter sideroad you are vulnerable, prime pickings. Some streets straddle the two. They are more real and local, but don't always lead where you are going. I pass through the medina gates, like a portal into the edge of the maelstrom. The street ahead is a main artery of the souks – no way, so I take a left and pass alongside workshops and local hangouts instead, a much better bet. Eventually, I have to take a right turn towards the souks and recall the golden rule of wandering alone in the medina: move with purpose and navigate on the go and you will not attract attention.

Sometimes a spot will present itself for finding your bearings, but it is best to plan ahead. Ponder for just a second and in some corners of the medina a dozen faux guides will thrust their services upon you. Halt to check your GPS and you are dead meat. Stopping is an invitation to be approached and shaking a persistent local can give a solo traveller a very hard time, as soon I shall learn the hard way … many, many times over. Faux guides are now illegal in Morocco, but the informal trade is a major employer and just like the impromptu tour guides and parking attendants that we have met, pestering tourists is the only feasible livelihood for many, and so the challenge is unlikely to subside soon.

Yet as I wander through this technicolour quarter of the souks north of the Jemaa el-Fna and west of the madrasa, the scene is one of cordial afternoon calm. Merchants relax outside their cluttered stores, each an Aladdin's cave of eccentricity, and some call you in. Few persist: "Can I show you a jacket? You need a djellaba!" Others amuse: "Sir, come back. Where are you going monsieur?" until the sound dies out behind you. Admittedly, many of the trinkets are the same – decorative tagines and tacky lanterns, wooden camels and vibrant scarves – but, as in Fez, this medieval maze is not a remnant of a bygone age preserved for the enjoyment of tourists. Rather, local women are out shopping for bags and leather babouches, an old man across the way is bartering for dusty antiques and young men are sipping tea at the edge of the carpet souk.

I wander liberally in the rough direction of the madrasa, but soon I am lost in the hustle of the souks. A Western man with shaggy hair had followed me close, but now, amusingly, he wanders by in the opposite direction, us both in likely pursuit of the same elusive goal. I must be close; the madrasa is on my GPS, but when I near its vicinity, the vibe of these streets changes abruptly. All of a sudden, tourists are hustled in doorways, hurried up staircases, and young men eye the passers-by.

Refusing to join in, I employ the golden rule of medina wandering and keep on moving, but soon I find the souks passing me by in a blur of colour and noise as I am funnelled, increasingly disoriented, through the warren. I seem to be on the M25 of Marrakech, except lined with chaotic store fronts, while the only real speed restriction on the narrow twisting streets seems to be the dawdling locals. Fumes choke as bikes blitz past, carving around me and darting past donkeys and rusted taxis. What would be a near miss back home occurs a dozen times over, until you numb to the madness and block it out, figuring it best to let them avoid you.

Eventually, I am lined up with the madrasa on my GPS and go for a home run. 'Muslims only,' a sign on a door reads. It this it? Tourists take photos, but surely – it can't be. It cannot be this hard to find! This was once the largest Qur'anic school in North Africa, built deliberately grander than any other in the land by the sultans of Marrakech to snub the imams of Fez, their erstwhile rivals at the Islamic heart of the king-dom. It is said that this very rivalry is the reason why the modern-day capital of Morocco is Rabat, rather than the grander imperial cities of Marrakech or Fez. To favour one over the other would have provoked uproar, so they chose neither. Faux guides linger around the corner, so I retreat, and make an approach from the opposite direction. But then, in my hastiness, I make a critical error. I stop.

"This way is closed, brother," a helpful young man tells me. "The madrasa is not open for tourists today, Muslims only." I double check. "Yes, not open for tourists," he says. "See," he points in the direction of two Australians taking photos, "no tourist." Okay, I say, willing to believe him, as he looks ready to head on his way.

"I will show you a leather market instead," he continues. "Berbers have come down from the mountains *just* today, you are very lucky. A colour festival! Every tourist is going there instead. Come, I will show you." Only a fool would agree.

"Okay," I agree. "Yallah!"

Before I know it, I am thrust back into the maelstrom of the souks – headfirst, tearing at warp speed through an unfamiliar corner of the medina, far from where I had intended to be.

"I must leave soon to catch my train!" I remind my new friend for the umpteenth time, as we dart towards the Berber festival. "It departs for the north in just a few hours."

"Relax, my brother!" he says again. "We have so very much time, it is amazing! You must come stay with my family in the Atlas one day. Five, maybe six nights."

Maybe, but now I have a train to catch. Kaleem is just a little older than I, maybe 23, compared to me aged 21, and he wears a black, blue and white tracksuit, which is as common among the youthful here as a djellaba is for the more mature. His skin is quite dark and more akin to the region I have just travelled from. He is a migrant from the desert, he tells me. He came here for opportunity.

"The Berbers are in town from the Atlas just today," he says again. "A Berber festival where they sell their hides."

Kaleem's family is at work in the tannery where we head. Some of them live in Marrakech, while others journey in from the desert every few weeks. Even today, this city is a centre of trade for goods from the east. Several young men linger at the roadside. He greets them, though some don't seem to notice him, their eyes all animated, darting about, examining the passers-by. Others look on with a knowing suspicion. I think I know what's coming. I should not be committing to this, but I am naïve and intrigued. For now, I'll play his game.

As we time warp through the souks, I express rising concern about the time again.

"How much further?" I urge him.

"Two minutes," is his laboured reply. Pah! I cannot help but laugh. Two minutes has been a recurring theme on this trip. Every location is just two minutes away, food takes just two minutes to prepare, a tour takes just two minutes to complete.

"Look," he says often, pointing to a half-empty street of dawdling locals, "all tourists heading to the Berber festival, just today! So lucky you are, John."

I feel no need to correct him. Two minutes have become ten, but now I am miles from anywhere I know. I consider darting down a side street, but turning back now would be futile; I may as well get a 'tour' from this debacle and anyway, Kaleem is keeping me at close quarters. Eventually, I am led to a gate saying, quite officially, *tanneries.* Kaleem points me to another man who grabs at my arm to haul me in, but first I demand a price for the inevitable performance to follow.

"What you want, what you want ... we relaxed," says another man unconvincingly at the gate. Mint leaves thrust into hands and a gaggle of guides of various shape and age grouped around me, I oblige.

My next guide is older, in his 60s, and he has short hair, a stubbled face, and extremely yellow front teeth. I can see them well, because he stands disturbingly close to me. He looks just like one of the Chuckle Brothers. Once more I demand a price for this tour, knowing too well that nothing in Morocco comes for free.

"Nothing!" he insists, urging me forwards.

Before me are the lines of tanning pots, which smell nowhere near as repugnant as the ones in Fez. This tannery must be at a different stage of the tanning process.

"All this leather – Berber. Not Chinese!" the man begins, pointing furiously across the tannery as if his arms have malfunctioned. "And in the market out there? All Chinese leather. All of it! This ... all Berber. Understand?" I do, and I believe him.

Berber Chuckle leads me to a small and darkened side room, where I am reassured to see a man working hides on a roller. This place seems to be genuine.

"This," he points to a heap of hides, "goat and sheep skin for bags. Next, this way ... here! A good place for a photo." I note, partly with relief and partly in pity, that three mildly bewildered Western couples are also being led at pace by other guides as I am ushered up some steps to a platform overlooking the main tannery.

"Cow, cow, cow, camel, camel, camel," the man begins, moving his finger frantically across the scene in front of us, where stinking hides drape over the edge of tiered yellow buildings. "Camel, camel, camel, up there, camel, goat, goat, sheep." He continues, "Belly of camel for jacket, goat and sheep for rug. And now, we go down." I take a quick photo. "Sheep skin, sheep wool," he continues as I point my camera at two murky coloured vats. "This – touch it! Cow. Not a Chinese cow! Berber." Reluctantly, I touch the treated hide.

A scattering of tanners are toiling across the site under a harsh afternoon sun, some up to their knees in tanning pots, while several others work treated hides in side rooms. Now the temperature hovers around

25°C, but come the summer it will soar to the sweltering forties. This is the work for the young and athletic. Fifty families work here and all the produce is sold locally. Berber Chuckle comes here with his family almost every week and most of his relatives work in the tannery, while he herds up tourists to make an extra buck. They are from the Ourika Valley, just 30 kilometres south of the red city, and he helped to set up the cooperative next door, of which tourist touts and tanners alike are members. In around 20 days, an animal hide can be transformed into a fine leather product, ready to be sold in the surrounding souks or transported far beyond the kingdom.

"This, in the water," Berber Chuckle is still in a hurry, "you call it pigeon sh–. Here, take photo! I am led in front of an American taking a photo. "This is the main tannery. Okay? We are done. Now, we can move on."

I feel like I am riding a high-speed conveyor belt, being processed through the system. Just fifteen minutes ago, I was trying to locate the madrasa, but now I am embroiled in a fast and furious tour of the back-end of town, where women and kids are virtually non-existent and all men appear to be working for one another as, of course, they are. The atmosphere is toxic. Tourists and guides eye each other with a knowing suspicion. As it happens, the tanneries are open daily and a market here is held every Tuesday, and I do not doubt for a moment that Amazigh from the mountains do indeed flood into the red city each week to sell their genuine local crafts and peddle hides to the tanners, as is the case right across this kingdom. Many of the tanneries in this city have been open since the 11th century, when leather goods from Marrakech were transported by caravans across the Sahara and were considered, simply, the finest in the world.

But as I am hurriedly led back outside and thrust into the hands of yet another guide, I do question the ethics of this particular trade. Still I wonder if the madrasa really *was* closed for tourists today … and now I must work out how this debacle is going to end.

14

Dark Arts of the Red City

Marrakech

O ut of the tannery gates, my instinct is to flee. I do not have a clue where in the city I am, how far the train station is, nor how long this 'tour' will continue. But refusing their service does not seem like an option; you are ordered to follow the next guide who will tug at your arm and insist that this *is* how you wish to spend your afternoon. Like quicksand, I am lured dangerously deeper.

Next stop on my whistle-stop tour of the back-end of the medina: a shop down a quiet and dingy alleyway, the so-called 'Berber Factory.' Through the door, I am handed over to yet another guide, my fourth of the half hour, older still and … rather generously proportioned. He is the warmest and most genuine yet, this the money end of the ordeal after all. I hope, as I am led upstairs, that an optional purchase, like was the case in Fez, is how this circus makes its money.

"Welcome to my store, brother!" my guide says, clutching both of my hands. "Please, allow me to show you my leather jackets. Winter is cold in England." I tell him that is why I am here, although I make it clear that I am not interested in buying anything today.

"My friend, don't panic yourself!" he reassures me. "You not want, we just smile and leave."

The jackets that he shows me are made from camel belly, they are *not* Chinese and I am told they make an excellent investment, because they last for years. I am scorching already, but he urges me to try one on, the thick black leather clinging horribly to my skin. It's disgusting.

"Very nice. How much is it?" I ask for some reason.

"Just 2,300 dirhams!" he booms in reply, around 100 pounds. Ha! I cannot help a laugh, not because his exchange rate is far off the mark, but because it is way too much for me.

Monsieur Nice Guy isn't too impressed when I suggest something smaller, so after a few more jackets are politely turned down, he shows me jewellery. "These are very pure. The very purest, actually. There is nothing purer," he tells me, channelling his inner Donald Trump. I am met with a face of disdain when I once again suggest something small. Perhaps ... a wallet?

"Slippers!" he bellows before thwacking his belly. "Tell me, friend! Who doesn't need leather slippers?!" I shake my head.

Eventually, I navigate our way to a wallet. Departing this afternoon fiasco without a small purchase seems an improbable end to this 'tour,' so I offer him 30 dirhams, going in low.

"You think I am a fool?!" he laughs deeply and at length, so much so it triggers a short coughing fit. "This is *Berber* leather! The finest!"

"Oh ... do you have any Chinese?" I ask him, angry with myself for how I ended up here.

"Come," he rebuts, "one hundred and fifty, but *only* for you." He puts a hand on my back, ready to whisk me off to take payment, but I cannot afford it. I do not have the dirhams. I offer him 50, but all of a sudden, the tone of Monsieur Nice Guy, *we just smile and leave*, starts to change.

"Okay." He ushers me closer. He is a real Amazigh, going through the motions to secure a deal. "You like to make things hard, huh? Tell me – what is your *realistic* price?"

I am now irrevocably in this exchange. I honestly don't have a clue how the afternoon has led me here, but I have been playing *his* game by *his* rules and the passing of time and the toil of this whole fiasco has ensured I am leaving with something. And I don't care. I will buy the wallet and get out of here. I have a train to catch.

He pauses. "Okay, listen to me. I do it for 60 … but you must not tell *anyone* out there that I have sold you *anything*." He points towards the dingy alley. "Do you understand?" A little confused, I nod and put the wallet deep in the pocket of my jeans.

"No, no!" he retorts in a whisper. "Zip it in your bag."

We shake hands and as I depart his store, he instructs me to pay the guides who will be waiting outside and to tell them *nothing* about our deal. I do not understand why I must remain silent, nor why this gang of supposedly busy tannery workers should still be lingering in the alley outside. But sure enough, waiting to meet me as I walk out the store is Kaleem and Berber Chuckle, who must have been lingering there for the duration of my time in the Berber Factory. They are ready to whisk me off on the next leg of the tour, but I flat out refuse.

"Here, have this for the tour, shukran," I say, placing 30 dirhams in Berber Chuckle's hand.

"What? No, no, you fool!" he growls with a face of thunder. "That is nothing!" He is not wrong, but I have few left and I know too well that this whole setup is a scam.

"At least 50," Kaleem rebuts, "give me 50 dirhams – now!" I have given them enough, I retort, *and* I spent money in the Berber Factory.

Berber Chuckle is outraged. "No, no! Give me another 10 dirhams at least, now!"

I concede, but now Kaleem demands his payment.

"We don't even get commission!" he protests. Ah – now it makes sense. Around here somewhere, a big boss must be collecting earnings from these supposed tannery workers. Perhaps its Monsieur Nice Guy, who didn't want them to know of my purchase. It's yet another cruel twist in the shadows of the informal economy. These migrants, one of whom has only recently moved from the desert, have been courted to play a dodgy backstreet game.

"Give me the money."

Berber Chuckle looks on with menace, his yellow teeth gnarly, as they both close in on me. The alleyway is dim and empty. Here we are at a dead-end; the only way out is back towards the tanneries and there are no other tourists about. Still the late-afternoon heat is immense and its weight bears down on me. The sun is raging a scorn and my entire face drips with sweat. The journey today has been long, the kilometres under my feet have taken their toll. This whole fiasco has crushed my spirits and worn me down.

Kaleem makes his demands again. I begin to walk away.

"Okay!" Berber Chuckle yells decisively with a thrash of the hand, ushering one of two children who were stooped on a step throughout the proceedings into action. He instructs the young boy, aged around 12, to lead me to 'the square' and orders me to follow him. Pah! What is this?! My afternoon is gone, I have handed out my remaining money, purchased a wallet I really did not need, and now I am being led wayward by a little kid. Still, it's either walk with the boy out of the deadend or head back into the Berber Factory.

At first the child speaks in French, but then remembers I have been speaking English.

"China good?" it sounds like he says.

"What? No, Berber is much better," I respond. He looks innocent enough and only half up for the game. Clearly, he has done this many times before. He reminds me we are going to the square, so I place my hand on his back and tell him that I am going to the train station and I do not need his help.

"Where are you going?" he enquires. Tangier, I tell him. "Oh, it's this way!" he says, pointing towards the square.

Still he walks with me, facing me, snug to my side. He is obviously undergoing his faux guide apprenticeship. He is the next generation of this pesky trade, an unfortunate but inevitable outcome of the booming tourist sector, coupled with a dearth of formal work. Every one of the faux guides I have met today is from the countryside – from the desert or small Amazigh communities high in the mountains. They have been lulled here by the false promise of opportunities and pushed from their homes by a warming climate and changing world. Many are Amazigh. These people marched in the Arab Spring and others just like them are rallying right now, on the streets in the Rif where I am supposed to be heading tonight. It was the self-immolation of a desperate street vendor that lit the spark for the Arab Spring and it is the failure of this regime to deliver hope and aspiration that will lead to such protests again.

It is a delicate reality the king and Makhzen are all too aware of. In early 2011, during the heat of the Arab Spring, tensions on the nation's streets looked set to boil over as thousands of informal workers joined the February 20 Movement to rally against their harsh socio-economic reality. The king was forced to step in and defuse the situation as near-by regimes tumbled, and so a deal was hastily struck. Informal workers would be allowed to freely conduct their activities without hassle from the police, but only if they promised to not join the protests. It worked and while regime after regime crumbled around them, the elites of the kingdom had managed to keep the peace. Yet just a few months on, it was as if nothing had changed at all. As soon as the rebellions subsided, the authorities resumed their crackdown, halting the movement of the street hawkers and demolishing informal dwellings that had sprung up in the brief truce. Constitutional changes were hastily made, promising basic social rights and raising state subsidies for staple foods and cooking gas, but they have been far from realised in practice and many urbanites still rely on the sheer goodwill of the Makhzen. It means that less than a decade on from the Spring, waves of popular unrest are beginning to simmer once again.

It is a challenge that looks set to endure. In the 1960s, only a third of Moroccans lived in urban areas. Today, around 60 percent call cities home. Come 2050, it is estimated that three quarters of the nation will reside in urban spaces. Many are forced here by environmental change. As Lahcen and Rahman had told me, while tourism has thrown a life-line for some, many others struggle to heat their homes and place food on the table. Agricultural yields are plummeting, torching summers are draining freshwater reserves, oases are running dry, and coastal fishing communities are battling with rising sea levels and soil salinisation. The result is a mass exodus to the cities. But urban life is not always what it promises to be. Between 10,000 and 30,000 street children occupy the streets of the kingdom, many forced from their homes by rural poverty and family breakdown, or the lack of educational opportunities. Then, on their arrival, they are faced with the threat of violence, and various forms of trafficking. Unemployment is rife for older teens too, forcing many to seek out informal work. Paradoxically, those with good educ-ations and university degrees have even higher rates of unemployment than those without, owing to the dearth of high-skilled, formal work.

Once more I bring us to a halt. I tell the kid firmly that I am fine. I do not need his help and I know what I am doing. With a short smile, at last, he is gone.

I take a right turn. Finally, at long, long last, I am solo again. Aghhh … wait. Immediately I have taken a wrong turn and there, at the side of the road, is Berber Chuckle, his eyes flicking once again in the hunt for new prey. I catch his eyes in the corner of mine.

"Go that way, now," he demands flatly, "to the square."

I ignore him and walk on. Where the hell am I? I am so lost. The heat is immense and once again I mop an ocean of sweat that ribbons off my brow as my ridiculous backpacks pull at my neck and shatter my weary spine. For a few minutes I walk aimlessly to evade the tanneries and this uneasy quarter of town, but eventually a moment arises to halt and check my GPS. Oh my … I am miles away. How on earth did we walk so far? I am right in the north-eastern corner of the medina, tight against the far city wall, whereas the station is in the extreme west. My planned time of return is now impossible and more than an hour's hot walking awaits me through pesky streets under a beating evening sun.

I feel angry. This city of alluring chaos and eccentric charm has now bitten me in the back. Unfortunately, I am far from alone. A quick on-line search reveals the sheer scale of such practices in this city, especially around the tannery quarter of the souks. There are simply hundreds of accounts filling the internet forums, recounting unpleasant experiences near identical to that of mine. 'Tourists beware,' 'Avoid the Marrakech tannery scam,' 'Don't go near!,' 'Scams, faux guides and more scams,' their headlines read. People speak of their fear and embarrassment they feel when led astray and the verbal aggression that they have faced from faux guides who rule these streets on a policy of intimidation.

Each and every time, the story is the same: a street is closed, but do not worry, there is somewhere better for you to go. It's only open today, you are lucky. Then, as you are lured deeper on a false promise of local advice, an extending tour is thrust upon you and becomes harder and harder to refuse. Before you know it, you are filtered through the system and passed from guide to persistent guide at speed, disoriented and far from the place where your fiasco began. Then, once the circus is over, money is demanded of you in a quiet medina back-alley, away from other tourists and surrounded by the congregation of guides that you have assembled over your last half hour.

Now they close in on you, like hyenas waiting to prey on a fruitless antelope, demanding *dirham, dirham*. By now you are dead meat and an outrageous sum will be demanded of you. Should you refuse, they will move in closer, faces will scowl and mouths will chatter in Arabic, voices raised. You are betraying them, they will inform you, and then, at the end of it all, you will concede. The heat, exhaustion and tension will have beaten you down, you will part with your dirhams, they will win and then the very next day, they will do it all over again. It seems that in this corner of the medina, faux guides, pesky touts and bewildered street kids leading naïve tourists astray are as prolific as the artists and craftsmen who put this city on the map. They are masters of their own craft, a dark art, and operate in networks of scammers who work in sequence across these streets to gather tourists and efficiently extract their money. Some online have compared the practices here to that of the Italian mafia. The tourist police are not visible here and the scam artists do rule these streets, but I wouldn't go so far.

Faux guides exist because of challenges that exist far deeper in this society. Those I have met today are from rural pockets of the kingdom. These are poor people, trying to use whatever skills they have to make money from wealthy outsiders. The informal sector is, for many, a way out of poverty, a path to a better life, the only way to cut a living, and so soon my anger subsides. And then there is me: prime pickings. I am young, travelling solo, hauling two ridiculous backpacks and sporting a face drained from the passage of a long journey and sweltering from a high-speed dash across the medina under a horrible, beating sun. I may as well be carrying a banner high above my head, reading 'come scam me, habibi!' And as the evening draws on, yet more vultures will soon swirl above my head, picking at my wounded body.

It is all rather unfortunate. While such pesky practices are especially prevalent in this quarter of the souks, encounters with faux guide still characterise many a visit to the red city and the kingdom at large. Such practices create an unfortunate distrust of locals, which makes it hard to recognise genuine hospitality when it does commonly occur across the kingdom. When a local has genuine advice, or wishes to share stories over tea, an indelible suspicion lurks in your mind, questioning 'why?'

Forever in Morocco, I am waiting for a hand to shoot out, demanding *dirham, dirham.*

The heat refuses to relent as I pace wearily towards the station. I've made good ground, but eventually I come across a fork in the road in an unfamiliar quarter of the souks. I do not know the way. Two young men, who are sat on bales watching the world pass on by, call to me as soon as I halt.

"Where you going, brother?" one begins. "The square's that way." Without looking up from my GPS, I tell him I am fine. I have neither the time nor energy to be accosted again. I have a train to catch.

"Need a riad?" they come again. No, I am fine. Just trying to find my way. "No, brother, chill," they insist. "We don't want money, we are just trying to help. Where you going?"

My mind is flooded with confusion. I think of Lahcen in Imlil and how badly I had misread him at first. I recall the wry smiles of the scam artists at the tannery gates, preying on my youth and naivety. My tired and drained emotions, coupled with the gruelling heat and distance that my feet have covered, are obviously clear to see. The station, I oblige, the Gare de Marrakech.

"You need to go down there, across the square, then take the third street on your right," they reply. They have been genuine and helpful, so I thank them sincerely.

I power back onto the M25, passing more tourists being led astray by faux guides as I time warp along twisting streets where motorcycles clatter around me, choking the air with metallic fumes. After following the route set out for me by the young men, I walk with purpose to try and avert further attention and begin an urgent search for water. Eventually, I have to stop again to recheck the route, but immediately I am approached by a young man. I turn him away flatly; I have no energy for this anymore. Where are you going? Do you need a riad? I'm fine!

"Show me! Where are you going?" the young man insists, pointing at the GPS open on my phone. I am heading out of town and reassure him that I have the route on my phone and know the way. I'm going to Tangier, but first to the station. Once more, I am conflicted.

Still the young man walks with me, increasingly distant from where we began. We have walked together for more than five minutes. He is not with me for an afternoon stroll, but I am unable to shake him. He is from Merzouga, on the fringe of the Erg Chebbi. He is another man from the geographical and societal edge. I tell him I have stayed there and ask if he knows Hamza.

"No way," he says, insisting that he does. He tries to find a photo of them together on his phone, though he fails. He tells me that this is his first time in Marrakech. I joke that I am therefore leading him. He is a migrant like many here, but he has a more secure job. He works in the medina, not in tanneries but in wood. Along the road, bustling and smoking workshops hustle with evening life. Tourists frequent this end of town. I know that he has been drawn to me by more than curiosity. Whenever I stop to check the GPS, he says no – it is easier if he shows me the way. I say right, he says left. Eventually, he realises he is trying to guide me to the bus depot, not the train station. He adjusts his bearings, as I again reassure him that I know the way better than him. But how can I shake him? Maybe I'm just too British. I am fighting to give him no reason to demand my dirhams, no service from which he may seek a payment. I ask where he is going. He says a café, to smoke after dinner; he smokes hashish every day. He is true to his desert roots.

But still he goes my way. Why? He is miles from where I met him. Ten minutes have passed. "Berber Ferrari," he jokes, as a donkey and cart clatter by. He is switching from guide to entertainer. I'm not sure even he knows why he is still following me. He is not going to make any money. Eventually, his phone rings. It is 'family,' so he answers the call and I slowly power off. I do not look back for some time, when I confirm that he has gone.

Jostling back through the medina, I care little for the myriad motorbikes that tear past me intoxicating my lungs with fumes, nor the sweat that stings my sleep-deprived eyes. Now I have walked for more than 15 kilometres, but finally I pass back through the medina walls and pace through the bustling fruit market and across a taxi rank.

"Where are you going?" a driver asks as I pass on through. I ignore him. "Tell me!" he grabs at my arm.

"Hey! I know where I'm going," I tell him firmly, adding that I'm heading to the station.

"You're heading for the Majorelle Gardens," he shouts back. He is right; I am veering off course, but I want to clear the medina. I straddle bullets of traffic that dart towards me as I cross a perimeter road that is awash with an ensemble of horns. A laugh slips out of my mouth. This city … what a draining rush of emotions. I wait for a moment to cross another road. A well-dressed man in his 60s stands beside me.

"Ça va?" Surely, *you* are above this. I look at him and try to think of French. *Bien* comes to mind, but he has already said "how are you?"

I'm good, I say, adding it's a beautiful evening. I am going to play this one cool. He too is fine, but where am I heading? He tries to slow me down before I cross the road. The main station, I say. He knows a quicker route and will show me.

"I'm fine," I insist, "just enjoying an evening walk."

As Marrakech is flushed with the mesmeric pinkish hue of evening, this morning's slow bus journey across the High Atlas could have been a month ago. I am drained and parched as hell. My face is arid, clothes sodden, and hair greasy enough to support its own small ecosystem. As I power into the outskirts of town, passing a quiet café on a street corner where locals sip tea on the pavement and a kitten curls by the feet of an elderly lady, I am unsure how to process the day. My mind floats back to Aroumd, the tranquillity of the mountains and valley, and that movingly clear night sky. I flash back to the desert, the crackling of the campfire, and the timeless plod of Hamza and his animals through the unbroken void of night. Back then, the passing of time was care-free. I recall my conversations with Yassine, how he had left behind this city of madness for a simple but hard life in the red dust rock of Dadès. And then I reflect on today.

Deep down, I know that I have relished every lasting second of it. I have met a dozen locals, whose lives are so different to my own, and delved to the heart of some of this nation's most bonkers and troubling realities. I have been dragged headfirst through a hectic melting pot of heat, colour and noise, my senses completely overwhelmed, and now I have emerged on the other side with a story to tell and only a few less dirhams to hand. I am unsure which – the landscapes of sheer serenity, or the maelstrom and noise of the medinas and souks – better captures the truer spirit of Morocco. That's because, I suppose – it is both. And now, as I once again near the superb façade of the Gare de Marrakech, I am readying to board a sleeper train to another corner of this simply fantastical kingdom.

The sun dips beneath the horizon as I devour a McChicken Burger and reconnect with the outside world while sipping sweet Americano. What a crazy day. I was in another world this morning, I've been torn through a circus today, and when dawn breaks tomorrow, yet another world awaits me. Then 20:40 rolls round and as I step onto the platform edge, I could be back in Ouarzazate, on a filmset in the Atlas Studios. Swooping palms frame the late evening sky, which is akin to the canvas that had blanketed that very first night in the red city one year ago: an alluring royal blue, smudged with deep purple. Before me in the dusk is the sleeper train, shaded in lime green but trimmed with black. Neat double lampposts dot the platform edge, completing a neat and elegant scene.

The sleeper train thunders into life and once more there is an energy in the air. Suddenly, I am feeling quite awake as I find my carriage and clamber aboard. I'm on a sleeper train, solo, about to journey over 500 kilometres north to the last land of lawlessness, the final bastion of the *Bled es-Siba* and the heartland of the Amazigh cultural movement: the Rif. I do not care that my clothes are sweat ridden. My exhaustion has been superseded by the anticipation of what lies ahead. I'm wide awake now. Come at me, Morocco. I'm ready to do it all over again.

15

Last Land of Lawlessness

Tangier, Chefchaouen

Miracles can happen. Last night I managed to sleep, and really rather well. Finally, it seems I have conquered my inability to sleep on any form of public transport. I mean, sure – on this occasion I did enjoy a surprisingly comfortable bed. Oh, and clean sheets. And I was lulled to sleep by vibrations of the train carriage after a day of carnage and exhaustion. But I rest my case: last night I slept in a very noisy, shaking box that I shared with three Moroccan men, who did not speak a word of English.

Not that this minor language barrier deterred one of my roommates on the top bunk opposite from trying to converse with me for most of the evening. In French. Yes, exactly. I don't speak French. In fact, this gentleman had one very long and seemingly jovial monologue with me that must have lasted a good couple of minutes. In a fruitless attempt to convey my cultural ignorance, I had mustered the words *je non parlez vous*, which I have since learned translates as *'I do not talk to you,'* but he continued unabated. At the time, it felt impolite to do anything but sit there and smile sweetly, with a few shoulders shrugs to suggest that

I wasn't quite making sense of it all. Why does everyone think I speak French?!

But anyway, back to my point. An unexpectedly good night's sleep has left me feeling somewhat revived as I'm deposited in a very gloomy and foggy Tangier at 6:15 in the morning. I'm not too sure what time the guard came through the train last night to slam shut our cabin door and turn out the light. I think it was 23:00, but my phone battery had died giving me no excuse but to catch up on my travel diary. With the amount of scrawling I did last night, my roommates would be forgiven for suspecting that I was a spy. But my first sleeper train experience had been a good one. Above my feet there was more than enough space to stow my backpacks and stinking shoes, while out the window I could watch the kingdom at night race on by.

In fact, the only thing that was missing from my second-class cabin was a charging port, so priority this morning is to source some power. And breakfast. But even at this earliest of dawn hours, my first task as I set foot in Tangier is to bat away the hordes of taxi drivers who swarm en masse at the station exit, their chorus insisting that every imaginable destination is an unwalkable distance away. At first glance, the Tangerines, who inhabit this corner of the world, are just a little less persistent than their brothers down south. Or perhaps they, like me, just need an early morning coffee.

Clear of the station, I find myself alone on some foggy, eerily quiet and rather sparsely furnished roads, leading towards the north of town. Unfamiliar with the area, I can't help but feel a little uneasy. Certainly, as I pass a stagnant river that smells discernibly worse than the tanneries of Fez (I forgot to pack mint leaves), I wonder if I should have taken a longer but more interesting route into town along the coastal esplanade. But what for it? Some 20 minutes and two laps of the bus terminal later I locate the entrance to the Gare Routière de Tanger in the city's north east. Already, it is bustling.

Today I am journeying east of Tangier to the very blue settlement of Chefchaouen on the northern shores of Morocco, an intriguing and long-secretive town perched on a rise in the lawless Riffian mountains. Early tomorrow, I am flying home from Tangier, so today is going to be an in-out assault and I am crossing my fingers that African transport continues to pleasantly surprise. My bus departs in just 15 minutes, so I head outside and onto the forecourt. Buses in Morocco often depart at capacity and timetables can be rather academic, so I am surprised to see that mine is already packed. Certainly, I am the only tourist attempting to clamber aboard and unlike my bus over the Atlas, I have no allotted seat number, so I force myself right to the back. Three seats remain, all dotted across the back rows, but they are 'reserved.' I appear to be out of luck.

Trapped in position by my oversized luggage, I am forced to reverse back down the bus the way that I had come. As fortune would have it, a beggar chooses his moment and climbs aboard the bus in the middle of my precarious reversing act. I therefore advance forward once again while he works his way along the aisle, requesting *dirham, dirham* from everyone. Few oblige, but now I am trapped in the aisle facing the wrong direction, with my enormous backpacks held in front of me. The driver fires up the engine and ushers the beggar off. I'm not sure that I am going anywhere today. Having endured yet another awkward reverse down the bus in front of the same three dozen locals now averting their gaze in pity, I approach the man at the door about the lack of available seats. He appears to be the only official able, or willing, to speak a bit of English. At first he shrugs in disinterest, but a few waves of my ticket later he is back onboard and heading to the rear. Yet again, I am squeezing down the aisle.

As we near the back, the official taps a young man on the shoulder and boots him off. Feeling a little guilty, and slightly perplexed, I drop my backpacks and take his position, hoping the young lad was a non-paying friend of the official. As I settle down, yet more locals arrive at the bus door. There are no seats left, but to my bemusement they too clamber onboard and sit on cushions placed on the floor along the aisle, which is rapidly filled by some half dozen locals of various age and size. As the driver engages reverse and edges the bus backwards, two more passengers run to the bus and load their bags on board. They fit inside, though I have no idea where.

On the journey ahead, glorious vistas over the foothills of the Rif provide some solace from the rather less pleasant environment inside. Oxygen is at a premium and as the windows steam up, the lady to my left fills yet another sick bag with remarkable efficiency and power. In fact, the entire family around me appears to be suffering, hopefully just from the roughness of the journey. Yet as we venture deeper into the Rif and the windows clear, the view is one of outrageous beauty. Unfurling is yet another landscape unlike any I have seen across this land. Cacti trim the roadside, mist rolls low over the swooping green foothills and birds circle like silhouettes in front of the dull and misted sun. Atop weathered trees, tall white birds perch proud and majestic, while soaring above them, darker birds jostle in flight and play. They are unlike any I have seen before.

These northern mountains are known as the last land of lawlessness, the last hurrah of the *Bled es-Siba*, and from the terrain that surrounds us, I can understand why. Distant from the central authorities of Rabat and close to the key smuggling gateways of Gibraltar and Ceuta, these isolated mountains lend themselves to banditry, while an agreeable climate and harsh terrain is virtually ideal for the undisturbed cultivation of cannabis, or kif as the Arabs know it. For centuries, the Rif has been home to rebels, hash-peddlers, outlaws, pirates, smugglers, thieves, and warlords, the latter of whom have always held more sway here than any central authorities. The word 'Rif' means 'margin' or 'edge,' ode to the fact that these mountains define both the edge of cultivated lands, and indeed the point beyond which the *Bled el-Makhzen* would have once become the *Bled es-Siba*.

Even the Riffian coastline was a place that many have feared across the millennia. From the 16th to 18th century, the shores of the Rif were among the most pirated waters in the world. Over a million slaves were taken to Africa through the Barbary slave trade, many acquired in raids on ships sailing the Mediterranean, although some are believed to have been captured as far north as Cornwall and even Iceland. England alone lost 466 merchant ships to raids by Barbary pirates over just seven years in the early 17th century, when the outlaws would loot cargos and take non-Muslim crews hostage to sell as slaves in Africa.

It is from these mountains too that opposition to Morocco's ruling elites has typically stemmed. Centuries of disdain and conflict between warring Amazigh kingdoms later spilled into wars and rebellion against the French and Spanish in opposition to regional colonial rule. Indeed, just along the North African coast, near the Spanish enclave of Melilla, is the site of an infamous battle between colonial Spain and the guerrilla forces of the Rif's Amazigh tribes. It took place almost one century ago, in 1921, when a small army of Riffian tribal fighters charged across the northern hills and killed more than 10,000 Spanish troops in the Battle of Annual. It was part of the Rif War, a long and bloody resistance against Spanish occupation of the region, and it inflicted upon Spain the largest loss of troops in one single day suffered by any colonial force in Africa during the 20th century. Back in Spain, it was considered to be a disaster of such magnitude that officials came close to abandoning their colonial mission altogether. For the Amazigh of the Rif, however, the battle is remembered less for the toll inflicted on the Spanish, than for what was soon to follow.

Commanding the Amazigh tribes in the Rif War was Abd el-Krim, a legendary military leader and notorious Riffian rebel, whose guerrilla tactics are reported to have later inspired Ho Chi Minh, Che Guevara, and Mao Zedong. El-Krim had succeeded where most before him had failed: uniting the restless and diverse Riffian tribes as one. In doing so, el-Krim was able to declare independence for the Republic of the Rif just months after defeating the Spanish, and the new republic set about forming a military and institutions, codifying laws and collecting taxes. Despite their differences, el-Krim had managed to find unifying ground among the tribes: resentment to colonial rule, a pride in independence, and belief that resisting colonial rule would serve as jihad, to secure the eminency of Islam in the north. It didn't last long. Just four years later, the French and Spanish deployed more than half a million troops along with air support to defeat a Riffian contingent of just 12,000 men. The republic was over before it had begun, but the legacy of independence and resistance to outside meddling endures to the present day. Stories, songs and poems continue to be passed down the generations, heralding el-Krim and remembering the days when a small Riffian army defeated a colonial power many times its size.

Since then, the Rif has never let its reputation slide as a defiant and proud region with a penchant for rebellion. No sooner had the Spanish been booted out, the Riffians continued to revolt against the Arab sultans and kings of the Alaouite Dynasty who took their place – including in the present day. Independence saw the Rif marginalised as Hassan II ruled with an iron fist, describing the Riffians as 'scum and thieves' who should watch their backs or expect unimaginable violence should they rebel. Rebel they did, as through Hassan's reign the Rif was neglected and barred from the new halls of power, which only served to confirm the idea that the Rif was detached from the rest of the kingdom. It was perhaps no surprise, then, that the two attempted assassination attempts against Hassan are believed to have originated from within the Riffian interior. Seldom has belonging to a greater political entity mattered to the tribes of this region. Instead, their history has been defined by pride in independence, loyalty to the clan, freedom from central authorities, and the steadfast defence of Tamazight and Tamazgha. Unsurprisingly, it is from within these remote, misted hills that the Amazigh movement has found its heart.

While travellers can journey through the Rif with comparable ease today, this remains a region on the geographical, political and cultural edge. A reputation for rebellion was rewarded with several decades of neglect and economic isolation under Hassan II, and so the lawless and disorderly north has been left behind as the rest of the kingdom moves forwards at pace. The predominantly-Amazigh Rif has the highest rate of poverty, female illiteracy and maternal death in Morocco, as well as the slowest economic growth in the country, which has only sown the seeds of strife. After years of neglect under his father, the reigning king set change in motion with a tour of the north early in his reign, as well as a programme of infrastructural development along the coast, his so-called 'Plan Azur.' But it has only gone so far. Poverty remains rife and decades of neglect and isolationism have allowed Wahabist ideology to flourish around the cities of Tetouan and Tangier and kif plantations to infest its foothills.

Journey just 100 kilometres east of Chefchaouen to the small town of Ketama, nestled deep in the mountains, and you will be at the heart of kif growing country. There you will encounter the largest region of cannabis cultivation on Earth, reaching over 1,200 km^2, an area larger than Hong Kong and doubling in size every three to five years. While the Moroccan government has sought to promote alternative schemes for agriculturalists, more than 800,000 Riffians make a living from the production of kif, with an estimated 80 percent of all hashish sold over in Europe believed to have come from this ribbon of isolated country-side. Lucrative profits from an illicit trans-European market, as well as the levying of EU tariffs on legal Moroccan produce, mean that despite its illegality, kif is, unofficially, the kingdom's largest earner of foreign currency. No country in the world exports as much kif as Morocco.

On a visit to the Rif, you will almost certainly be offered hashish, and should you dare to journey deeper into the lawless mountains east of Chefchaouen, you should expect to encounter roadblocks set up by both customs officers and roadside drug traders, who have a reputation for leaping into the path of oncoming car traffic to try and force a sale. Tourists should not stop. Many accidents and breakdowns are arranged as traps, while armed men are said to guard the slopes around Ketama, which is certainly not a place for an overnight halt. The so-called *Bled es-Siba* may be little more than a notion of history throughout most of the kingdom, but here in kif country the remote mountains to my east remain virtually lawless lands.

As we near Chefchaouen, the road starts to climb and the bus smells hot as it strains around the steepest bends. I hope we are going to make it. The limestone peaks around us are now shrouded in mist and soon tall forests of cedar and pine will give way to plantations of kif. Ahead of us, eight burly men stand in the back of a pickup truck; it too appears to be disliking the terrain. For now, there is no sign of blue.

Bah! Finally. Almost two hours later, I haul my body and my excess baggage up the final steps and into the main square of the medina. At last, I can see other tourists and sights that vaguely resemble the sort that I have been double-tapping on Instagram for years. Since departing the bus depot, which seemed to offer no real pointers for tourists, I had been trudging around a district of Chaouen that was neither interesting nor blue while rapidly consuming my precious supply of bottled water. Eventually, I had to rest up in a park where a kind Spanish lady pointed me in the right direction and advised where I should go this afternoon. A plan – hurrah. I really should have thought this excursion through.

I am entering a walled town where less than a century ago, I would have been a most unwelcome outsider. It is said that prior to 1920 only three Christians had ever managed to penetrate the walls of Chaouen:

a Frenchman who disguised as a Rabbi, a correspondent from the New York Times, and an American, who was poisoned among the streets of blue. What they all discovered was a medieval settlement strung across a jagged limestone ridge where Jews resided, descendants of the Jewish settlers who founded this town, having fled the Spanish Inquisition. Its occupants spoke Castilian, a language that had been extinct in Spain for more than 400 years, and worked leather just like their ancestors from Andalusia had done centuries before. Yet today its distinctive blue hues, which were first daubed in their iconic shades by the Jews, have placed the Rif on the tourist trail and lured infidel like me into its fortified and long-elusive interior.

Judaism may not first spring to mind when you think of Morocco, but across the kingdom, Jews do indeed have a long and proud history, especially on these northern shores. Before the Arab Conquest and the arrival of Islam, some Amazigh tribes embraced a local interpretation of Judaism known as Karaism and, over time, the Jews would come to be among the most trusted advisers to the sultan, as well as merchants and artisans who claimed an entire monopoly on the trade in gold. Today, the Star of David can be found emblazoned on many Amazigh rugs and crafts, while proud at the heart of every major Moroccan metropolis is a mellah, the Jewish quarter, which was always positioned close to the palace to ensure the respected Jews enjoyed royal protection. From the 11th to the 15th century, many Jews arrived in Morocco following the Christian Reconquista in nearby Andalusia, then more in the Spanish Inquisition, and even in cities as far south as Essaouira near present-day Agadir, over half the population of several major Moroccan cities were Jewish prior to the end of the Second World War.

Everything changed in 1945 when the return to peace marked the end of more than 500 years of peaceful cohabitation between the Jews, Arabs and Amazigh. With Morocco's realignment with the Arab east and the creation of the state of Israel, sentiments towards the Jews in Morocco began to sour, while calls for Moroccan Jews to journey east to build the new nation saw their numbers in the kingdom plummet. Of some 200,000 Jews who lived in Morocco in the mid-20th century, around 7,000 remain today, though here in Chefchaouen, their legacy is daubed on each and every one of its walls.

Last Land of Lawlessness

With yesterday's fiasco still fresh in the mind, I revel in the calm of these easy streets. I am rubbing shoulders with locals on the maze-like medina streets, but they're just going about their everyday business; few seem remotely interested in my passing. And yes, it's true – everything here is very blue. Fantastically so. Like a brilliantly abstract painting. In fact, almost every street and tucked-away square is shaded its very own blend of cobalt, azure, indigo or sapphire, one thousand shades of blue, brushed tastefully with the odd dash of white for balance. Lawless the surrounding hills may be, but here in Chaouen there is a distinct feeling of Riffian freedom. The air is spiced with a cocktail of mint tea, tagine smoke and kif that wafts from windows and side-alleys, and here your ears do not ring to the buzz of raucous barter and thunder of smoking bikes. Instead, stray cats curl around your feet and merchants wish you a pleasant day from the front of their jumbled stores. What a respite!

A local calls me over.

"Amigo," he calls from somewhere. I can see no person, but I must have been spotted, for the pile of babouches to my left now rustles and motions on its own accord. Eventually, a stocky man donning long red robes with teeth as messy as his store behind bursts through the piles of babouches, beaming a smile of mild insanity. His hand is outstretched, so I shake it and wish him a good morning.

"What, oh … you are from where?" He is perplexed by my choice of language. Nassim is a jolly man, aged around 50. His belly rolls and animated eyes grow bigger as he speaks. He refuses to believe that I am not Spanish.

"But you have Spanish grandparents," he insists, "no, no, no … yes, must have. Yes, absolutely." He has convinced himself, so I assure him he's probably right. By this stage of the journey, my skin is quite tanned and most tourists who flock to this Europe-hugging end of the country are, indeed, Spanish. I cannot blame his confusion.

I tell Nassim that I am from London and he proudly tells me of his British friends who work in the embassy in Rabat. He will be visiting them soon in London, near the casino in Piccadilly Square. It is heart-warming to meet an everyday Moroccan who can afford to visit lands beyond their own. I have met few. I tell Nassim about my country. He is curious and eager to learn more. He is a fan of Britain, and then …

"Lubbly jubbly, mate!" Nassim remarks with a shriek of laughter. I join him in hysterics. He has nailed a London accent, heavier than my own, which he finishes with a bit of a dance and a wiggle of the belly. I tell him that he will be just fine when he visits my country.

Before I know it, a handshake with a local has become an extended stay and a folder is whipped out containing printed photos and business cards from all the people Nassim has met. He offers me Berber whisky, but my stay here is short so I politely decline. For a long time we chat cordially; Nassim has friends from around the globe, but soon enough and sure enough, the conversation swings to business. A long chat can make it very difficult to extract yourself from a Moroccan's store. Elsewhere in the kingdom, I may have felt guilt-trapped into handing over dirhams in exchange for such an *experience*, but no such bother here. Nassim offers me an Amazigh rug and a djellaba; I own both and have no space in my backpacks. With a disappointed frown, Nassim has one parting message for me.

"See ya later, alligator!" he exclaims with a massive grin as we shake hands to part ways. He tells me to stop by again. Perhaps I'll see him in London, I say.

While the day is young, I head east out of the medina and towards a hike recommended to me by the Spanish tourist earlier today. On my way through the cobalt streets, an angry old man confronts me. He insists that I buy a djellaba out of respect for the locals and to ensure that I am not bothered by anyone. Locals in Chaouen dress conservatively, like those from Fez. Men wear djellabas with pointy hoods up and only the faces of most women are visible, but I tell him that no-one, in fact, has bothered me here at all. As I approach the edge of town, I pass by another old man taking his ostrich and peacock for a walk. After a while on a journey like this, sights of such strangeness become ... somewhat normal, but I avert my gaze to avoid being charged for looking at these beautiful but out-of-place birds.

Not for the first time today, I am also offered hashish. As per usual, it is offered by a young man, around the same age as me, who appears from nowhere. Hash is made from the cannabis plant, or kif, which in Arabic means 'perfect bliss.' In some corners of town, a rather pungent and piquant aroma wafts from open windows and floods through side-alleys. While illegal and though the penalties for its use are high, some tourists travel here to enjoy its easy access. This was, after all, a bastion on the hippy trail and, judging by some of the characters around here, some of them never quite found their way home. It's not at all unusual for accommodation, food and hashish to be offered in a single breath.

"Amigo, hey, friend. You need a riad no? Let me show you a good café down the road. Want some hash, brother?" A polite but firm shake of the head and they have vanished back into the cobalt blue as swiftly as they appeared. Deeper into these hills, shaking off the hash peddlers would prove a much more troublesome task.

A small, gushing waterfall known as the Ras el Maa marks the start of the trail, which leads up the dusty shoulder of the hillside to an old Spanish mosque, the Jemaa Bouzafar. The hike is not long but steepens towards the top and those who walk it are torched by a fiery afternoon sun. With my heavy backpacks, I roast. With height and vista, the blue sprawl of town becomes ever more apparent. The entire town is awash with blue, even the graveyard and many of its gravestones. Chaouen is a mosaic of sapphires and diamonds scattered across the rugged terrain, behind which a tall and abrupt rock face towers. It contrasts so vividly with the rolling, misted green of the Riffian hills behind. Cacti sprawl in the foreground, their large spiky pads clinging to jagged roots. They trim the edge of the trail like barbed wire along a precipitous edge, over which exotic trees peer.

I must stop and rest. I have not had a shower for some 42 hours, so I care little for the sweat that streams down my face. Travel across this kingdom can take its toll, but as the call to prayer begins and shudders through the valley, the reason for my journey here makes perfect sense. One by one, the mosques of Chaouen begin a collective cry. A subtle beginning is superseded by a rising thunder that overpowers all around it, reverberating from the midst of an ocean of blue across shimmering green foothills of the misted Rif. You cannot fail to be moved by the sound. It pulses through the air, pinballs through your entire body. The reason for Chaouen's many shades of blue is contested. Some argue the blue is to keep away the mosquitos, others to keep cool, or merely to bring in tourists. Others say that the Jewish blue is a reminder to look to the skies, to the heavens, or to wade off evil spirits. The Amazigh of these northern hills, a majority of whom are Muslim today, are known for their reverence of marabouts and Chaouen, for many, is a holy city.

In a moment like this, in a land so different to my own, any one of the reasons seems feasible.

The trail kicks again as I near the mosque. All around me I can feel Chaouen's past and present. To my left, veiled women wash clothes in the stream as above them, high on a precipice, young Australians shout to each other at either end of a climbing rope. Behind town I can now see a turreted wall, which snakes around the edge of Chaouen like the border of a painting, flowing and zig-zagging over the contours of the terrain. This has always been a place of reason: a fortification, to defend against the encroaching Portuguese; a refuge, for the Jews and Muslims expelled from Spain during the Reconquista and Inquisition; a mecca, for the devout and now the Instagram generation who flood Chaouen in their hordes to glimpse its famous blue, myself among them.

And as I reach the Jemaa Bouzafar, which is small, understated and quite shockingly un-blue (it is white, with tasteful, reddish brickwork), my journey too feels one of perfect reason. This is a day so different to yesterday, in a land so different from my own. I have not showered in days, last night I slept on a train, but like the settlers who founded this town, I came here to escape. I came here to experience a place where I could contrast my own life. I journeyed here to find another contrast in a kingdom of so many fascinating guises. I found it.

16

Sands of Africa

Chefchaouen, Tangier

With rising concern, I glance at my watch again in the hope that time has slowed down. The last bus of the day should have arrived around forty minutes ago, but there is still no sign of it. I have a flight out of Tangier at first light in the morning, but there's still a helluva lot of travelling to be done first. As the unyielding sun weighs down heavily on me, my weary mind weighs up the various options: wait for the bus, which may never show up; flog an expensive taxi, which I cannot afford; or find a job in a local hostel and stay for a few months. For now, I go with the former.

I am stood at the edge of the Gare Routière forecourt, with its very colonial-looking terminal building behind me. It, of course, is blue and white. Buses come and go, except for mine, though I have reasonable confidence in my timings as a few other tourists linger near me for the journey back to Tangier. As I wait, a man across the forecourt catches my attention. Rude as it may sound, the sheer sight of him gives some merriment to distract from the monotony and worry of this long wait. Earlier in the day, I saw him resting in the main medina square, where I presumed he was some kind of guide. But now it seems that he too is heading west.

The man is aged around 60 and is certainly a Westerner, though his head is adorned with a round and archaic patterned hat, which fits him snug and makes him look distinctly like an African dictator. A long and beaded necklace drapes around his neck, hanging low in front of loose local robes. On his wrists dangle bracelets, on his feet flop dirty sandals. Standing at the forecourt edge, he stands with his hands clasped by his front, his neck tilted back and his eyes closed, basking in the late afternoon sun. I cannot work out whether he looks biblical, like a Victorian explorer, or just a hippy from the '60s who never found his way home. Eventually, he strolls over.

"Do yer speak some English?" he asks. I'm not surprised to hear an American accent. I *am* English, I say, as he double checks that I too am heading west to Tangier.

"Forty minutes late?" he responds to a question that I have not yet asked. "Pah! This is Africa. If it arrives within an hour, it's basically on time." He beams, before closing his eyes and tipping his head back into the sun. "That's the charm of these parts. Oh, Mother Africa."

Then, as if woken abruptly from his slumber, he shoots his hand in my direction. "Jim," he introduces himself. He is an American, he reiterates, or, at least, that is what his paperwork says. Because, while he is from New York State, he hasn't liked a US administration for some 20 years, so he has been travelling across South America and Africa instead. His only recent journey home was to visit his elderly mother in hospital. His daughter is flying out tonight to meet him.

"I'm meeting her in Tangier," he says. "She absolutely loves all the local attire. She actually asked if I could kit her out like the indigenous people, just like me." Jim grasps a large suitcase and taps it with a grin. Today he has filled it to the brim.

"Just a little worried I won't find her," he sighs. "We haven't made arrangements." I assure him that mobile reception will be much better in Tangier, but he tells me that he hasn't owned a mobile in three years.

"Chaouen's a gem, don't yer think?" Jim continues. "Mind you, I wouldn't spend the night here. Not in hash country!" he howls. "Nah, who am I kidding? I feel a billion times safer here than in New York. I'd gladly see the month out here, but we're moving on south." Jim is setting out on a reverse journey to me, overnighting on the sleeper to Marrakech, before pushing south into West Africa.

"So, where exactly do you live?" I ask him.

"Live? Pah! God gave me feet." He kicks off his sandals and stands barefoot in the dirt. "I'm a wandering nomad."

I am the first Brit he's met on his travels in Morocco. He is the first American I have come across.

"Huh, surprise!" he says, sarcastically. "Most Americans would die in horror if they saw a turbaned man in slippers out in the street. I tell you, most Americans don't even know this country exists. They think Africa is a song by Toto, or an invention of the Lion King. The US ... it's an island, I tell you, brother. An absolute bubble. So, I beat it outta there soon as the Bush's became a dynasty.

"You know," he rambles on, "Morocco was the first nation in the world to recognise the United States as a country?"

Before I can utter a reply, the bus shows up and we both clamber aboard, relieved to take our rest ... but our seats are taken.

"16B?" I confirm with the man who occupies my seat. He returns a blank stare, so I show him my ticket.

"Meknes," he replies. "Meknes!" I don't understand, but then Jim chirps up.

"Meknes, oh, oh really? Darn it," he says. "Alright, come on Mike, we're on the wrong bus." We shuffle back down the bus, Jim running a commentary as we squeeze past those boarding the other way. "I am so sorry, ma'am. Sir, please accept my apologies."

More buses come and go but still not ours. The sunset adhan pulses across Chaouen and the day's last light fades with it. Tomorrow I have a flight at dawn. Only a few other tourists still linger around us.

"Okay," says Jim decisively. "I think that's enough. Let's get outta here."

I nod in approval, as Jim leads the way to the dusky roadside where the headlights of a grand taxi spear towards us in the looming darkness. "What about our tickets?" I remind him.

"Never mind those, Mike. We'll be splashing more on a hostel in a few ..."

A roaring thunder and plume of dust bears down on us before he is able to finish. A bus tears past the taxi and bounds across broken earth, shuddering to a halt in the forecourt. It is ours.

Jim snores his way back to Tangier, as we space across a bus that is palatial compared to that of my outward leg. Night has now fallen, the last light of my journey across Morocco lost behind the foothills of the Rif. As we charge west in the moonlight, the blues of Chaouen fade to the reds, creams and pasty whites more typical of this country. Just this morning I had departed Tangier, this great northern city, a harmonious clash of Spanish Europe and Amazigh Africa, in the mist and gloom of dawn, and now, on my return, it is once again hidden behind a veil of elusive night. Even by African standards, though, we have arrived back in Tangier really late and the bus company has dumped us at their very own terminal, as opposed to the Gare Routière from which we departed earlier today. A twenty-minute stroll along the coastal esplanade to my hostel has therefore become a city-straddling trek of over an hour. Or, I could always …

Our late arrival and weary legs have pushed me to the brink of the unfathomable. For the first time in my life, I am going to flog a taxi – all for myself. I have never been one for personalised transportation. I'd be all down for riding a taxi with friends, or driving the distance myself – but employing someone to drive you, and *you* only, to a destination of your choosing? That's just preposterous! Back home, I'm more than happy to sit at the top of a London bus, stopping off at everyone else's destination on route to my own, feeling like one of the common folks. But needs must and, mark my words: I'm gonna barter the price of this luxury blommin' hard as well.

Omar, my taxi driver, is full of conversation as we dart towards the old town at speed. As Tangier at night hurries by, I ponder what kind of fool would consider walking such a distance. We discuss his Dacia – it's a reliable workhorse – and the politics of the local area, specifically Gibraltar and Ceuta, the latter a disputed Spanish enclave that juts into Moroccan territory – how dare they! Omar tells me about his dislike of the French, "Their accent, it bothers me," and the Chinese, whom he can't understand. Fortunately, he doesn't seem to have any issues with the British. Or, at least, none he's willing to say to their face. Omar has driven people from around the world, but he's never left Morocco. He can't afford to; the visa is just too expensive. He wants to see Paris, and Barcelona where his favourite football team plays. It's the cost of a visa to Europe. It's simply out of reach for the ordinary Moroccan. And, as any Brit in a taxi would, I ask if he's had a busy day.

No. As it happens, his shift is just beginning. He works through the night, when this frenetic and enigmatic sprawl strapped to the northern shores of Africa is less busy. And I do not blame him. As we race along Monte Carlo-esque streets of the old town and slalom around donkeys and dawdling pedestrians that block the way, I can understand why he prefers to have these outrageously narrow roads lined with buildings to himself. My £4 ride has been an all-round good show, so I take down his number and tell him that I'll be in touch later if I cannot better his rate for a ride to the airport tomorrow. Omar must think that I am one petty bargainer.

Throughout the journey, Omar has been on the phone to another taxi that follows closely behind. Its occupants are two Americans, who are heading to the same hostel as me, so Omar deposits me in a square and imposes my new travel buddies upon me. Fortunately, they know the way rather better than me. The Americans are a young couple who are beginning a pan-African journey that will culminate, all being well, in their marriage in Kenya in a few months from now. Shockingly they claim they have never even heard of Toto's Africa, so I commend their taste in nightclubs and suspect that these worldly West Coasters will be set for life if they are still keen to marry one another after a journey like this.

On arrival at our hostel, we are forced to play a guessing game as to where our host is from. I'm gutted, having lived in Denmark for some time, that I fail to identify that he is, of course, a Dane. Even by Danish standards though, he seems a little uneasy in conversation – but then it all makes sense. The Americans have just been checked into *my* room, and, aside from a bed in a shared dormitory, which after some 50 hours without showering and a night on a train I turn down, there is no room in the hostel. So, my hopes of rest are scattered as I am handed over to a young Moroccan man, who whips me through Tangier in a blur to a different hostel, whom my Danish 'host' has gotten in touch with. My legs burn as we tear through the night at pace. Right, Tangier in a nut-shell, I think to myself. This is all you're getting.

As it happens, this last night doesn't get much better. My route into town for dinner takes me through an unavoidable and very shifty park in total darkness and down a street buzzing with nightlife, patrolled by exceedingly heavily armed guards, unlike any I have seen in Morocco outside of the airports. In fact, I have never seen so many guns before in a public space. Tangier has recently been the beneficiary of generous government investment, which has transformed the city into a hip and vibrant destination, but while its infamously edgy and dangerous past is mostly behind it, at night these streets feel quiet and uneasy. In winter, few tourists are about and only the odd local lingers shadily by the dim roadside. I am not at ease.

Then, on return to my hostel, passing through the same park that I crossed on my journey out, I feel the least safe that I have done on my entire journey across this kingdom. A dozen shouting youths pound a-long gloomy streets beneath the park and charge down darkened alleys, chased by yet more youths and traced by the aggressive barking of dogs that booms through the cool winter's night. Fortunately, I memorised the route before leaving my hostel so I have no need to check my GPS on my phone, but my heart pulses as I hurry along eerily quiet and un-easy streets towards my new hostel. Perhaps I just don't know Tangier, or it comes from the drain of another tiresome day, but the easy energy that is endemic to the cities further south, and certainly Chaouen to my near east, is starkly absent here at night.

Throughout the 20th century, Tangier was an edgy and sometimes dangerous metropolis, known for its markets, but also as the domain of smugglers, criminals and spies. Prior to independence in 1956, Tangier held 'international' status, falling under the shared administration of the sultan and several nations, including Portugal, Belgium, Italy, the UK and Netherlands, as well as Spain and France whose colonial reach ex-tended across the rest of the country and region. The international days are often regarded as Tangier's golden age, when the northern port be-came a hip and liberal city at striking odds with the rest of the country, where anyone could come and do pretty much whatever they wanted. This made it a haven for artists, musicians, writers and the jet set, but it also rendered Tangier a global capital of espionage and mecca for spies, exiles and arms dealers.

Matisse was among many artists who decided to call Tangier home. The Rolling Stones were often in town too, lured south to the northeasternmost point in Africa for its deviant reputation, amicable climate and eccentric neighbours. Independence brought the party to an abrupt end, at which point the expats and artists headed for home as the aura of freedom ran dry along with the alcohol, and so this northern enigma faded with time into a mundane and dreary port city. Like most of the north, Tangier was starved of investment and neglected under Hassan II and so many Tangerines found themselves poor, isolated and jobless, the legacy of which endures today.

But now Tangier is an entirely different city again. Cheap air travel and close proximity to Europe has made it an easy city break and once more the expats are returning, lured south to a dynamic and enigmatic city that has always struck a different chord to the rest of Morocco. It's too bad this hasn't been the last night I hoped for. There's an intriguing old city beyond these dingy backstreets, but time has simply deprived me. Still, as I enjoy a much-needed shower and kick back for the short night ahead, I take solace in the fact that I made it back to Tangier and this excursion to the north has been a success.

Once more, Tangier is in the darkness. Tangier, it seems, is always in the darkness. Before the dawn has arrived, Omar clambers out of his moon-struck Dacia and paces towards my hostel in the gloom.

"How are you feeling?" I ask him.

"Restless!" he replies with a half-smile, half-stifled yawn. He is yet to sleep, and I can see it in his face. In fact, I did not sleep much either. The street outside my first-story room seemed to sporadically spring to life through the night and no sooner had the 2am delivery men cleared off and taken their diesel generators with them, the binmen showed up to clang their cymbals and pound their drums. Shortly after, a donkey-drawn cart convention kicked into life along the city streets, at 4am, as every donkey owner in the Rif bounded along on cart wheels made of wood. And so, I take it back; Omar looks decidedly fresher than me.

"Last ride of the night?" I ask Omar.

"Inshallah," he says with a huff. "But if someone calls, I'll take it." He laughs briefly. "You can rest when you're dead!"

"When's your next day off?" I ask him as I clamber inside his Dacia and we depart for the airport.

"Tomorrow. I will go to Tetouan, to see my parents. They are old now and it has been a long time, so I'll take a day off. Actually ..." he ponders out loud. "Yes, good plan. I will go to the bus station and see if anyone is going my way and wants a ride. Business!"

"You never rest!" I tell him.

"We do not rest in the Rif," he laughs again.

Tetouan has been at the heart of recent protest in the Rif. It is deep in the hills, sandwiched between Tangier, Chefchaouen and Ceuta.

"I hear there has been unrest in the Rif in recent months," I say to Omar. "What do you make of it?"

"It is normal," he replies. "But last summer, it is true – the protests were bigger than they have been for a long time."

"Why?" I ask.

"You know, things never change. It is the same reason that people protested before. People in the Rif feel they have been ignored. They are fed up. When I was young, my parents told me to never even speak of the king. 'They will come cut your tongue,' they said. But now, the people don't care anymore. They are angry, because nothing changes. Many protested in Tangier back in 2011, in the Square of Nations, by the port. There were too many protestors for the police to stop, so the king told them not to beat them. And so more people came and joined in. And now people protest again. Because they know they can!"

Last summer, in 2017, protest rocked the Rif once again following the tragic death of a fishmonger, Mohcine Fikri, who was crushed in a garbage truck while trying to recover his swordfish that had been confiscated by police. He had been accused of selling his fish out of season on the local market. What begun as isolated anger in the coastal town of Al-Hoceima soon sparked life into a much broader wave of popular unrest that swept across the region. It came to be known as the Hirak Rif Movement, and its embers are still alight today.

Many in the Rif considered the tragic events to be just another example of hogra: the sheer neglect of public officials, the lasting impact of economic isolation, and the bane of endemic corruption, which has caused many to feel angry and humiliated. In 2010, a comparable event sparked riots in Tunisia and kick-started the Arab Spring and while the Hirak Rif Movement begun with peaceful protests, last summer it was met with violent repression by the authorities, which fanned the flames of disdain across the kingdom. Thousands have marched on Rabat and in growing unease between protestors and authorities, more than 1,000 people have been arrested on political charges since 2017, including the leader of the Hirak Rif Movement, Nasser Zafzafi. While the February 20 Movement fizzled out as reforms were promised, many in Morocco feel that nothing has changed, and so isolated anger has morphed once again into a far broader movement. Thousands of Moroccans are taking to the streets yet again.

"They are brave, bold people," Omar says.

"Free people," I comment.

Omar tugs at my shoulder playfully with a beaming grin. Dangling around his neck on a beaded necklace, shining polished silver, hangs an emblem. It is unmistakably a Yaz symbol.

"Exactly, brother," he says. "Exactly! We are 'free people' because of our fighting spirit! We never give in." The boom of his voice seems to usher in the first spearing rays of day. Now, on the far horizon, the Mediterranean shimmers in the misted gold of dawn, as I brace for departure. Somewhere, distant in the haze, is Europe. "We do not rest," he continues, "except, maybe tomorrow!"

Just like the Arab Spring, the protests that rumble today are diverse and plural. They are not about usurping Arab rule, or pitting Amazigh against Arabs, just as the French had tried to do. Those that I have met on my travels have spoken with pride in their diverse origins, not prejudice, and almost all Moroccans can claim lineage from both an Arab and Amazigh past. This nation has a proud dual identity, shaped by the eastern winds of Arabia, but bound by something else that runs much deeper, a shared heritage, an African conception. Being a 'free person' is not about race or history. It is about a shared fighting spirit and a refusal to give up despite the odds. The protests are not about Tamazgha at all. Instead, they are about unsettling the status quo and demanding reforms that transcend identities and histories.

Once more I dwell on the changes that simmer beneath the surface of this kingdom. I think of the Draoui, the Aït Atta and all the nomads fighting the odds and a warming world. I think of jumbled Fes el Bali, that medina at the crossroads, and the many abrupt clashes of a modern and ancient world that can at times seem irreconcilable. But then again, I realise that the story of this land is one of East meeting West, Europe and Africa, Arab and Amazigh, tradition and modernity, serene hinterland and spellbound medina, an almighty clash of worlds. I do not see a paradox anymore. I am convinced that one world cannot thrive without the other.

That is why the inhabitants of this enchanting region have come to know themselves as 'free people.' Through strife, struggle, suppression and Spring, their unyielding spirit has endured intact. I have sensed it in the Sahara, witnessed it in the mountains and felt it in the city souks. The spirit that rallied the Moroccans in the Arab Spring and in the Rif today is the same spirit that has ensured the Amazigh would never truly be conquered. Despite the odds stacked against them, their defiant and rebellious spirit has endured. It is the quandary of the Arab elites who endeavour to unite this region today as it was for the conquerors who tried and failed before them. While few have ever managed to conquer the formidable geography of North Africa, none have broken the spirit of the region's free men.

After all, Tamazgha isn't real. Everyone knows that Tamazgha only exists in the imagination. But who you are runs much deeper.

GLOSSARY

Adhan – Islamic call to prayer, recited by the muezzin of a mosque five times per day and usually projected across an area with loudspeakers.

Adobe – Durable mudbrick building material, composed of earth and organic matter such as straw or clay.

Aït – Tamazight word used principally by tribal groups to denote the 'people of' a common homeland or ancestor.

Alaouite – Ruling dynasty of Moroccan monarchs, who have reigned as the nation's royal family since 1666.

Amazigh – Indigenous people of North Africa and some of northern West Africa. Often known as 'Berbers,' they use the name 'Amazigh' themselves, which is believed to mean 'free man.'

Arab Spring – Series of mass protests and uprisings across the Arab world that lasted from 2010 to 2012, mostly against corruption, poor living standards, government repression and in favour of democracy and human rights. Results varied across the region, resulting in partial democratisation, the removal of regimes and triggering of civil wars.

Arab world – Collective term for Arabic-speaking countries, located mostly in North Africa, the Middle East and the Horn of Africa, which are members of the intergovernmental Arab League.

Arabism – Arab culture, identity and language. Arabism has been a key component of North Africa's post-independence identity. Arabisation refers to its spread.

Babouches – Pointed slippers of Moroccan origin that have no heel, typically made of leather.

Berber – see 'Amazigh.'

Bled el-Makhzen – Historical term denoting the supposedly governed and law-abiding lands of Morocco where the sultan could gather taxes and provide security. Typically included the cities and lowlands.

Bled es-Siba – Historical term denoting the supposedly lawless, unruly and tribal lands of Morocco that were beyond the sultan's authority in the early 20th century. Typically included the rural hinterlands.

Caliphate – Islamic state ruled by an Islamic leader called the caliph.

Caravan – Group of people who travel together, often for the purpose of trade. Historically, travelling in a caravan would have helped defend the party against bandits and enable economies of scale.

Dahir – Royal decree made by the King of Morocco.

Desertification – Process by which fertile land turns into desert.

Djellaba – Long, loose, woollen robes with a pointed hood worn by both men and women across North Africa.

Erg – Desert landform comprised of large wind-blown sand dunes and almost no vegetation. Loose and shifting sand makes them notoriously difficult to cross.

Fondouk – Medieval inn and stabling, typically located in a medina, where merchants and their animals could halt for the night and store goods while visiting a city for trade. Also known as a *caravanserai*.

Gîte – Guest accommodation available for rent. Many were originally a farmers' traditional rural lodgings.

Hamada – High, dry, barren and often rocky desert plateau with very little sand.

Hammam – Moroccan public baths, often consisting of steam cleansing in progressively hotter rooms, followed by a massage. Given that the cost of hot water for cleansing at home is beyond the budget of many, hammams are commonly used for ablutions: ritual purification before prayer, and many Moroccans will visit the hammam weekly.

Hogra – Maghrebi word that captures the feeling of contempt, anger and humiliation over the neglect of public officials, corruption and the denial of human rights. Such sentiments kickstarted the Arab Spring.

Imam – Leader of worship in a mosque, also used to refer to the leader of an Islamic community.

Infidel – Non-believer, or someone who follows a religion other than that of the majority.

Informal economy – Workers and enterprises that operate beyond the regulation of government. Most, but not all, are legal and contribute significantly to public life and the alleviation of poverty, but informal livelihoods are untaxed, unprotected and can be deeply insecure.

Inshallah – Arabic expression of hopefulness that something will come to pass, translating as 'God willing.'

Islamism – Political ideology or form of government where principles of Islam provide the legitimacy for governance and are used to guide social, political and often private life.

Jinn – Genie or magical spirit that can appear in human or animal form and influence humans.

Kasbah – Either a North African citadel to provide defence for a city and housing for a local leader, or a prominent square home with four turreted corners where an important and wealthy family would have resided. Many have now been converted into hotels.

Ksar – Fortified village for sedentary populations, often built close to an oasis. Original purpose was to defend inhabitants and their harvest from bad weather, raiding nomadic tribes and bandits. Typically made up of tightly-packed earthen clay homes and facilities, surrounded by high walls. Most common in southern and desert lands.

Madrasa – Islamic school that teaches subjects such as Arabic, law and history in line with Islamic principles. Often located next to a mosque to function as an important cultural and social setting.

Maghreb – Predominantly Islamic part of the western Arab world that encompasses much of the Sahara Desert. Typically includes Morocco, Algeria, Tunisia, Libya, Mauritania and disputed Western Sahara. Egypt and Sudan form part of the Mashriq, the eastern Arab world.

Makhzen – Governing elites of Morocco, the 'establishment,' typically including the royal family, high-ranking military officers, civil servants and security officials. Serves to maintain the status quo and reinforce the monarch's power.

Marabout – Hermit, mystic or holy man who is believed to possess the ability to heal or hold other supernatural capabilities.

Medina – Old walled part of a town or city made up of narrow streets, colourful souks, palaces and mosques. Owing to their labyrinthine and densely-populated nature, many have struggled to adapt to change and so have preserved their ancient characteristics.

Minaret – Tall and slender tower of a mosque, from which the faithful are called to prayer.

Muezzin – Mosque official who recites the call to prayer five times per day, often from the minaret.

Oud – Pear-shaped stringed instrument, much like a modern lute.

Oued – Seasonal river, valley or ravine that contains water in the rainy season, but is otherwise dry. Also known as a wadi.

Political Islam – see 'Islamism.'

Riad – Traditional Moroccan house with an open-air central courtyard or a garden in the middle. Often used today to refer to any Moroccan guesthouse or hotel with private rooms and shared common areas.

Rghaif – Crispy Moroccan pancakes, served at breakfast or for tea with sweet or savoury treats, such as honey, jam, butter or cheese.

Salam – Arabic greeting meaning 'peace.'

Shukran – Arabic word meaning 'thank you.'

Souk – Outdoor market in North Africa or the Middle East. In bigger cities they will typically specialise in a particular kind of product (spices, carpets, jewellery) and form a large network of specialist souks. Known in some countries as a bazaar.

Sultan – Muslim sovereign. Morocco opted to replace the title 'sultan' with 'king' in 1957 to emphasise the monarch's secular authority under the rule of law.

Tagine – Clay or ceramic cooking pot with a distinctive dome-shaped lid placed upon a shallow circular dish. Also refers to the slow-cooked meal that is prepared inside, typically consisting of meat and vegetables.

Tamazgha – Imagined homeland of the Amazigh, encompassing lands originally inhabited by their ancestors. Straddles North Africa from the Canary Islands to the Siwa Oasis in Egypt and from the Mediterranean to the Niger River. Derives from Amazigh nationalism and widely used in the Amazigh movement.

Tamazight – Group of closely-related languages that are spoken by the Amazigh people, written in the Tifinagh script. A written tradition has existed for around 2,500 years.

Tifinagh – Ancient script, used to write Tamazight. Originally written in symbols, it received a modern alphabetical form in the 20th century.

Transhumance – Nomadic practice of moving livestock seasonally from highlands in summer to lowlands in winter.

Tuaregs – Confederation of ethnically Amazigh people, most of whom live as nomadic pastoralists in the Sahara and Sahel. Often heralded in the Amazigh movement for preserving ancient Amazigh traditions that have been diminished elsewhere in the region by foreign influences.

Ville nouvelle – 'New town,' built under colonial rule to provide the colonists with a European-styled space for administration, governance and living, while preserving the ancient medina for the local people.

Wadi – Seasonal river, valley or ravine that contains water in the rainy season, but is otherwise dry. Also known as an oued.

Yallah – Arabic word meaning 'let's go.'

Yaz (ⵣ) – Letter in the Tifinagh script that features at the centre of the Amazigh flag and represents the 'free man.'

Zellige – Colourful mosaic tilework and form of Islamic art. Appeared in North Africa around the 10th century and flourished under Almohad rule. Forms an important decorative feature of Moroccan architecture.

Printed in Great Britain
by Amazon

53792334R00137